Scratching the Surface

Scratching the Surface

Impressions of Planet Earth
from Hollywood to Shiraz

Jeff Greenwald

NAGA BOOKS

ALSO BY JEFF GREENWALD

Mr. Raja's Neighborhood: Letters from Nepal
Shopping for Buddhas
The Size of the World
Future Perfect: How Star Trek Conquered Planet Earth

Library of Congress C.I.P. forthcoming

ISBN 1-58790-018-1

Cover images: Replogle globe factory, Illinois
© 1998 Andrew Sacks

Manufactured in the U.S.A.

Naga Books
6020-A Adeline
Oakland, CA 94608
To Order: www.jeffgreenwald.com

For Ruthie

TABLE OF CONTENTS

Where there are humans
You'll find flies, and Buddhas

— Issa (1763-1827)

INTRODUCTION

⤸

It was a hot, bright afternoon in August, just a few days before the total solar eclipse. My friend Sam and I had broken away from our small, nervous group of Americans, and wandered the streets of Teheran alone.

Earlier, we had been looking for trouble: shooting surreptitious videos of the former American Embassy (now an Iranian military training camp) and sneaking into seminary courtyards to pose for pictures with naive young *mullahs*. Now we were looking for lunch. Nothing fancy; we'd had it with the glitzy hotel restaurants preferred by our tour agency's insurance company. Our goal was to find something local, the kind of no-frills eatery where work-a-day Iranians might stop in for a bite.

It didn't take us long. Halfway down a nondescript city block, a stairway descended into a large, white-tiled room lit by rows of buzzing fluorescent lamps. A Coca-Cola wall clock ground its teeth on the wall above the cash register, flanked by images of severe ayatollahs. There were a dozen cafeteria-style tables, most of them filled with bearded, black-eyed men bent over rice plates and newspapers. The waiter observed our entry with a resigned expression, and seated us at the one empty table, rather near the door. He handed us menus, printed entirely in Farsi.

Sam flipped through the pages, which looked as if they'd been written by an inchworm on absinthe. "Do you think there's an English-language version?"

"Unlikely," I replied, conscious of sounding like Mr. Spock on an away mission.

"Do you have any idea what to order?"

I shrugged. "It's all good."

"Seriously. I don't know where to begin."

"Try the Coca-Cola."

We looked around, craning our necks, trying to see what the other patrons were eating. It was difficult to do so with discretion, as we were still the center of a very subtle, but very definite, attention. I glanced a few tables down, at a rather alluring plate that seemed to be covered with meatballs and beans. The customer glared at us, then turned to find the waiter, who hurried over. He grunted something, and motioned at us. I reddened, and returned my gaze to the indecipherable menu.

"We seem a shade less than welcome," Sam observed. "Do you want to stay?"

"I don't know. The food looks good... all we need to do is find something we like, and point to it... I really don't think anybody is going to give us any trouble."

He whispered, "Do you think they know we're Americans?"

"Of course they do." I closed my menu, and scanned the room with as much discretion as possible. "We look just like our pictures."

The waiter arrived, pad in hand. We ordered Coca-Colas. He asked us something in Farsi; we shrugged. Some of the locals snorted in agitation. All eyes were upon us, judgmental and severe. A second man motioned to the waiter, and, staring at us, made a few gruff comments; so did a third, jabbing at the table with his finger. The waiter disappeared, and returned with our drinks. By now a low murmur filled the room, as the patrons began sharing their reactions to our presence. The word "America" percolated darkly through the room. Heads nodded; newspapers were folded. My travelers' radar, tuned to crystal clarity by twenty years on the road, signaled high alert. Somehow, an unseen barrier had been breached. The atmosphere had shifted from edgy discomfort to imminent danger. Sam and I regarded each other.

"Not exactly Marie Callender's" he observed.

"How much should we leave for the Cokes?"

"Plenty. And a big tip, too."

We placed a few bills on the table, gulped down our drinks, and rose to leave. Halfway out of my seat, I felt a large hand on my shoulder. It was covered with black hair, and pressing downward with sufficient force to overcome my escape velocity. The expression on the Iranian face behind it spoke the universal language: we were going nowhere.

The truth dawned on us simultaneously: we were about to become hostages.

This was a grim turn of events for Sam, whose software start-up was shooting ahead like a greased marmot down a water slide. For myself, however, it was fabulous news. A year in captivity, perhaps, with sporadic episodes of anxiety, boredom and despair; then our inevitable release, triumphant homecoming, and a six-figure book contract. Plus movie rights, of course; unless the numbers looked better from HBO....

I had barely started spending my advance when the door to the kitchen burst open. The Iranian waiter charged toward us. He carried no weapons; just a filigreed tray. On the tray rested a half-dozen small plates and bowls, bearing *kuku* and *kofté*, *kebab* and *khoresh*, *dolmé* and *mast*. The men, looking stern as ever, nodded piously as one dish after another was placed before us, followed by *lavash* bread and a vast tureen of rice. Each customer, it seemed, had sent over his favorite dish; and each offered the slightest smile as I began—after swallowing my disappointment—to devour this Persian cornucopia.

We ate until we could eat no more; about half our portions. The waiter brought our bill, charging us only for the drinks. And as we finally rose to leave—unobstructed, this time—I flipped sheepishly through my guidebook, and offered the only phrase that seemed appropriate: *Chub kari nakon.* Your generosity puts me to shame.

• • •

This story is offered not as a plug for Farsi lessons, but as an example of how strange and enlightening travel can be. No matter where we go—even just a few steps off the beaten path—we risk having our preconceptions shattered, and a new world view implanted in their place. It's not always an entirely safe or comfortable process, but it's a process that many travelers relish, and one that travel writers roam the world to cultivate.

I very much love to travel, and love equally to write. Combining the two has shaped my career, lifestyle and personality since 1979, when a ten-week trip to carve marble in Greece (I was studying sculpture at that time) bloomed into an eleven-month, around-the-world odyssey that took me from the coast of Crete to the sands of the Sinai; from the Pyramids of Giza to the bazaars of Bombay. It was an unplanned journey, which is often the most magical kind. Every mile brought new revelations, new scents from the spice box of Earth. But the ultimate prize was yet to come. For it was on that voyage that, pursuing a doomed romance across three continents, I found my way to Kathmandu: the sacred valley that would be my second home for the next twenty years.

Ever since that time, the alchemical gift of travel—the opportunity to shed my stale skin, and molt into an entirely new creature—has been an obsession.

When I took my very first trip abroad, just out of high school in 1971, the Vietnam War was still raging; World War II had ended only 25 years ago. Back then Europe itself seemed exotic, even menacing. I remember finding myself in a Munich beer hall, listening to two drunken ex-Nazis—they must have been in their forties—proclaim their undying love for Hitler. The Cold War was frozen solid; the Berlin Wall was impenetrable. The maps of Africa, and Russia, were completely different than they are today. Apartheid was law. Greece was a dictatorship. And Turkey, Iran and Afghanistan were still the gems of the overland bus circuit, which began in London or Amsterdam and culminated at the cobblestone plaza near Kathmandu's Freak Street, and the Eden Hashish Centre.

These were the years when the vagabonding Tony and Maureen Wheeler published *Southeast Asia on a Shoestring*, launching their Lonely Planet empire; they were the days when even the beaten path was trampled with flip-flop prints, rather than Vibram soles.

By the time my own travel writing career began, in the early 1980s, the world had changed completely. The Vietnam War, at least as far as most Americans were concerned, was over. The Cold War was thawing, with both SALT treaties signed. Afghanistan (besieged with Soviet troops) and Iran (scene of the hostage crisis, which destroyed Jimmy Carter's presidency and brought Ronald Reagan into power) had closed their borders. Hashish was no longer legal in Nepal. Though South Africa was still a racist mess, political consciousness about apartheid, and support for the boycott, were growing. Idi Amin was history, and Anwar Sadat had, miraculously, made peace with Israel. More subtly, but equally significant, a tsunami of kitschy globalism was beginning to inundate the world. American icons like Coca-Cola, Mickey Mouse and McDonald's (soon to be followed by Rambo, Madonna, et. al.) began appearing everywhere. On top of that, most revolutionary of all, the Neosilicate Age was beginning. The first clunky personal computers had emerged, with the Apple Macintosh—heralded, at its 1984 release, as a thumb in the eye of Big Brother—poised to unleash a worldwide plague of mice.

It was into this world that I launched myself, first as an artist, and later as a writer/photographer. My spontaneous 1979 trip was followed, in 1983-84, by a residency in Kathmandu as a Journalism Fellow of the Rotary Foundation. By that time I'd been writing for a while. My very first published gig had come in 1972, when I covered the launch of Apollo 17—America's last Moon mission—for my college newspaper. Through the late '70s and early '80s I'd worked with a number of weekly newspapers and small magazines, and started a limited-edition art magazine called *eye*. But the pay was poor, and it was necessary for me to rely on photography, graphics, and editing as well.

With the Rotary Fellowship, journalism became my career. Travel

writing moved to center stage, inaugurating a hand-to-mouth exist-
ence that I have sustained, to the amazement of myself and the dismay of my mother, until this day. But there are advantages; my last
day job, as the Cultural and Features Editor of the now-defunct *Santa
Barbara News & Review*, ended in 1980. And if the years since have
not covered me in glory, they have more or less kept my name in
print. At this point, after five books and some 200 articles, with my
stories appearing in more than 15 travel anthologies, I might mod-
estly argue that, in the hearts and minds of a few, I am the best-
known obscure travel writer—or the most obscure well-known travel
writer—in America.

• • •

Scratching the Surface is an offering, in part, to the many people
who read my books and/or visited my website, then wrote to ask
where they might find more of my work. It's not been easy to direct
them. Unlike books, magazines and newspapers have a pretty short
shelf life. Any friend or fan discovering my work after 1990, for example, probably missed the stories I contributed to magazines like
Image and *Equator*; even my most intimate associates (with one or
two exceptions) have never read *Very Alive*, which tipped the first
domino in my professional writing career.

Another reason I'm putting this anthology together is to place
myself, and my work, in context. Like all travel writers, I'm a product of my times. And just as it has been said, of nations, that "geography is destiny," it's equally true that, for many turn-of-the-millen-
nium travel writers, technology is destiny.

One of the most significant aspects of my career is that it coincided with the PC, laptop, and Internet booms. Science has always
been a passion of mine, so it's probably not surprising that technology has had so great an influence on my work. This relationship
really took off in 1993, when I began writing for *Wired* magazine. My
most profound partnership with the new technology, though, began
in December 1993—when, in celebration of my 40th birthday, I set

off to circle the Earth without the use of airplanes. It is now acknowledged, though not widely known, that I was the first travel writer to circumambulate the world while sending back real-time dispatches for the Internet ("The Paradise of Wind Roses," "Across the Persian Gulf," and "Live from the Yak Hotel" were among those essays). The story of that nine-month journey, of 27,158 miles across 26 countries, is told in *The Size of the World* (Ballantine, 1996). In the years since, scores of fellow travelers have called and written to comment on the book, and (more to the point) take me up on the offer I so recklessly made, while thirstily marooned in some Qinghai backwater, to buy every one of my readers a beer.

But technology has its limits. I write these words, as fate would have it, just days after the terrorist attacks that toppled Manhattan's World Trade Center. The effect this calamity will have on travel, and travel writing, is impossible to gauge. For the time being, people (Americans, at least) may prefer to stay closer to home, and explore the transcendent beauty of our own shorelines and national parks. Before too long, however, our panic and self-protective isolationism will subside, the deck of possibilities will be reshuffled, and we will be footloose again. Because there is nothing about us more human than our curiosity; and there is no way to satisfy that curiosity, short of exploration.

Earlier in this introduction I mentioned the beaten path, and how valuable it can be to stray from it. As many of us already appreciate, that's getting much harder to do. During the past 25 years we've seen that path grow ever wider, with tendrils sprouting off toward villages, beaches and enclaves that were off the map a few decades ago. In Peru and Cambodia, Tibet and Mauritania, locals who once pulled at our arm-hairs in wonder are now streetwise and blasé, checking their Swatches as they await our arrival, with knick-knacks polished and soft drinks on ice. I was especially stunned by this phenomenon in North Vietnam where, after staggering to the crest of a small mountain in the blazing sun, I found a half-dozen old women cheerfully hawking Fanta. A dramatic contrast is the Kingdom of Bhutan, a once isolated Buddhist aerie that now protects its culture and environment by rationing visas, charging a small fortune in daily "permit" fees, and chaperoning visitors along well-worn trekking and touring routes.

A radical measure—but as every corner of the world becomes more accessible, we're likely to see more of them. This opalescent planet, which our Moon-bound astronauts so easily blotted out with their thumbs (from only one hundred thousand miles away), is being webbed within a shimmering grid of highways, airline routes, and backpacker circuits. Nothing is going to change that; and no one can begrudge the thousands, even millions of others who will continue to seek, consciously or unconsciously, the elusive grail that travel still offers: transformation.

I'll continue to look for it myself, and to find it now and again. The world will get more crowded, and long-hidden places will be trampled. But there will always be that unmarked restaurant; those enigmatic eyes; the thrill of being utterly, ecstatically wrong.

The Earth is still an enormous, surprising place. I make no pretenses about being an accomplished traveler. To the contrary, I'm continually disheartened to realize that all I ever see of our planet is a narrow band which, defined by the limits of my vision, meanders with fractal abstraction across the landscape. Any illusion of depth—in my perception, or in these stories—comes not from looking without, but from looking within.

In terms of the larger view, I have a single observation to offer about travel in general, and humanity in particular. Nowhere, at any time or in any place, has any human being refused my direct and sincere request for help. If there is anything I have learned in my travels, it is this: we must learn to ask for help when we need it, and to offer help where it is needed. Once we have mastered this, the entire world will be open to us all.

Oakland, California
January, 2002

ON MAPS

I've always loved maps, and this essay—written for *Great Escapes*, a bi-annual travel magazine published by the San Francisco *Examiner*, in 1987—is still one of my favorites. For one thing, it features some pretty good anecdotes about Nepal (one of which would appear again, eight years later, in the opening chapter of *The Size of the World*). For another, it demonstrates the wonderful writer/editor chemistry I shared (and share still) with Donald W. George, the former *Examiner* travel editor who assigned the piece.

MAP MEMORY FROM early childhood: the jagged outline of Treasure Island. A compass crowned with an ornate *fleur-de-lis*, pointing due north. Black lines radiating across parchment; roughly drawn hills peppered with crosses; skulls and crossbones. Pirate treasure. My brother and I used to dig up the backyard with plastic shovels, looking for our share. What did we know from the Caribbean? They could've buried it anywhere.

The first maps that most of us encountered were keys to a world of fantasy. Captain Flint's led to a fabulous cache of gold and jewels—but equally compelling were the maps that escorted us over the mountain ranges of Middle Earth, through *The Phantom Tollbooth's* "Land Beyond," and along Marco Polo's route to the Court of Kublai Khan.

And then there were the maps that led to real places—like the giraffes at the zoo, or the Dumbo ride at Disneyland.

My relationship with those early maps was pretty one-sided. I was basically a tag-along, following the leads of courageous others. Directions were simple, rewards were great, and wrong turns were next to impossible.

Then came high school, adulthood, and the necessity to navigate one's own course through the world. My relationship with maps abruptly reversed. Before, they had been crude sketches of ideal, imaginary worlds; now, they were idealized portraits of sloppy reality.

It was a difficult transition to get used to. I recall blithely studying a map of Bombay—a clean grid of meticulously ruled avenues and British place names—as our 747 descended toward the Indian metropolis. Leaving the airport was one of the rudest awakenings of my life; nothing in that map had prepared me for the gnarled streets, riotous bazaars and sprawling slums of the city itself.

At that moment, the famous words of semanticist Alfred Korzybski hit home: "The map is not the territory." You can read all the how-to books you want, I realized, but you don't know a damned thing about boxing until you've climbed into the ring.

. . .

Growing up on Long Island, I had map fever. It was more than a compulsion to cover my walls; it was a need to possess the places those maps represented, to accumulate destinations. In the tribal rituals of the ancients, a boy was elevated into manhood through a vision quest, or by bagging a powerful pelt. My American initiation, a coming-of-age in the land of consumerism, combined aspects of both. I wanted not only to experience mysterious new places, but to collect them as well.

Above my desk hung a map of the United States, stuck full of pins, heavy with the destination voodoo of the post-Kerouac generation. *On the Road* was practically mythology to me; I charted Sal Paradise's route through bop America as a scholar of ancient Greek might try to trace Odysseus's travels.

In 1974, after two years at the local college, I set off for the west coast at last, attempting to duplicate Kerouac's journey and follow that "one long red line called Route 6 that led from the tip of Cape Cod clear to Ely, Nevada, and there dipped down to Los Angeles." Needless to say, my path across the country took its own shape. It included some of the cities Sal Paradise visited, like Chicago and Denver, but for the most part I wound my way through territories unknown, an eager disciple of the Fates that steer young travelers into unexpected—but always strangely appropriate—encounters and experiences. Maps, I discovered, always seem immutable at first; it's only later, in the heat of an intimate relationship with them, that one realizes they can be re-drawn to suit new priorities.

Thinking it over now, I wonder if what inspired Kerouac—and possessed me—to steer our lives westward, full of blind faith and optimism, with only a printed page as rudder, was that illusion of immutability itself: the notion of the map as God.

Consider that my Sinclair highway map of the USA provided all of the following: a sense of direction; an escape route from suburbia; a supportive companion and unwavering guide; an object worthy of profound faith; a bounty for the imagination; and a tiny symbol of something vast, intimidating and (so it seemed then) immortal. What more could anyone ask from a deity?

. . .

Howard Sacks was a buddy of mine in Nepal. He was inner-city, street-wise and bluntly honest, but with a wild, impulsive streak that sometimes frightened his friends. He lived his life in a seemingly haphazard fashion, without any discernible plan. As I think of him now I recall two things: his passion for poker, and the pride and pleasure he took in correcting maps.

Since WWII, technology has given maps, like parachutes, an awesome degree of reliability. As a result, most of us have come to take the accuracy of maps for granted. As we leap out into the world, huddled against the headwind of possibilities, we rely on them absolutely.

But on the maps of some remote parts of the world—like the north-

ern border of Nepal, where the Indian and Eurasian plates collide—
much is still relatively uncertain, or changing. One town will have
three different names, based on how each surveyor heard it; earthquakes, glaciers or erosion will have sliced off a hillside, permanently erasing a major trail; a well may have moved, and only the
collapsed stone walls of a recently thriving village remain.

Howard enjoyed nothing more than pressing into the Himalayas,
usually alone, always in sneakers, into obscure regions where the
caprices of the earth play havoc with the accuracy of maps. For some
of his destinations, the only maps of any integrity were decade-old
topos, drawn from satellite data by the Defense Mapping Agency.

Defense maps are not for public sale; you can only get them by
writing to the Agency and "justifying your need." How Howard got
his first DMA map is uncertain. Maybe he had used his credentials
as a lawyer, or his connections with the Tibetan autonomy movement. Maybe he had won it at poker; the man was a shark. At any
rate, he brought it back from his first solo expedition full of correc-
tions, and mailed this edited version to the Defense Mapping Agency.
They wrote back on official stationary to thank Howard, and offered
him a freelance assignment to correct other maps, of his choice, in
the future. The payment for each job would be the coveted map itself.

Howard showed the letter to everyone. It was as if he had been
given a dare. After some deliberation he followed up on the offer,
requesting a series of maps showing the landscape north of a mountain called Dhaulgiri, which lay very close to the prohibited Tibetan
border. In March of 1984, shortly before leaving Kathmandu, he
encountered an expedition of Japanese climbers who were going to
attempt an ascent of Dhaulgiri and somehow talked them into letting
him come along. They left in mid-March, 1984.

I left that spring too, on a relatively well-mapped trek up the Arun
Valley. When I returned to Kathmandu in April, dreaming only of
pizza and a hot shower, I was stunned to hear that Howard was dead.

Nobody seemed to have any concrete details; everything I know
came by word-of-mouth. According to Singh, his housemate, the expedition had been driven back by inclement weather. Howard

decided to continue northeast, toward the border, into the shady portions of his maps. As he climbed, whole Sherpa families passed him—going the opposite direction, fleeing the ice, warning him to do the same.

Somewhere, sneakers on ice, he slipped off the trail. The fall didn't kill him; he was apparently able to call a passing porter, who took his SOS and ran it to the nearest village by evening. The following day, a rescue helicopter from Kathmandu was turned back by the weather. The day after that it managed to fly in, but only Howard's body could be recovered.

I would like to see a map which commemorates the spots where those who have tried to correct maps have perished. A map to mark the sunken vessels of discovery; the beast-eaten expeditions; the blackened launch pads. The last stands of people like Howard, who dare to collar territory that turns to bite the leash.

. . .

Sometimes, in the lonely parts of the world, a strange kind of love will blossom between the traveler and his map. He will come to admire the map more and more, and defer to it constantly, until he is completely seduced by it and utterly lost without it.

In truth, of course, the traveler has fallen in love with the territory. But in the constant process of bouncing between one and the other, that distinction has blurred and vanished. Korzybski's warning has been tossed to the winds.

To see a person thus smitten is a beautiful thing—especially in the autumn, as red leaves fall over the Himalayan trails and yak dung, damp with dew, steams in the brilliant morning sun.

In preparing for our three-week walk into the Khumbu—the region of the Himalayas that includes Sagarmatha (Mt. Everest), Lhotse and Nuptse—it was decided that Bill, my trekking partner, would be responsible for the map. Why didn't I get one, too? That's easy: weight. Like an obsessive bicycle racer who shaves his legs to cut wind drag, I thus managed to trim a good half-ounce off my 40 lb. load.

Although I hardly noticed the few grams, I was compelled to

watch—with no little envy—the budding romance between Bill and his colorful, beautifully scaled topographical map of the Everest Valley. They were like young lovers; by the end of two weeks Bill was intimate with every soft swell and lush contour of that map. He had admired it in sunshine and by candlelight, mastered it in every position, and—love for a map hath no greater deed—even learned to fold it up properly, along the original creases.

In spite of all the hardships we encountered on the trail, the only times I ever saw Bill wince were the rare occasions when some misfortune befell his map. A leather Sherpani cook spilled a bit of *dhal* onto it; I, in the numbing cold, lost control of my mouth and dribbled coffee onto it; an ember leapt from a crackling firepit like the finger of God and touched it, burning a tiny hole. At each incident Bill dropped everything and sprang into action, a model of efficiency and damage control.

This vigilance paid off in spades when we reached our destination: the crest of a round black hill called Kala Pattar. Over 18,000 feet high, surrounded by an army of rumbling glaciers, sublime white peaks and cracking, deadly ice falls, Kala Pattar hung above the clouds like an island in the sky. The panorama was staggering, and we were immediately seized by a desperate longing (so uniquely human!) to identify every landmark in sight.

As we set about slaking that thirst—orienting ourselves, guessing heights and distances, and deducing the name of each unique mountain—the landscape underwent a profound change. Before, it had seemed aloof and anonymous; now it was imbued with personality. It had soul. It had a *plot*—we could see where things had been and where they were going. There was even a hint of celebrity in it all, as we let our eyes wander up the flanks of Everest, finding the paths used by the great mountaineers.

It was a giddy afternoon, wide-eyed in the cold, thin atmosphere. Gaping at the wind-swept peak of Everest, 10,000 feet above us, the three of us (Bill, the map and myself) had literally reached the highest point of our lives.

A couple of weeks later I returned to the richly aromatic air of

Kathmandu, obsessed with the desire to buy my very own Schneider map of the Everest Valley. It was hard to find, but I finally dug one up in an obscure bookshop. I ran back to my hotel and opened it at once, eager to re-experience our fabulous voyage; to recapture, vicariously, the thrill of standing upon Kala Pattar with the high, thin wind beating against my ears.

It was no use. The map seemed the same; but something was terribly wrong. Where was the smudge of dried Spam on the western face of Nuptse? Where was the ugly coffee stain, meandering recklessly along the banks of the Dudh Kosi? Or the jagged grin, burnt at the edges, in the contours of the mighty Chhukhung Glacier?

Where was the *soul*? I tossed the new map aside as if it were a cheap impostor, painfully aware that nothing I could do—short of repeating the entire trek—could imbue that piece of paper with the power and magic of the map that Bill had hung, like a lover's portrait, on the wall above his desk.

. . .

Is it fair to think of maps as perfect journalism? Like that related art, they attempt to objectify, to inform, and even to influence the course of events. But maps have one thing going for them that journalism can't touch: mathematics.

Because of their celebrated precision, maps are not traditionally subject—as is their brash and opinionated cousin—to the banter of public outcry. They are held to be sacrosanct, the products of undeniable physical truth rather than mere mortal contrivance.

This almost universal subservience to maps has given them substantial powers, benign or deadly, over humanity. For hundreds of years, for example, conventional wisdom that the world was flat stifled exploration. When Columbus at last sailed west, he mistook North America for the East Indies; our Native Americans are "Indians" to this day. On the other side of the world, more than 500,000 Indians in India itself (a country whose national, racial and religious names were invented by western invaders of the Indus Valley) died in the chaotic uprootings of 1947-48, when a British cartographer rewrote the map of their country to establish East and West Pakistan.

These are severe, and obvious, illustrations. But there is something else; something far more subtle. Maps, since they are rarely questioned, can also be subliminal tools for propaganda. How many people realize, for example, that a common Mercator projection—your typical classroom world map—is skewed to show the northern hemisphere, which includes the United States and Europe, in twice the size and detail of the southern hemisphere, where lie most of Africa and South America?

Any attempt to represent the round world as flat is bound to end in some degree of distortion. The point is, cartographers can choose which distortions to make. For years they've been making the mistakes in favor of their home addresses: the colonizing powers. The choice hasn't been malicious; since 1569, when Gerardus Mercator's map was first printed, the overwhelming percentage of world travel and commerce has been conducted in the northern hemisphere.

As South America, Africa and Australia emerge as world powers, though, irritation over the bias inherent in the old view has inspired several new world maps. The best example is the recently released Peters projection, designed in the early 1980s by German historian Arno Peters. The Peters map, unlike Mercator's, shows all countries, continents and oceans at their true relative size. You can clearly see, for instance, that Europe—which appears larger than South America on traditional maps—is actually about half the Latin American continent's size. Greenland, looming so enormous on the maps we grew up with, looks like a shriveled fig compared to China. And Africa, so manageable by Mercator's scale, dwarfs both Europe and the United States completely.

The Peters projection simply strives to attain greater accuracy. Other new maps are more combative; they *keep* the old, biased Mercator scale, but literally flip everything upside down. North and south (which are arbitrary anyway, since there is no "up" or "down" in space) are switched, and Antarctica becomes the north pole. This satirical reversal of the generally accepted "missionary position" (colonists on top) gives South America, Africa and Australia plenty of room to stretch out; and it gives the northern hemisphere countries, which suddenly find themselves cramped into the lower third of the map, plenty to think about regarding maps and self-image. This is not to disparage maps, or cast doubt on their credibility. Quite the contrary. The very thing that makes maps so fascinating as journalism is their ability to reflect (usually in retrospect) the deeper currents of elitism and allegiance that flow beneath periods of human history. At the moment a map is published, it is as accurate as the prevailing world view will allow, taking in all the changes that have led up to that point. To study it is to see a mirror of that world, frozen in its epoch.

. . .

Map memories, 1989: a guide to the Tokyo subway; a floor plan of the Bangkok National Museum; a map of the Martian moon Phobos, radioed back to earth by a fleeing spacecraft.

Up in Num, a small village in the Kanchenjunga Himal, I watched a bunch of schoolkids play volleyball—with neither net nor ball. Not one of them had ever heard of Phobos. And even if they (and most of Num) were familiar with more populated places like Tokyo and Bangkok, I would venture to say that few of the villagers had ever seen a map of the world.

This would explain why, unfolding the trusty wall map I had brought from home (Mercator, unfortunately), I was immediately approached by two teachers, who politely requested an informal guest lecture about Where the Hell Everything Is.

First, of course, we found Nepal—they blanched at the sight of their own land, wedged between the geopolitical monsters of India and China. They nodded respectfully at the elegant landmass of North America, and bit their lower lips sizing up the Soviet Union.

The teachers were surprisingly well versed in current events, and, like tourists at Mann's Chinese Theater, delighted in spotting the "celebrity" countries featured so frequently on Radio Nepal. First they hunted out the most volatile areas of the world—like the Philippines, Korea, Iran and Iraq—then broke off to search gleefully for

Mexico and Thailand. Coming back to the Middle East, they looked around in puzzlement, and gaped when they found the tiny sliver that is Israel. "*Kasto sano!*" they cried, astonished. "It's even smaller than Nepal!"

The volleyball game ended, and we were surrounded by children. Their eyes and fingers centered on Asia, then fanned out to find India, Eurasia, America, Australia. Observing their faces observing the map, I felt as if I were watching two mirrors probing each other's depths. One reflected the physical world of landmass and ocean; the other, the world of hope and imagination. The images bounded and rebounded, disappearing into the future.

VERY ALIVE
IN A CAMBODIAN REFUGEE CAMP

In December 1979, I returned to the U.S. from my first trip to Asia: an 11-month odyssey that completely shattered and reshaped my worldview. A friend in Santa Barbara invited me to house-sit while she flew home for the holidays. Alone in the house, reeling from culture shock, I wrote a story about my still-fresh experiences on the Thai/Cambodian border. When the piece was done, I submitted it to the local weekly: the *News & Review*. The story appeared in January, 1980. One week later the paper's chief, Charles Rappleye, offered me the position of Cultural and Features editor.

I lived in Santa Barbara, the "Versailles of the Pacific," for the next four years. It was a highly creative period, and led to many important associations, both personal and professional. Santa Barbara, for example, soon became the birthplace of *Islands* magazine.

The Cambodian situation, of course, changed dramatically during the course of my writing career—a fact I would observe first-hand, some 14 years later.

In early November of 1979, I was traveling as a tourist through Thailand. At the tail end of a year-long journey, I went to Bangkok to purchase an airline ticket for my return trip to California.

At that time the border conflicts between Vietnam and Cambodia had escalated severely, and displaced Cambodians had begun to flood the small camp at Sakaew. Thai newspapers seemed to be vying with each other to print the most pitiful and horrendous photographs of the refugees.

The actual situation inside of Cambodia was unclear to me. I was simply a tourist, happy to make the rounds of Bangkok's spectacular temples and bask upon the white beaches of Koh Samui. After a year of travel, the notion of a few weeks rest prior to my flight home appealed to me.

My situation was about to change. After only a week in Thailand I met up with Dorothy, a friend with whom I'd traveled intermittently through Greece, India and Nepal. A Harvard medical student, Dorothy claimed she would be unable to relax or enjoy herself in any fashion until she offered her skills to the United Nations or Red Cross. She encouraged me to continue my travels alone—but her own path was decided.

My conscience immediately began to nag me. If there was a need for volunteers, how could I ignore it? Just as visitors in the vicinity of a forest fire are required by law to help quell the blaze, so I felt that the war in Cambodia represented a vast human conflagration. Although I was unsure what skills I might offer at the camps, it seemed clear that on some level my presence could be useful.

After making a few queries and scrambling through a mass of red tape, Dorothy was able to arrange transportation for herself and ten other volunteers to a then-unknown camp. Situated right on the Thai/Cambodian border, the Khao-I-Dang camp had barely been mapped out; nonetheless, refugees were already arriving by the thousands.

The first camp, at Sakaew, was officially a disaster area. The opportunity now existed to set up an alternative camp, much larger but also much closer to the fighting. Since the Khao-I-Dang facility had just opened its gates, skills of all kinds were needed: everything from surgery to latrine-digging. If I could not define my own skills for the camp, the camp would no doubt provide those definitions for me.

And so, when Dorothy's bus left Bangkok—on November 20, 1979—I was aboard it.

...

November 21

"If you find you can't take it," Chris, a veteran of Sakaew tells us on the bus, "go back. No one will think any less of you. A lot of people come here totally unprepared for what they're going to see. It's terrible; beyond anything they might have expected."

We arrive at the bamboo gate of the Khao-I-Dang refugee camp after passing half a dozen military checkpoints, where bored guards wave us on after one look at our Caucasian faces. The embryonic compound consists of a vast spread of hasty shelters and medical facilities; only 5,000 of the expected 200,000 Khmers have yet arrived. As we drive along a dirt road in search of the volunteer coordinator, Cambodians grin at us from their shanty lean-tos of bamboo and plastic. A few shout phrases in English; greetings. But aside from a handful of pathetically sick children (one, her distended bowels a lurid red, stares blankly from the roadside) most of the refugees look healthy, actively engaged in the construction of shelters and campfires. This new camp, so perilously close to the border, is not the chamber of horrors we expected after viewing photographs of Sakaew.

Though only one day old, Khao-I-Dang seems remarkably established, almost livable. The paralyzing rush of refugees has not yet occurred. Many Khmers, in fact, have been refused permission to migrate to this camp from their hideaways, just inside Cambodia. Their leaders fear that in the sunny, open camp they'll be "sitting ducks" for an attack—for once the Khmers cross the border into Thailand they must surrender their arms, forfeiting their soldier status. As a result only women, children, the elderly and sick may come to the camp. Able-bodied soldiers remain in Cambodia—as the men clearly seem to prefer. There is much to defend.

Just on the Thai side of the frontier, buses supplied by the UNHCR (United Nations High Commissioner for Refugees) await the fleeing Khmers and transport them to Khao-I-Dang. It is the official nightmare that, on a busy day, a dozen buses an hour might arrive, bringing in 6,000 new refugees. But even this may not be fast enough; there is talk of Thai military units escorting 10,000 Khmers a day along their eight-mile exodus.

We arrive late in the afternoon and are given time to explore the camp on foot while the authorities—as confused as ourselves—decide what to do with us. A short walk takes me through the populated section, a tiny percentage of the total available space. Smoke rises from myriad small fires; plastic flaps in a steady breeze. Children, as ever, have found the tools of play and chase each other around. Laughing brightly, they seem the embodiment of hope.

Clusters of Khmers squat around their austere tents, forking boiled vegetables over rice. One family gestures to me, offering to share their food. Along the periphery of the settlement, young men with machetes hack at scrawny trees while a gleaming backhoe scrapes the earth. Pick-up trucks, bearing sacks of rice and rations, form the heads of long queues while relief workers distribute cabbages, oranges, potatoes and dried fish.

The refugees, new to this system of linear distribution, line up with gleeful ceremony. Standing at rigid attention, they form perfectly straight lines.

More chaotic is the "line" for building supplies. The man in charge of distribution needs 50 arms to police his bamboo poles, which snake off in all directions as he howls for cooperation. In equal demand are posts, plastic buckets, and tarpaulins.

The sections of the camp allotted for water supply and washing are horrendous, thrown together without care or intelligence. Already there exist vast swamps, through which Khmers wade waist-deep in muck toward cubic steel water tanks. Each day, 70 water trucks empty a total of nearly 40,000 gallons into these tanks. Without proper drainage, the ground beneath them has become a muddy lagoon into which the tanks collapse, often rupturing. Unless this problem is tackled soon, the swamps will breed malaria and cholera epidemics of devastating proportions.

We are at last recruited, albeit for grunt work: loading a truck with plastic tarpaulins, so they can be removed from the camp grounds and placed under guard at the supply depot. The man recruiting us, familiar to me as the helpless victim of the bamboo pole fiasco, urges

us to board his truck "as goddamned fast as you goddamned can"—
he's left his station unattended in order to locate us. As we pile onto
the open flatbed, Tom, the volunteer coordinator, rushes up. He tells
us that our living arrangements are "uncertain," but that, tonight at
least, the twelve of us will sleep outside the UNHCR house in the
nearby town of Aranyaprathet. A Land Rover carrying three four-
person tents will meet us there "within the hour."

Thus relieved of our most basic worry—sleep—we hop aboard
the pick-up and ride toward the distribution point. Eager Cambodians of all ages are being chased away from the precious plastic by
shouting Khmer leaders. The bamboo itself has completely vanished.

Just before we reach the loading area, our truck becomes helplessly mired. The worst of the water-tank swamps has completely
claimed the roadway. As our driver spins the wheels in desperation,
a geyser of mud shoots up through the truck's missing floorboards.
The crowd of curious Khmers roars with appreciation as the volunteers are instantly coated with slime. After long minutes a bulldozer
tows us from the muck, and we set to work.

By the time we arrive in Aranyaprathet it is dark. The moon gleams,
iridescent with earthlight, the stars blaze, and neither the Land Rover
nor our tents are anywhere in sight. The UNHCR house itself, mutely
official, seems elite and out-of-bounds. Four of us—Dorothy, Richard, Carol and myself—hike into town.

Dinner is a fiasco. We wait well over an hour for a meal that,
unfortunately, arrives... and then we see the bill! Aranyaprathet's
merchants, it seems, plan to take full advantage of their foreign guests.

November 22
This morning the 12 volunteers are gathered together and assigned
tasks based on our skills. Dorothy, a medical student, joins the American Refugee Committee; Richard, a Civil Engineer, is assigned road-
building and heavy equipment operation along with his wife, Carol.
Eight of the volunteers have no special skills, and are distributed
amongst the distributors. Reluctant to be a supply shoveler, I tell
Tom that, as a sculptor, I'd acquired a number of engineering skills.

He regards me warily. "What kinds of 'skills?'"

"Well, I've built playgrounds... and designed a few fountains." I doubt that any engineering job within the camp is terribly complex; it all looks pretty mechanical. And I desperately wish to avoid passing out buckets.

"Okay," Tom says, briefly considering. "You're on water."

"Water?" I await a more specific assignment.

"Yeah. The water systems. This camp is going to have ten sectors, and each sector will need at least six water areas. Have you walked around? Have you seen what's happening at the water points?"

I assure him that I have.

"Well, those swampy areas have got to be drained, and new ones with drainage have got to be built. And we have to build a lot of them and we have to do it *fast*, because we're expecting an emergency rush of about 80,000 people—within the next three days."

"Sure," I tell him. "Who do I report to? Who do I see?"

"*See?*" He looked at me with incomprehension. "You don't *see* anyone. This problem has just developed, and it's your job to solve it."

"Me? Alone? For the whole camp?"

"No. We'll get you some workers." A worried pause. "Look, if you don't think you can handle this, say so now and I'll find someone else."

"I'll do it," I declare boldly, regretting my vanity at once. I feel as if I've just leaped forward to volunteer for guillotine testing.

I gather up a dozen Khmer workers, led by a wizened man in a straw hat who introduces himself as Mr. Sony. "Like the radio," he says. Working from scattered bits of rumor, it takes half the day to locate hand hoes and start the men clearing brush; I want to begin a fresh area. Towards three in the afternoon the men become restless, demanding water. "Wait here," I say, and run off. When I return with the water only Mr. Sony remains, standing sheepishly beside a pile of abandoned hoes. We wander off together in pursuit of our workers— but by the time we retrieve five of them, all the hoes have been stolen.

At the end of the day, as the volunteers ride back into town, Dorothy tells us she was interviewed in the medical tent by CBS.

"You wouldn't *believe* those journalists!" she growls. "Every time you look around, somebody's breathing down your neck with a camera."

"What did they want to know?"

"They asked me if I realized that today was Thanksgiving."

This brings a murmur of pure astonishment, for we had all forgotten.

November 23

I am given a large group of actual Thai laborers, who are paid at 5 p.m. for their day's work. The eight women and twelve men are led by a self-appointed foreman, eleven years old. The boy's command of English is limited to two words: "Okay," and "Disco!" I quickly teach myself how to count to ten in Thai. Through hand-signals, drawings and ambitious pantomimes we succeed in clearing off one new area and setting up two dozen water tanks.

No sooner have the brass spigots been screwed into place than the water trucks appear. With their arrival, pandemonium ensues. The lengths of bamboo we'd laid down as flooring are whisked away in the melee, while scores of bucket-toting refugees—kids, mostly— make it impossible for my crew to dig the drainage ditches. I find myself racing off for aid, as the laborers savor American cigarettes. But no help is available, and frankly, I'm not even sure what kind of help I need. A guard? A bullhorn? The military? By early evening, the site is well on its way to becoming just another swamp. The pre- teen foreman has managed to dig a single, narrow channel, which directs a thin trickle toward a dry riverbed. His effort, though he- roic, seems but a thumb in the dike.

I visit Dorothy in the ARC hospital during lunch. It's a complex of long, airy tents, roofed with translucent blue nylon. Cots butt against each other; straw mats cover the dusty dirt floors. Each In- ternational Red Cross team, I learn, has its own specialty: the Ger- mans provide surgery, French doctors administer in Obstetrics, Gy- necology and Pediatrics, and the Americans serve Acute Adult Medi- cine. Few specialized drugs are available; simple antibiotics, aspi- rin, re-hydration mixtures, malaria treatments and vitamins must suffice. Most of the adult cases involve malaria or dysentery, though

there are a few wounded soldiers, and a number of elderly patients
with serious illnesses. Children are seen everywhere, munching on
high-calorie biscuits, their swollen bellies and matchstick limbs illustrating the advanced stages of malnutrition.

Thanks to a constant flow of international donations, there is plenty
of food at the camp. Some are absurd: like the palette of bittersweet
chocolate that, donated by the government of Israel, has melted into
an ant-covered hillock. Fortunately, the UNHCR supplies basic nu-
tritional needs, while merchants from Aranyaprathet infiltrate the
camp and enjoy a handsome black-market profit in bananas, cigarettes, Coca-Cola and popsicles. At first, I can hardly believe the
refugees are willing to waste money on such junk—but by late afternoon, I am not above waiting in line for a frozen jackfruit bar.

November 24
Many of the relief workers staying in town claim they've heard
fighting during the night: mortars and M-16s. I must have been dead
asleep. It just reminds us how tenuous our position really is; only
international attention on the camp (thanks, ironically, to the intru-
sive media) prevents the war from spilling over the border into Thailand, and into the camp itself.

Today, using the same Thai laborers, I try out a new system: digging the drainage pits *first*—then placing the square tanks upon long,
flat boards, which keeps their legs from sinking into the wet earth.
Richard and Carol—the heavy equipment team—suggest that, in
the future, we should map out exactly where the water tanks will go
in advance. They'll bulldoze those areas flat, clearing the rubble. I
add that we might want to gravel those areas, and slope them along
lines of natural drainage.

We discuss these strategies during an engineer's meeting. These
now occur three times each day. Khao-I-Dang is growing at the rate
of about 5,000 people a day, and coordinating the roads, toilets and
water systems is a full-time task in itself. Somehow, the very desperation of our situation seems to produce a startling level of com-
petence, and the wheels of progress steadily gain speed. There is no

competition between minds in the tent; room for such concerns does not exist.

My workers do well this afternoon. We're beginning to understand each other intuitively, and they clearly enjoy teaching me bits of Thai (though what they enjoy most, I suspect, is my hopeless mispronunciation). I find myself acting like a Boy Scout troop leader, which amuses them enormously; they love watching me enact typically American stereotypes. Still, there is much mutual respect. Between the Thai workers and Cambodian refugees, I note, there is only a benevolent curiosity. There, too, lies a language barrier.

During a break I approach a group of refugee children sitting in a circle. To my horror, they are playing merrily with a sack of used hypodermic needles. I race off to the medical tents, where Dorothy acknowledges the problem: the hospital has no proper disposal system.

"And if they see us burying them," she says, "they'll just dig them up. It's like a game."

I mention the problem at the five o'clock meeting; a couple of others have also seen kids playing with needles. Rob MacDonald, the camp's chief engineer, grunts in agreement. "They use 'em as squirt guns," he says.

Carol pipes up with a wry bit of intelligence. Though we westerners refer to Khao-I-Dang simply as "the Camp," it now has an official title: CHUNK I. The "Crisis Holding Unit for Nationalist Khmers." I wonder who was paid to come up with that fanciful acronym, and how much.

We all remark on another abomination: this afternoon, incredible as it may seem, a caravan of Japanese tourists arrived. They dismounted from their tour buses clutching tiny cameras, and wandered in a chatty group through the medical compound. There, they posed alongside the wretched and the weary, grinning broadly for the lenses. The volunteers watched, astounded; we had thought nothing could be worse than the international media.

"It's not just the Japanese," says Chris, who had accompanied us on our maiden trip to the camp. "In the early days of Sakaew, buses full of western 'volunteers' arrived daily from Bangkok—a three-hour drive. They spent they day wandering through the misery with their Nikons, before boarding the evening bus home."

That information partially explains why volunteers—and there are now more than 50 of them in Khao-I-Dang—are on the lowest rung of the ladder. Told in Bangkok that food and shelter would be provided, many of them arrive here ready to work, but with little or no money. And then they learn the expensive realities of the situation. At this point Dorothy, Richard, Carol and I have been permitted to crash on the floor of the UNHCR living room. But the "unskilled" volunteers share a dank, claustrophobic cement room that, infested with stinging red ants, lies within the compound of the local military prison. With two primitive toilets, and no food provided, their privation approaches that of the refugees themselves. I complain about the situation to Tom, but it seems doubtful that anything will be done. The plight of these good-hearted people fills me with bitterness; the official U.N. "presence" is enjoying every creature comfort, and drawing six-figure salaries as well.

And if I see another damned tour bus, I swear I'll slash its tires. Let the Japanese have a *real* thrill: "I Spent the Night in a Refugee Camp."

November 26
The noon meeting in the engineer's tent revolves around toilets. Carol, and an uprooted Peace Corps volunteer named Larry are working on that together.

"We've got four latrines completely dug out with the backhoe," Carol says, "and we're almost out of Sector Three. Tomorrow we should get as far as Sector Five, which is only populated to 40% capacity."

"Give it all you've got," Rob MacDonald says. "The refugees just keep coming."

"We *are* picking up speed," Larry adds. "The problem is, we've got one very good group of workers, but the second group's just really slow. Always bullshitting. I want to ask you about firing the foreman. What's the policy?"

"Thai or Cambodian?" MacDonald asks.

"He's Thai."

"Go ahead then, fire him. But let's keep that good group going. Pick two foremen, and raise their salaries to 75 *baht* a day. Give the rest of the workers a five-baht raise. We've got to hang on to the ones who can work together."

MacDonald asks me how the water systems are going. "Pretty good," I admit. "We were given two trucks this morning, and managed to hold onto them. Also, gravel has started coming in; enough for four complete sites. We'll finish all four of those today, maybe get another one done just for kicks. My workers are a good team, too. But it takes them forever to spread all that dumped gravel with their hand hoes."

This is discussed, and MacDonald grants me the services of a road grader. "That'll save you guys a tremendous amount of time," he reflects. "But go ahead and give your workers a raise anyway."

I am empowered to raise the laborers to 55 baht a day. One baht is equal to five cents. It's a handsome increase.

My group, God bless 'em, is already at work when I return from the meeting. After finding a translator, I tell everyone about the raise. I also pick two new foremen; a muscular young guy who speaks basic English and wears a Singha Beer T-shirt, and a quiet old man, chosen for his seniority. The group listens attentively, almost solemnly. The raise has inspired their confidence; I can almost *see* them gel into a more cohesive working unit.

I pass out cigarettes—always a celebratory gesture. As I'm about to light my own, an old woman with raven-black eyes and a woven bamboo hat jumps to her feet and jogs up to me.

"Boss, boss!" she shouts, "Disco dance! Disco!" She grabs my hands and, with amazing expertise, performs a brief repertoire of steps and spins. I am not up to her talent and she is not up to my chest, but we succeed in creating a brief air of hilarity amid a landscape of shattered lives.

All through the day the backhoes work, surrounded by fascinated throngs of Khmers. Under Carol's direction, the hoes dig huge trenches to drain away the swamps via underground ducts. By late afternoon the deepest lagoon is only moist mud, cracking beneath the Asian sun.

Dorothy shows up at our engineer's meeting at the end of the day. Over the past week, she reports, there have been seven deaths—compared to fourteen a day at Sakaew. Seven deaths, and eleven births in a village of 30,000. No different, really, than any American city.

MacDonald asks what will be done with corpses. The U.N., Dorothy informs us, in its own inimitable way, has the situation covered. A cultural "task force" has been sent from Bangkok, to determine whether the bodies should be buried or cremated, as per Khmer custom. The experts made their call; a graveyard was set aside for burial.

"But what I came for," she says, "is this." She leans over the table, and opens a canvas sack. Inside are scores of used hypodermic needles. "Every time I see a child with one of these, I offer to trade for a sweet. Well, word got around that I was buying needles at a good rate, and about 50 kids came running up to barter. But I ran out of candy, so a bunch of them are coming back tomorrow."

"Oh, no!" Carol says, only half amused. "By that time...."

"I know," Dorothy whispers. "There may be *thousands* of them."

"A good opportunity," observes Richard, "to get rid of that chocolate."

November 27

What did the Khmer refugees do before they became refugees?

They were doctors, professors, Ministers of Agriculture, housewives, college students, journalists. Mr. Sony, manager of my Cambodian volunteer workers, was a plant geneticist. Mr. Longnam, my best drainage man, was Director of Advertising for Cambodian Airlines. Mrs. Hue, the disco-dancer, was a French teacher before Pol Pot's Beijing-backed Khmer Rouge killed her husband (a veterinarian), their children, and her seven brothers and sisters.

The "progressive" Pol Pot regime, bent on the destruction of the Khmer intelligentsia, killed people who wore glasses for fear they could read. Possession of photographs was punishable by death. So many doctors have been killed that the Cambodians, in desperation, now resort to faith healers. Scores of Khmers will always wear the scars of those "healing" rituals.

The "Free" Khmers at Khao-I-Dang fled their homes as Khmer Rouge and Vietnamese forces began battling within Cambodia. Caught in this communist crossfire, many of them crawled through the forests of the frontier toward the dubious shelter of the camps. Some carried infants; most survived without food or water for many days.

Cambodia is in the middle of a genocide that may approach the figures of Hitler's Third Reich. But the most startling thing about it is that the refugees themselves, living in mud, dust, and complete austerity, maintain a calm humor about their situation. At Khao-I-Dang, both Khmer Rouge and Khmer S'ri (Pol Pot's Red Khmers and the Free Khmers, respectively)—bitter enemies inside Cambodia—live and work together without incident. And, from the smallest child to the most aged adult, no one ever seems to complain—about anything.

This afternoon, a Cambodian man emerges from the plastic sheets of his tent, dressed in a business suit and black tie. He carries a small packet in the palm of his hand. I question him, and he explains in excellent English that today is a special occasion. He is bringing color photographs of his family, smuggled from Phnom Penh, to show a group of Red Cross volunteers in the Refugee Reception Tent.

I join him on the short walk to the "processing" area. A small crowd of silent volunteers watch silently as this man, who spent four years studying architecture at Boston University, leafs through his memories.

"Those are my three nephews, at Angkor Wat. And here I am, you see, with my wife and her brothers, at Rockefeller Center in New York City." He pokes the images with his finger. "Dead," he says. "Him, him, him. My wife also, dead."

At that point, incredibly, he smiles. "*I* have very much luck," he says.

November 29

The water sites are flying together. By the time I get my workers to each sector, the drainage is dug and the gravel spread. It's almost as if there's not *enough* work now. We've seen no swamping yet, on any of the graveled sites. I tell this to Rob MacDonald, who shrugs. "It's only a matter of time."

"The big joke," Larry adds, "is that all the refugees are supposed to move to another camp further inland, right?" He gives a wry snort. "So this is theoretically just a 'holding camp': Temporary Residents Only."

"The actual theory," Richard says, "is that they'll return home, to Cambodia, when the fighting stops."

"That's always the theory. But the truth," Larry concludes, "Is that they'll be here forever. For a million years."

"Boy," Rob mutters. "I'd hate to see this place after a million years!"

This invites laughter, but we all agree that it would be a real mess— and that it wouldn't take a million years.

Official estimates now put the population of Khao-I-Dang at more than 35,000 people. Outrageous as this may be, it's a mere trickle of what we can expect at the first new offensive.

Our engineer's meeting waxes philosophical. The problem at Khao-I-Dang is not space: we have plenty of that. The problem is setting up facilities with assembly-line rapidity, keeping one step ahead of the advancing throngs. This, in itself, is theoretically possible. What is impossible is to build such systems so that they will *last*.

We finish early, and ride into town on the school bus reserved for the volunteers. Thanks to Rob MacDonald's efforts, Dorothy, Richard, Carol and I now reside in comfortable hotel rooms, right in town. The unskilled volunteers are still encamped in the prison. They have been supplied, however, with roll-up mattresses and mosquito netting. Inspired by the refugees, they have not complained. To the contrary, thanks to a powerful *esprit de corps*, they've turned their situation around. A few guitars, a bottle or two of Mekong whiskey, a co-ed dorm; our hotel rooms now seem almost desolate in comparison.

November 30

Tom, aware of my imminent departure, assigns me five bright-eyed U.N. volunteers this morning: new blood. "Train them," he orders.

It is my last day at the camp, and it's a hectic one. We're frantically working in two sectors at once, far out by the bordering hills.

The morning is spent teaching the new recruits the finer points of drainage digging. At 11 a.m., it occurs to me to ask the volunteers how long they plan to stay on at Khao-I-Dang. Not one of them is staying through the week! I storm back to the noon meeting, full of piss and vinegar. After lunch, Tom finally finds a single individual who will replace me: a man named Steve who, until yesterday, was a temple-hopping tourist from Great Britain. We're introduced in the engineer's tent, and I bring him outside to meet the crew. I like him, and—far more importantly—so do the workers.

The Thai government, obscenely, will not allow U.N. volunteers to renew their visas in Bangkok; they must leave the country and return. Thus even Steve must leave in a couple of weeks. A few days in Malaysia, then back up over the border with another two-month stamp. It'll be nice when the bureaucracy catches up to the realities of this dire situation.

Steve learns fast; he's had more experience than I in the engineering field. Once he's operating on his own, I leave him in charge of the team and wander around to shoot some pictures. The sunlight, as usual, is harsh and grating, and I keep my palm tightly over the lens as clouds of fine dust blow across the camp's unpaved roads. But I'm grateful for the few hours; at last I have an opportunity to relax, walk about, and record a visual homage to this remarkable community.

Above all, I enjoy a feeling of great satisfaction. I never dreamed, when I reluctantly left Koh Samui an impossible ten days earlier, that I could do so much good in such a brief span of time; or that I'd have to wrestle such a crucial set of responsibilities. By now, of course, the water system installations are routine. The creativity has evaporated, and now it's a simple matter of coordinating the assembly teams and graveling crew. Steve's intensely committed, and should have few problems.

Exploring the camp on foot, I'm amazed at the growth rate since our first busload of twelve volunteers arrived. Modest tents disappear into the distance, as far as the eye can see, and a constant whirl of activity fills the roadways. "Veteran" refugees, who have lived at Khao-I-Dang since its conception two weeks ago, gossip around cooking fires or joke by the food distribution points. Many relax in hammocks, smoking cigarettes and writing hopeful letters to friends and relations in Europe, India or the United States.

Meanwhile a constant stream of beleaguered survivors, carrying tattered duffle bags and starving children, flows off buses and into the lines at the Reception Tent—and then into the ever-more remote living areas of Khao-I-Dang itself.

I watch a few families set up their perfunctory shelters. They build fires, and send their children with buckets to carry water from distribution sites completed only hours before. The children make a wild game of it, shrieking with pleasure as they splash and shower each other.

"Take picture!!! Hello, hello, take picture!" The parents yell to me, grinning and pointing to the antics of their kids. Some things, I suppose, are eternal.

My original image of the Khmer people, as a doomed race beyond hope or salvation, has evaporated. Here in this camp I have witnessed little else but hope. Hope, tremendous dignity, and a vast equanimity, an acceptance of the present moment completely unparalleled in western behavior. All of this, plus the pure joy of simply being alive—very alive, in spite of unspeakable suffering. And in spite of the statistics.

THE GREAT WHITE WAIL

During my 1983-1984 Rotary Fellowship in Nepal, I wrote some 450 letters to the friends and artists I'd left behind in Santa Barbara. Every single letter was typed on the "portable" Smith-Corona I'd carried to Kathmandu in my backpack, and copied with a sheet of carbon paper. Upon my return to the U.S., Santa Barbara typographer Jim Cook published a dozen of these letters in his bi-monthly arts and literary journal, *ConneXions*. The following year (1986), working with publisher John Daniel, Cook spearheaded my first book: *Mister Raja's Neighborhood: Letters from Nepal*. Many still consider these fearlessly personal vignettes my best writing; and though I dare not agree, I'd give just about anything to recapture the raw, reckless style of my late twenties.

NIGHT MOVES... in a plush living room with the mosquitoes buzzing, the sound of bells outside, always bells even if they're only voices, the dogs that never stop barking, the horns of the nouveau-riche, sound of my own breathing, arrogance of the man alone. My senses are sharpening as to what's going on around here and I'm keeping good company, though none of it stays the night. Only the 'skeeters....

What do I see? Gods and clouds reflected in scummy puddles; my reflection in a bowl of *mo-mo* soup; the brown faces with white teeth and a weird sense of what's funny that I seem to share; the holes burned through my stack of typing paper by the smoldering incense I forgot about; a tree stump hammered thick with ten thousand nails, each one a prayer to the goddess of smallpox; rainbows every evening as the sun breaks under the thick belly of the sky and shoots to where it's been raining.

But it hasn't rained for two days now. It's impossible to move from point A to point B without a thin scum forming on your body. No amount of the parasite-polluted water can clean you for long. Scratch mosquito bites and worms of dirt roll under your fingers.

. . .

Write me a letter and you're in my world, but I know damned well it's a stranger world than any of my friends out there can speculate. We carry sticks to fend off rabid dogs, boil the buffalo milk for 20 minutes before daring to drink it. The flowers that grow here eat human flesh, and all our peanut butter is imported from India. Twice a day the electricity fails, plunging us into darkness or silent light.

As I came out of Narayan's Pie Shop this evening I saw an odd scene in the center of the blacked-out intersection just outside the restaurant's front door. Someone had built a weird little shrine on the ground—complete with clay figurines, incense, a burning candle, an offering of cooked rice and about a dozen five-*paise* coins. It was all right out there, on the scrambled pavement, miraculously spared by the wheels of the rickshaws and bicycles hurrying by in the otherwise dark. I crept up to have a look, then asked the teenager running the pharmacy next to Narayan's for the story.

"For coots," he said cryptically.

"Coots?"

"No, no, COATS!" He started to laugh. "Like night-time they are coming: bad coats."

Suddenly I understood. Everything in Nepal is understood suddenly, or not at all. "Ghosts!" I shouted. "You mean ghosts!"

"Yes, yes! Goats!"

We had established that the bizarre construction somehow related to spirits, but my further attempts to draw the boy out proved futile. By the time I glanced back at the shrine a dog had appeared and was gobbling up the rice. A few ragged kids came by and stole the coins. A passing rickshaw smashed the figurines. Still, the candle did not go out.

Rode home past the unimaginable stinks and the hulking shadows of sleeping cows, the racy panic of barking dogs, black alleyways illuminated for blinding instants as gigantic buses heave by spewing clouds of diesel, black on black, to the posh safety, the rugs and warm lamps and wicker of this house. Sometimes I just want to bolt the door behind me, although there's nothing and no one to fear. It's an E-ticket ride out there.

· · ·

Everything you have heard is true, and I'm sure that by now you've heard everything. Sacred cow shit on my shoe, inundating even the laces, still disgusts me, nor have I grown accostumed to the malign belches of the diesel buses, so thoughtfully donated by the Japanese. But such things would repel me anywhere. The fact is that I have come to take the city of Kathmandu at face value. I never cease to be amazed by the color and contrast, but I'm no longer reduced to gaping when I stumble across a burning body, or see a little boy dressed like an elephant. Don't know if I'm going native, or becoming the Perfect Spectator. Sometimes, though, it works against me—like when a friend and I visited Dakshinkali, one week ago.

Dakshinkali, the "southern shrine of Kali," is where the local Hindu goes on auspicious Saturdays and Tuesday to make a wish, to ask a favor large or small from that particular goddess. Ah, but everything has a price. Kali/Durga is the goddess of wrath and destruction; in order to petition her, one must make an offering of some sort. And there's only one sort she'll accept: blood.

The bus wasn't as cramped as some others I've been on—my groin grinding against the round, virginal rump of an otherwise unapproachable Nepali sylph—but the lack of human company was compensated by a preponderance of goats and chickens, all marked on the head with red *tika* powder. Outwardly calm, the goats farted incessantly. Ever experienced a goat fart? At any rate, we all "made nice" to these animals, for they were to be greatly honored, and destined to bring great luck to their households.

Uphill all the way. The monsoon clouds drew back a fraction, and we could see the impossible flanks of the Himals rising beyond the northern wall of the Kathmandu Valley. It's a sight to make your heart leap. Nothing on Earth compares, literally or spiritually. We crested ridge after ridge, and switchbacked down to a parking lot full of other buses.

The air was thick with smoke, and rancid with the odors of boiling flesh and freshly spilled blood. Along the river, beneath a maze-like confluence of bridges crowded with gorgeously dressed devotees, squatting men scooped entrails out of decapitated goat bodies and washed the whitened viscera in the clouded water. We descended into an area where the separate queues of men and women converged. That place—where visitors entered the sacrificial pit—was densely packed, and I couldn't see a thing. But patience won out. After hanging around for a while the crowd shifted, and I found myself pressed against the metal bars of the shrine, telephoto lens in hand, staring with fascinated revulsion at the black stone idols utterly bathed in thick crimson; at the tiled ground ankle-deep in blood; at the rows of smiling, chatting women with flowers and incense and bare, blood-spattered feet.

As I stood waiting, two men—obviously the "executioners"—led an unresisting goat to an altar not six feet from my face. They carried curved blades, dulled from much use. Two gruesomely abluted idols, of Ganesh and Kali, waited expectantly. They sprinkled holy water on the animal's neck, scratched it with deceptively gentle fingers— then grabbed it by the legs, pulled the head back, and began sawing.

I was fine while I snapped the photos. I caught the first few slices, the blood spurting onto the deities, the goat's struggles, the headless body kicking on the ground. Snap, snap, snap. Then I backed away, and as my lungs filled with acrid smoke and the smell of death, I

sank onto a bench. My ears were ringing, and I felt the blood draining from my face. Every pore opened, and I was instantly drenched
with sweat. My vision began to blur and, realizing that I was about to
faint, I plunged my head between my knees and tried to breathe
deeply. It worked, thank God. Fainting at Dakshinkali would have
been a pretty humiliating experience, though I'm certain it's happened before.

As Tom Wolfe was told by Ken Kesey: "You can't fool around with
this stuff without getting some of it on you."

Even now, the memory of what I witnessed fills me with loathing.
You go through your life here, dodging cows, smiling at the monks
with their new quartz watches, stopping at the import stores to buy
the latest Elvis Costello cassette, and you forget how thinly the veneer of western influence is pasted over what is basically a very
superstitious and pagan society. It makes me think neither more nor
less of the Nepalese, but it sure opens my eyes as to where I really
am. This is *not* Middle Earth.

EROTIC WONDERS OF THE ELLORA CAVES

For a brief but glorious spell, the European magazine *GEO*—sort of like *National Geographic*, but with soul—maintained a foothold on the American continent. On a visit to Manhattan in 1983 I barged into the *GEO* offices, cornered the first editor I met (Richard Conniff), and lobbied for an assignment. It wouldn't cost much, I insisted; I was going to Asia anyhow, on a Journalism Fellowship with the Rotary Foundation. The big-hearted Conniff gave me a break, and this story was the result. It appeared on the cover of the final American *GEO*, in October 1984. The story was the first I ever wrote in Kathmandu—and includes my first published reference to the sly and sagacious Lalji, an India-born seer who would play a pivotal role in both *Mr. Raja's Neighborhood* and *Shopping for Buddhas*.

ONE AUTUMN MORNING, preparing to leave the kingdom of Nepal, I paid a final visit to my friend Lalji—a high-spirited mystic who had frequently (and always with great accuracy) advised me on matters both personal and professional.

"So you are off to Bombay," Lalji reflected. "You have been in that region before?"

I assured him that I had.

"Then there is no need," he continued with a smile, "to insist that you visit the Ellora caves."

"I'm afraid I've never heard of the place."

Lalji nodded, never altering his amused expression. This was obviously the answer he had expected.

"The caves of Ellora," he repeated. "Near Aurangabad. They are perhaps the greatest wonder of the ancient world. Until you have seen them, you have not seen India."

. . .

Stepping off a ramshackle Indian bus less than a week later, I discovered that the word *caves* is a mere convenience. Ellora is a strand of 34 magnificent rock-cut temples, hewn from a sweeping basalt cliff between the sixth and the 11th centuries A.D. The first thing that struck me was not the individual caves, but Ellora's situation as a whole. Clusters of half-hidden temples pock the domineering earthscape, punctuated by waterfalls and linked by rough stairways. Unlike their heavily trafficked neighbors at Ajanta, these monuments retain a musty aura of mystery and reserve. Wandering about the site, it is possible to feel that you've discovered them yourself.

Carved during an epoch when Buddhism's thousand-year grip on the subcontinent was slowly loosening, the caves span three major faiths. Buddhist hammers gave way to Hindu, then the Jain artists took their turn carving the weathered stone. More remarkable than its immense store of art, though, is the effect Ellora gives of an almost musical continuity. The ancient architects clearly enjoyed an inspired dialogue, drawing constantly from one another's creations.

Yet every cave is different, successive generations of artists having gleefully changed—or broken—the rules set by their masters. The Buddhists began in an almost claustrophobic vein. It seems the early monks were determined to bury themselves in the earth, the better to renounce the world. Their style gradually blossoms, though, climaxing with a vaulted cathedral where precise acoustics lend the human voice a tuba-like resonance. Deep in the half-light, demure stone Buddhas gesture with symbolic *mudras*, a concise vocabulary of hand motions. They seem to smile as one approaches; yet the effect is calming, not eerie.

The Hindu caves explode into life, a startling contrast. Galleries of gods and goddesses burst from the invaded stone, vigorously portrayed in scenes of dance, heroism and erotic love. A legend tells how the deities petitioned Indra, King of Heaven, for the privilege of spending a full-moon night on Earth. Mesmerized by the glowing cliffs of Ellora, the gods and nymphs failed to return home by sunrise. They remain clasped in the cool stone, frozen forever in their bawdy festivities. To enter these energetic temples after the sobriety of the Buddhist caves is like gulping fresh air after a long dive; perhaps it was this very playfulness—the hijinx of the Hindu pantheon—that lured central India back from Buddhism.

Sexual images are abundant in many of the Hindu caves. The Hindu gods—Brahma, Vishnu and Shiva—attained their full powers only when the energy of their female consorts was released. At Ellora, the most common expression of this sexual release is the *yoni-linga*, two sculptures that, together, symbolize the creative energy of the universe. The *linga*, carved as an erect penis, represents the power to create. The *yoni*, shaped like a stylized vulva, consists of a stone base that encloses the shaft of the linga—releasing its sexual/creative energy. Devotees honor these images with water, milk and butter: a ritual that celebrates the beginning of life.

The third and final group of caves was executed between the ninth and 11th centuries by the Jains, under the good grace of their Hindu rulers. Espousing an underdog doctrine similar to (but stricter than) Buddhism, the ailing Jains badly needed the high-profile advertising that an exhibition at Ellora would provide. Aiming to please, they fashioned five temples that combine the meditative qualities of the Buddhists with the exuberance of the Hindus. These caves, too, are filled with sculpted deities, some of which are reminiscent of the Buddha. Though the Jains eschewed the worship of idols, they evidently preferred compromise to extinction. But even if their priests were skeptical, their artists had their hearts in it.

. . .

Ellora hearkens back to a time when the great religions coexisted not only in harmony, but under the spell of mutual admiration. What made this possible was the enlightened rule of two vast dynasties that, together, spanned half a millennium: the Chalukyas and the Rashtrakutas. Still, it seems hard to believe that two successive empires found the strength of purpose—and funds—to support the efforts at Ellora; particularly when the religious sentiments of the artists happened to differ from their own.

"Yet perhaps," says Dr. T.V. Pathy, leaning across a desk cluttered with photographs and index cards, "it was this very tolerance that allowed those rulers to survive as long as they did." The head of the Department of History and Ancient Indian Culture at Aurangabad's Marathwada University, Pathy has devoted nearly a decade to solving the riddles of the caves.

"Those kings, you see, were governed by norms that are somewhat uncommon today. One of the major social duties of India's past rulers was known as 'the responsibility of the teacher.' It was the sacred obligation of the Chalukyas and the Rashtrakutas to not only defend the religious practices of their subjects, but to actively promote them as well."

Under the influence of this embracing patronage, Ellora became more than a complex of temples. It developed into a township, one of the great religious and educational centers of medieval India. Artists, architects, designers and religous figures flocked to the cliffs from the far corners of the subcontinent. While political intrigues and blood feuds etched their way across the land, the sequestered caves of Ellora remained an oasis of quiet.

· · ·

Of all the caves, the one known formally as Number 16 stands in a class by itself. This is the peerless Kailasa Temple, initiated in the eighth century by Krishna I, the first of the Rashtrakutas. He opened the dynasty with style. According to Hindu mythology, Kailasa is the Himalayan home of Lord Shiva, Lord of Creation and Destruction, Master of the Dance.

Doing justice to Shiva was not an easy task. Sculpted top-down from a massive outcropping of live rock, Kailasa is probably the world's largest monolithic structure. According to the blend of legend and fact that comprises much of the region's distant history, it took thousands of artists somewhere between 30 and 100 years to complete the job. Two hundred thousand tons of rock were excavated—but nothing was added. Every hallway, pillar and stairway was carved out from the existing escarpment. It was an ancient harbinger of Michelangelo's famous contention that the sculptures are already in the quarries—awaiting release from the stone.

The man-made chasm created by Kailasa is nearly 100 feet deep. In the center, the temple itself rests on a lavishly carved pedestal the approximate area of a football field. The whole structure is embellished with some of the liveliest stonework to be found in Asia. These include episodes from the great Hindu epic Ramayana, a virtual zoo of mythical beasts, and scenes from Shiva's rather active romantic life. I was not surprised to hear a legend that when Kailasa was completed, the gods themselves—Shiva, his voluptuous wife Parvati, and their elephant-headed son Ganesha—appeared at the opening reception to congratulate the artists personally.

Deep in the labyrinthine chambers of Kailasa, past the pillars and porticoes of the northern cells, it's possible to encounter an unlikely character with silvering hair, a silk scarf, and mirrored sunglasses. Kashinath Deore might be found reclining against a sculptured panel, arranging a display box of cast stone figurines. Appearances in India are often deceptive. This is no common peddler, seeking the fickle coinage of Kailasa's tourist trade. Deore, an alumnus of the famous J. J. Art School in Bombay, has worked at Ellora 27 years as the Government of India's Advisor for the Preservation of Sculpture and Painting.

"You might call these my hobby," he says, carefully wrapping the statuettes and fitting the lid onto his case. "How could any artist work in these temples, without receiving some small inspiration of his own?"

For nearly three decades, Deore has supervised the treadmill race against ther forces of decay at Ellora. "There's no question," he says, "that the condition of the temples has improved since the Archaeological Survey of India took over, just after independence." Stone may seem eternal, but time and the elements work their gradual damage. "Ellora's worst enemies are bats and water seepage," explains Deore. "You'd be amazed at how corrosive bat shit is. It does awful things to the walls and ceilings. We do what we can, but the best we can manage is preventive measures—screens and the like."

Deccan Trap, the geologic name by which Ellora's basalt is commonly known, is soft and porous. Water creeps through the site's innumerable fissures and invites vegetation and erosion. As the seasons change, the stone expands and contracts, emulating Shiva's terrible dance with ruinous consequences. "Without constant attention," Deore laments, "I wouldn't give this place more than another thousand years."

A natty figure amid the khaki-clad groundskeepers, Deore leads me past an area where workmen restore dilapidated pillars with a cunning mixture of cement and dye. We enter an elaborate chamber bristling with mythical figures. "But as you can see," he says, pointing with a fist to the shattered features of the deities, "the very worst damage has come from, shall we say, *unnatural* forces."

According to legend, the Mogul emperor Aurangzeb (the fundamentalist son of of Mumtaz Mahal, the concubine who inspired the Taj Mahal) was responsible for Ellora's worst vandalism. After seizing power in 1658, this Muslim despot waged an all-out war on non-Islamics, going so far as to remove the prayers from his kingdom's coins, lest they be polluted by the touch of non-believers. The emperor himself was said to have loved the caves, and often took his family there for outings. But worldly pleasures are fleeting, and the son of Shah Jahan took it upon himself to deface one of the greatest treasures of his kingdom—all in the name of Allah.

Journeymen, the story goes, under orders from Aurangzeb, set out to destroy the images at Ellora. The project was not approached systematically, however, and many sculptures remained untouched. The henchmen, dismayed by the seemingly endless scope of their task, began to content themselves with small bites. A cryptic smile; a regal nose; a provocative breast; the wrecking crews nipped selectively at Ellora's most delicate and expressive touches. That done, they lit brush fires in the caves. As bats poured shrieking from the dark chambers, black smoke discolored forever the lush murals and painted sculpture that had earned Kailasa the accolade *Rang Mahal*: the Palace of Colors. But despite their best efforts, neither the elements nor Aurangzeb did much to neutralize the magic of the caves. "After all," Dr. Pathy reflects, "an artistic imagination must always fill in. That is the way with history."

. . .

Having survived the caprices of its rulers, Ellora has become a quiet settlement, a brief stopover for tourists on their way to the more famous glories of Ajanta. No longer do caravans ply the ancient trade route between Paithan and Broach, resting at the caves for physical and spiritual renewal. The mesmerizing beat of tablas has been replaced by a frantic thumping at nearby Gunku School, where an old groundskeeper pounds a drum to frighten away the crows. But the creative life here continues; dancers, architects and painters still journey to Ellora to draw inspiration from its fount of vital stone.

Among this company is Deva Vasanthrao, an artist who visited Ellora to practice sketching and stayed for five months. "From the beginning, I've been fascinated with the ignored elements," Deva says, leafing through a portfolio of painstaking abstracts. "Let it be a broken flower, or a small rock that was left untouched by the artists; I'm confident I can evolve something."

Listening to the artist speak, I could not help considering the ambitions of the architects who first set eyes upon Ellora's naked cliffs—confident that they, too, could evolve something. "Evolution," in fact, seems to be the key word at Ellora. Lalji, as usual, was correct; nowhere else in the whole of India is the procession of the centuries cut in deeper relief.

POSTCARD FROM YOGYAKARTA

It was a great idea, suggested by the editor of *San Francisco*: write three tiny travel vignettes, meant to be read as postcards. Here's the first, set in "Java's Cultural Cauldron": Yogyakarta.

NIGHT ARRIVES FAST near the equator. The sun sinks, then it's gone: lost below the fast approaching horizon. Time enough for *gado gado*— a spicy salad tossed with boiled egg, veggies, and peanut butter— and then onto the motorcycle. The streets of Yogyakarta pulse in two-stroke harmony, filled with the mechanical crickets of a typical Javanese night.

I park my Suzuki outside the doors of a high school gym. Inside, thick clouds of clove cigarette smoke carry the riverbed rhythms of a gamelan orchestra. On a vast canvas screen, backlit by the yellow flicker of kerosene lamps, heroic shadows batter each other with staves while the audience howls approval.

The all-night *wayang kulit*, or shadow-puppet play, is the soul of Javanese art. Manipulated by a hidden *dalang* (puppet master), projected images of gods and goddesses loom and dissolve, filling the screen with escapades drawn from 30 centuries of Hindu and animistic mythology. Though the themes seem simple—good vs. evil— the deeper message is unsettling: we're *all* shadows. All of us are vivified by an enormous, unseen hand. Briefly illuminated, we loom large for a few precious instants. And then....

Back into the night. Riding back towards my lodge, I spy a crowd of rickshaw drivers clustered on an eerily lit veranda. Approaching, the source of the strange light reveals itself: a TV set, tuned to an American cop show. The mob cheers at every new scene, delighted by the antics of these imported puppets. How outrageously comic these blustering *wayang* clowns must seem—and how mysterious the *dalang*!

WELCOMING THE SPIRITS ON JANITZIO ISLAND

In September 1984, I flew back to the United States after spending 16 months in Asia. A friend picked me up at LAX, and when we got to his apartment I phoned my parents in New York. To my amazement, my brother Jordan—who should have been at college—answered the phone. "Dad is dead," he declared. "He suffered a massive heart attack two days ago." Three hours later, jet-lagged and in shock, I was on another airplane. It was all a surreal nightmare. My father was only 54; I'd called him from Hong Kong only days earlier.

One month later, photographer Cara Moore and I left for Mexico on an *Islands* assignment, which Cara had arranged while I was still overseas. The trip, which I'd initially dreaded, turned out to be a miraculous gift; and though I never mention it directly I spent much of my private time in Janitzio's cemetery, among the candles and marigolds and melting sugar skulls.

THE STORM CAUGHT me by surprise. In less than a minute, the fine rain falling over the island had turned into a downpour. I ran for the nearest refuge as sheets of water waved through the streets, finally ducking into a crude cement construction site on a high overlook. All around Janitzio, bolts of lightning sizzled into the steel-gray surface of Lake Pátzcuaro–so close by that no delay separated the visual jolts from their apocalyptic report.

There was another man in the shelter—a laborer, I supposed. He wore an open leather jacket over a white T-shirt, and leaned against a thick plank supported by sawhorses. He watched the storm with satisfaction.

I hopped about in the cold, cursing piously as the rain turned to hail.

"*¿No le gusta a usted?*" he asked with a grin.

"Oh, it's terrific," I replied. "But my hotel's on the mainland, and I've got to catch the ferry before dark."

"There will be no ferries in this storm."

"I think there will be one more. But I may miss it. Is there a place to stay here on the island?"

"I think not," he said, still smiling. "And why do you visit Janitzio?"

"I've come for *Día de los Muertos*, the Day of the Dead."

"*¡Muy bien!* Yes, that is very spectacular—as long as it doesn't rain!"

"Did it rain last year?"

"*Sí.*"

"Will it rain this year?"

"No."

"*Muy bien.*"

The storm had indeed subsided a bit, and I realized that it was now or never. A brief farewell and I was off, sloshing down the flooded steps. The sky, opening to the low sun, had turned a flaming marigold orange, and the final launch was sputtering to life at the landing.

Early the next morning I sat aboard a ferry at the mainland dock, waiting for the boat to fill with passengers. It was the 31st of October. Bolts of sunlight and pockets of shadow played across the surface of Lake Pátzcuaro—a rough crescent of silver in the heart of Michoacán. Pátzcuaro is a lake capable of exhibiting many moods simultaneously, but all signs of the previous evening's rage had abated.

As we roared off I kept my eyes glued to the island. Janitzio is a deceptively small hump of land, dotted with white houses and crowned by an overlarge statue of the patriot-priest Morelos—progenitor of

Mexico's constitution. About 1,500 Indians, descended from the fiercely independent Purepechas, live there. Long before the Spanish conquest, when the volcanic landscape of Michoacán was thick with jungle, the Purepechas settled Janitzio to escape the toll that tigers and other wild animals were exacting from their ranks. Using rude dugout canoes and distinctive "butterfly" nets—both of which endure to this day—the Indians began farming the lake for its delicate *pescado blanco*, a small white fish in great demand on the mainland.

Many impolite accounts had been written about my destination; I'd read that it was "unsympathetic" on approach and "uninspiring" on arrival. Perhaps these reviews were not entirely unwarranted. Janitzio, after all, seems to have only reluctantly ended an age-old tradition of barring mainlanders from its shores. But like a rough boxer who is somehow transformed at the ivories of a keyboard, so does Janitzio transform itself before the bones of *Día de los Muertos*.

Passage from the mainland to the island takes 30 minutes. I was accompanied on the short voyage by my guide. Señor Antonio Torres peered ruefully around the nearby waters, concentrating his gaze on the clumps of tall reeds by the receding shoreline.

"Mmmmm. Not so good," he said. "On this first morning there is usually a big duck hunt; maybe fifty or a hundred canoes. But I don't see any right now."

"Why might that be?" I asked.

He shrugged his shoulders. "We will have to ask on the island."

Día de los Muertos is one of the most unusual celebrations in the world. The pagan rituals of Aztec myth combine with somber Catholic dogma, producing a unique homage to death. Not only to the spirits of departed family and friends, but to Death itself: the grinning skeleton that awaits us all with gleeful anticipation. The holidays are spread over two days and two nights, varying slightly but generally coinciding with our Halloween. Unlike Halloween, the celebration is a fascinating paradox—an occasion both pathetically mournful and outrageously festive.

We docked on Janitzio. Torres led me up a narrow street, past rows of trinket stalls and restaurants. Everybody seemed to be cleaning up, repainting and preparing in general for the anticipated throngs—living as well as dead. We walked through the main plaza, past an overgrown bell tower and down a steep path toward the lanes where the fishermen live. Nets were hanging everywhere, weighted down by small stones. An old man came hobbling out of a doorway, slow of gait but otherwise quite fit. Torres accosted him at once.

"Don Luis Campos!" he cried, "Why is there no duck hunt today?"

"There is no duck hunt, Antonito, because there are no ducks."

Don Luis Campos was 82 years old, but remarkably spry. Although we could not hunt, he could still teach me *how* to hunt. He pulled the duck-spearing apparatus down from a makeshift attic and let me get the feel of it. It was a clearly lethal device consisting of a three-pointed spear, and a wooden handgrip for slinging it. I was glad I was not a duck.

"He is sorry about the hunt," Torres informed me, "but insists you come back this evening. Tomorrow morning, as you know, is the feast for the *angelitos*: the dead children. Tonight, a special ceremony is performed in the homes. The godfather of the child visits the dead one's family, and blessings are made over the offerings. It is very beautiful. Will you come?"

I told him I would. I had in fact found a modest lodge on Janitzio, so catching the ferry back to the mainland was no longer a concern.

Torres and I left Don Luis and walked along the well-maintained pathway that circles Janitzio. Entire families were engaged in preparing elaborate offerings for the spirits of the dead. Mothers and daughters sat in the kitchens, kneading dough for *pan de muertos*: the ceremonial "bread of the dead" that would be baked into fanciful shapes and placed upon the altars. Brothers wove brilliant yellow marigolds onto wooden trellises, punctuating the runs of flowers with an odd array of ornaments—animals, angels and molded sugar skulls. A feast was being prepared, meant to assuage the hunger and thirst of the dead during their annual homecoming.

As we circled back toward the lodge, a man in a leather jacket called to me in greeting. I recognized him: the laborer I'd met during yesterday's storm. Now he was escorting a cadre of photographers from

Michoacán State Television, which would be filming the festival.

"That man seems to know you," Torres said, evidently impressed. "Have you met him?"

"Only briefly, while hiding from the rain. Does he work here?"

"You might say that!" Torres laughed, slapping me violently on the back. "That is Señor Alfonso Séptimo, the Mayor of Janitzio!"

. . .

We'd had every intention of joining old Don Luis Campos for the godfathers' rite, but two things interfered. First, a heavy rain began to fall just after sunset. Then, at eight—the very time we planned to leave—a power failure plunged the island into pitch blackness. I steeled myself for a long, dull evening. As it happened, however, the proprietor of my lodge was himself a godfather. His family invited us to join them as they brought their flowered offering to the home of the deceased godchild.

It was a journey I will not soon forget. Stumbling along behind the procession, I literally clung to the shawls of the women before me as they navigated Janitzio's steep, rain-slicked and unlit paths. The word "path" is generous; I was sometimes scaling sheer rock. Rocket bombs exploded around me, lending a battlefield intensity to the sport. These, I later learned, were designed to guide the wandering spirits back home.

The souls of dead children are called *angelitos*; having committed no evil, they repair immediately to the heavens. As I staggered in from the storm, the scene inside the house seemed angelic indeed. Candles burned on the tables; the women, wrapped in dark shawls, sat meditatively against a wall. A dozen children, silent and well behaved, were also seated. Dominating the room was a towering *ofrenda*, the labor of many loving hours. Bedecked with flowers and draped with fruits, *pan de muertos* and sugar toys, it faced the mourners like an overgrown easel, surrounded by incense and flame. Efforts to please the child's spirit had not ended there; a model of a souped-up Chevy van stood among the other offerings.

An enormous quantity of food was served, but almost none was eaten. After a ceremonial taste we passed our plates forward, heaping the beans, tortillas and soup bowls before the altar. When the *charanda de caña*—a liquor distilled from cane—was placed before us, I took a sip and regretfully pushed them along. My faux pas was instantly corrected by the godfather, who reminded me that children don't drink liquor.

The assembly waited patiently for the man who would lead the recitation of the rosary; he finally stumbled in from his rounds about the island, drunk but reverent. The invocations that followed were mysterious and cathartic. He transformed the family gathering into an uninhibited choir of grief and prayer, and the house began to swell with lament. The mother of the *angelito* burst into tears. Rain drizzled in through the roof, soaking her offering and melting the little candy skulls.

. . .

I woke before dawn on the first of November. No alarm clock was necessary; rocket bombs had been bursting since the first hint of daylight. The spirits could afford an early start—they had not been up all hours drinking the deceptively mild *charanda*.

This was *Día de los Niños*, the Day of the Children, and the cemetery was the place to be. The offerings, blessed the previous night, would be placed on their respective graves, awaiting approval from the little souls. I scrambled into my clothes and climbed the long stairway leading toward the burial ground. In spite of the early hour there was much activity: a battalion of islanders soaped and scrubbed the plaza; women sat in doorways, pulling the heads off little white fish; shopkeepers arranged their displays. Clearly, many visitors were expected for the famous nighttime celebration.

The sun rising over Lake Pátzcuaro was blood-red, a fair approximation of my own eye color as I leaned over a low cement wall and stared eastward. The dormant volcanoes that ring the lake rose through the lowland mist. Like the jungles and the Aztecs and the Spanish, their ancient threats had long been plowed under the soil of Michoácan. There is but one eternal enemy, I reflected; but on *Día de los Muertos*, even Death can be cultivated.

Shortly past dawn, the cemetery filled with people. Colorful *ofrendas* were placed on the appropriate graves, their golden-yellow marigolds electric in the early light. The color yellow has long been associated with death in Mexico, and these brilliant "flowers of 100 leaves" are universally acknowledged as the favorite blooms of the dead. Tall candles flickered in the morning breeze. Little girls molded the wax with their fingers. Some of the graves seemed almost lively—boys wrestled in the dirt while their mothers, wrapped in pinstripe shawls, chatted softly. At others, a desolate silence prevailed. Every once in a while the mood was shattered by a rocket bomb, but by this time even the birds had ceased to be alarmed by the blasts.

Why do children die? I wanted to know the fate of Janitzio's *angelitos*, but it seemed inappropriate to conduct interviews in the cemetery. Later in the morning, as I strolled down toward the fishermen's launch, I met a woman who would speak to me about the children.

"Often they will die of bronchitis, or grippe," she explained. "And the whooping cough also takes many lives."

"Is there no clinic on Janitzio?"

"There is a small one," she said, "which opened in 1983. But the doctor is not always on the island."

"But the town of Pátzcuaro has excellent facilities," I said. "Why aren't the children brought there?"

"They are. But since most of these illnesses occur during the winter, it is often the journey itself that kills them."

I left the tiny quay and walked back to the ferry landing. Their morning vigil over, the Janitzians had launched themselves into an ecstasy of cleaning, baking and decorating in preparation for the Night of the Dead. In the midst of the frantic activity I spied Mayor Séptimo, darting from scene to scene like a tireless master of ceremonies.

It was not yet noon, but tourists were already combing the island in search of meals and souvenirs. Feeling claustrophobic, I decided to return to the mainland for lunch and a shower. Though the ferries were coming in fully loaded, nobody wanted to leave Janitzio; an hour passed before I found myself ashore, hailing a cab to the town of Pátzcuaro.

Pátzcuaro is a fascinating place, bustling with street life and visibly proud of its historic importance. In the 1530s, the venerated Don Vasco de Quiroga opened the first schools in the Americas in this lakeside village. His success in organizing cooperative craft communes—based on ideas from Sir Thomas More's then-contemporary *Utopia*—brought the native Indians a prosperity that has lasted half a millennium.

I showered at my hotel, lunched in a quaint pizzeria, and wandered off to explore the town's two large plazas. Both thronged with tourists and townfolk. The mainland was preparing for its own *Noche de los Muertos*, and the trappings of the holiday were visible everywhere: tables loaded with sugar skulls and toy coffins; stalls selling personalized *pan de muertos*; a modern drugstore festooned with paper skeletons and imported plastic jack-o-lanterns. I peered into a news stand to read the *calaveras*: a word that literally means "skulls," but also refers to special poems published on this holiday, lampooning public figures with premature (and often unflattering) obituaries.

Back at my hotel I was greeted by Señor Alvarez, the affable proprietor. He ushered me into the dining room. There was only one other guest, a distinguished looking gentleman immersed in a magazine. "I would like you to meet Señor Cámera," Alvarez chortled. "He is an architect, from Mexico City." Cámera stood up, and we shook hands. With his short gray hair and squarish jaw, he resembled a Mexican Perry Mason.

Cámera had come to Michoácan to admire the buildings; the magazine he held was an edition specifically about Pátzcuaro. He leafed through the journal, praising the structures but bemoaning their present straits. "Look at this photograph," he said. "This is the famous 'House of the Crooked Stairway,' one of the most unusual homes in the city. In its day it was an architectural marvel—do you know what it is now?" The place looked oddly familiar. I flushed, but held my peace. "A pizza parlor!" Cámera spat. "They've turned the place into a pizza joint!"

My brief encounter with Cámera resonated with me, as the fate of the "Crooked Stairway" house seemed an apt allegory for *Día de los Muertos.*

The Day of the Dead is rooted in ancient paganism and Aztec death rituals. These included the worship of Mictlanteceutli, god of the underworld inferno—a sinister skeleton whose homage required living sacrifices. Over the centuries the rites changed. The Purepechas dismissed the bloody Aztec traditions. When the Dominicans arrived in the 1500s, they found observances not unlike the ones seen today. Souls of departed ancestors returned to their native villages, and were honored with food and flowers. Back then, the ceremonies took place in August. But as an attempt to fuse the Indian customs with Catholicism, a parallel was drawn between *Día de los Muertos* and the church's All Saint's Day, November first. The syncretism was evidently successful, for today it is nearly impossible to determine where aboriginal traditions end and Catholicism begins.

Like the House of the Crooked Stairway—and many other dwellings throughout Mexico—Day of the Dead had been altered just slightly, to insure its survival in the modern age. My only hope, as I set off to return to Janitzio, was that the festival would have a more authentic flavor than the pizza.

. . .

The Janitzio-bound ferry was packed with passengers. Most were tourists from other parts of Mexico. There were even two mimes on the boat, hoping to extract a few pesos from the evening crowds.

Antonio Torres met me at the landing. He surveyed the crowded ferry with alarm. "I'll tell you what," he said. "All of the tourists think the big ceremony happens at midnight. But that is the *worst* time to be in the cemetery."

"What do you suggest I do?"

"Sleep until 3 a.m.," Torres advised, "and then go up there. By that time, all the tourists will have decided there is nothing to see, and will have gone home on the ferry." He lowered his voice. "But the late hours are the very best.... Oh, you won't believe how beautiful it is!"

I considered his words as we docked. The island was already

swarming, and more ferries were on the way. Three avenues led up and away from the dock; each one, I noted with amusement, had a sign reading *Subida Principal al Monumento*: Main Route to the Monument.

Halfway to the island's crest I found a man I'd been looking for. Padre Rubén Ruíz sat beside a collection box on the side of the wide stairway. He was a droll-looking patriarch, dressed in black robes and holding a fat cigar between delicate fingers.

Padre Ruíz had served on Janitzio for 36 years, and I wanted to question him about the twilight zone between Indian ritual and Catholicism. But there were too many people; every few seconds an ascending tourist would appear and kiss the padre's hand, derailing his train of thought.

"How long," I asked, "have tourists been coming to see this celebration?"

"Hmmm. Well, the statue was finished in 1936," he said, "and many people began coming to see that. The Indians were kind of glad, because it brought a little extra income. Before that there was nothing, and no one bothered to come here." A group of attractive women mounted the steps toward us, and Ruíz automatically extended his hand. "Mostly, though, tourism for *Noche de los Muertos* began in 1948. A group from Mexico City came and made a film of it. I guess a lot of people see that film, because every year there are more and more tourists."

"What do the Janitzians think of that?"

"In the beginning they resented it quite strongly, but now they're getting used to it."

"But how about the ceremony itself? Has the celebration changed?"

"The festival is the same," said Ruíz stiffly, and looked me in the eye. "The only difference is that now there are too many tourists. But I suppose you will see that for yourself."

By the time the sun set, Janitzio was crowded enough to pass for the French Quarter on Fat Tuesday. I hid in a corner of my favorite restaurant, dining on *pescado blanco* and *frijoles*. The scene outside was frantic. The television crew was running from place to place, turning the bright lights upon any sign of religious activity. Up the hill on the basketball court, a musical performance was underway; I could hear the bleating of trumpets.

Not much for crowds, I finished my beer and returned to the lodge. Perhaps it would be possible to sleep for a while. But when to wake? Ignoring the warnings of the well-meaning Torres, I set the alarm for twelve.

I rose at midnight, wondering if I'd slept at all. It seemed as though nothing had changed. Through my window I could hear the ferries landing in rapid succession, each one solidly packed with obstreperous tourists. The restaurants were overflowing, and the air crackled with the sound and smell of frying fish. Foot traffic up the main routes of town moved slowly, a bovine procession with its ironic end at the cemetery. Following the mob, I caught sight of an old Janitzian woman. She sat huddled in a doorway with her candles and flowers, reluctant to continue onward.

The cemetery was very dark, a sea of anonymous figures milling about in confusion. As flashbulbs lit the darkness I caught strobed visuals of the tableau: people frozen in motion with cameras poised; raised beer bottles; wide-eyed children gripping their mothers' hands. The TV crew seemed to be filming something by the ceremonial coffin reserved for the symbolic Christ child, but getting near it would have been like trying to reach the stage during a Grateful Dead show.

Then I saw something that broke my heart. A pop of light illuminated a huge ring of people encircling the center of the graveyard. My height was an advantage, and I was able to see within. It was the woman I had spotted in the doorway. She now crouched alone by a gravestone, surrounded by four candles and a tattered photograph of the man she had come to mourn. Flashbulbs exploded around her as she stared sorrowfully at the ground.

This was too much for me. I returned wearily to the lodge and flopped onto the bed, plagued by Malthusian nightmares until the alarm rang out at three.

Returning to the cemetery in the wee hours of the morning, my first thoughts were of Antonio Torres. The man was a genius. Never had I seen a more profound transformation. Nearly all the tourists were gone, and the graveyard had become an otherworldly landscape of flickering candles—hundreds of them—and spectacularly flowered arches. Bells tolled mournfully from Janitzio's venerable tower while small groups of islanders sang the rosary before the graves of their ancestors. The smell of marigolds spiced the air.

I hiked up to a vantage point overlooking the scene. Viewed from above, the cemetery really did look like an elaborate, ghostly banquet: a feast that only the most antisocial spirit could resist. Row after row of candles cast their glow onto flowered trellises and cloth-covered trays of food. It was a breathtaking sight, more lovely and reverent than anything I'd dared imagine earlier.

An odd thought struck me. Less than three days before, I had huddled in a nearby shelter with Mayor Séptimo as all hell broke loose around us. Had that furious storm simply cleared the air for the arrival of more benign spirits? I remembered the curious look of satisfaction on the mayor's face as he watched the lightning, and wondered how much I was willing to believe.

By 5 a.m. the graveyard was nearly silent, but as luminous as a vivid dream. I wandered among the offerings. Clusters of women, wrapped in shawls, nodded before the flames. Sleeping children lay curled in their laps. Once in a while a man would stumble in from the drunken revelry outside, knocking over a candle or two before collapsing against a wall. I hid myself away and kept my own vigil, mesmerized by the dancing lights, finally dozing off to the rhythms of a distant guitar.

Just before sunrise a velvet fog covered Janitzio. Dawn came slowly, savoring the last mysterious flavors of the night. One by one, the families gathered their offerings and left the cemetery. They would later dine upon the leftovers, but without enjoyment; the visiting dead, they knew, had already consumed the essence of the feast.

· · ·

The second of November was blindingly sunny. Down at the landing, an assortment of tourists and villagers waited for the ferry. Every-one looked vaguely stupefied. The restaurants, which had been open for 30 hours, seemed befuddled by any order more complicated than a beer. A mixed group of *mariachis* wavered on the dock, blundering recklessly through a ballad. I bumped against them and was engulfed by the crowd; a paper cup of *charanda*-on-the-rocks was pressed into my hand, and long arms were thrown around my shoulders.

But I wanted a last look at the cemetery before leaving Janitzio. Extracting myself from the musicians, I climbed up the wide, now empty stairway.

The damp ground was covered with crushed marigolds, all that remained of the night-long trance. It was difficult to believe that, only hours before, the enigmas of Life and Death had sojourned here. An Aztec verse ran through my mind:

> *We only come to sleep,*
> *We only come to dream;*
> *It is not true, it is not true*
> *That we come to live on Earth....*

I scooped up a few golden petals, and watched them blow away in the morning breeze.

INTO THE DENKI FURO

Originally written for *Equator*—one of the first, and best, of San Francisco's independent 'zines—this story is possibly my all-time favorite. One of my fondest memories is of reading it before a huge audience at the 1994 Book Passage Travel Writers' Conference in Corte Madera, clad only (truly) in a frayed Japanese *yukata*.

MY GOD, it was hot in Tokyo. The kind of heat and humidity that makes the jaw go slack. Morning was to stagger toward the newsstand, shielding my eyes from the glare off scooters and vending machines. Afternoons were spent careening through Tokyo in search of information, or prone dumbly on the *tatami* beneath an oscillating fan, listening to Tony Bennett on the Far East Network:

> *"The little boy lost*
> *will find his way once more*
> *Just like before*
> *When lips were tender...."*

Our apartment, like most in Tokyo, had no shower. But when the cool evening finally arrived I climbed gratefully into my *yukata* (robe) and made for the *sento* (public bath).

How I loved our neighborhood *sento*! Big bright locker-room-cum-gym, spotlessly clean. Please Leave Shoes At Door. Never crowded. A handful of Japanese men—I was the only foreigner—attended themselves naked and unselfconscious, rubbing their bodies with rough towels.

The walls were lined with low mini-showers. One must squat. Also, Please Turn Faucet On Slowly: those little Japanese showers can knock you across the room.

The entire back portion of the *sento* was occupied with baths. First there was an olympic-sized hot tub/jacuzzi. Next to that was a cold bath; then a green bath; and at the end a small mystery bath, perpetually empty, with an alarming lightning bolt emblazoned in red on the white tile wall above.

Glancing now and again at that placid final bath, the surface of which seemed supernaturally calm, I felt a nagging curiosity. For all I knew it might have been a device for sterilizing surgical tools, or hyper-cleaning jewelry. Why was I seized by a crazy intuition to climb recklessly in?

. . .

There are no beggars, few elderly on Tokyo streets. The city seems to belong to a youthful post-bomb generation that moves at ease among high, clean buildings and throbbing electrical billboards. As if there had been nothing before this. As if Tokyo had elected to submerge its history under canyons of steel and glass and especially plastic; infinite quantities of plastic. Flowers wrapped in plastic. Plastic eels in the windows.

Another day ended. I sweated and staggered from subway to subway, swooning in the unspeakable heat. Home at last and all I wanted was a bath. Collecting my toiletries in a plastic bucket, I set off for the *sento*.

There were men in the mystery bath.

Two old men, covered from neck to waist with outrageous tattoos. Their faces wore expressions of the purest transcendence, like samurai warriors under torture. One of them motioned to me with his head—a mere twitch really—in what seemed to be a gesture of invitation.

Silence prevails in the *sento*, but foreigners are expected to breach every custom and who was I to disappoint the Japanese? Pointing to the fateful pool, I inquired of the young man on my right.

"*Denki furo*," he explained. Electric bath.

There is a moment we have all experienced, on the edge of a diving board or at the threshhold of a bedroom, when we know that to take another step is to commit ourselves irreversibly. I walked, naked, to the wall of the *denki furo*. The water within pulsed invisibly, and I felt the fascination and aversion one experiences when bending over to touch a completely still animal that may or may not be dead. But to touch the water hand-first would be, I imagined, shameful, as if I lacked the strength of my convictions.

Every eye in the room was upon me as I swung my leg into the bath. Electricity swarmed up my calf, buzzing and stinging. I uttered no cry. Bracing on rubber arms, I swung my other leg in. Face be damned; this was as far as I was going to go.

But wait—the bath was doing something, not unlike love, to my loins. They were turning to *soba* (noodle). Wearing the resigned grin of a fall guy in some '50s comedy, I began to sink gradually into the water.

There was no point trying to escape; my feet would not respond. The most important thing, I understood, was to remain unflinching as my testicles went under. Every situation in Japan is a test. I would not disgrace myself.

Contemplating the *wu* (essence) of the white tile wall I sank, expressionless, up to my neck. The men in the adjoining bath watched my eyes, staring with an impassive, cat-like gaze.

What did it feel like? Imagine the howling physical rush of a blow to the "funny bone," generalized over your entire body. Or think of yourself as a silver filling, and the *denki furo* as a mouth full of foil. Did it hurt? The exquisite intensity went far beyond pain. My only hope was that there would be no permanent physical damage; that, like the cartoon cat whose tail is thrust into a wall outlet, I would sizzle for a while then reappear, unscathed, in the next scene.

. . .

I do not recall how I left the *denki furo*. Perhaps the two old men lifted me, a recalcitrant tumor, from their buzzing province. Perhaps I mustered a supreme effort of will and climbed from the tub myself, like Batman in a fix. Or maybe I never left the bath at all. Perhaps I'm still in it, existing in a Borgesian dream-state of compressed time. It often seems that way.

I live in America now, where the burgers are charcoal-broiled. People take baths at home. I have never met anyone else who has taken an electric bath. We have all seen movies or read newspaper stories of people getting electrocuted when their radio or blow dryer decides to take a bath with them, and I would go so far as to say that electrified water, like darkness or sharks, is a deeply rooted fear.

The men in the Japan National Tourist Board laughed when I asked them what I had encountered in Japan. *"Denki furo,"* they replied, unable to elaborate.

Still mystified, I called a shiatsu school specializing in oriental healing techniques. "It obviously effects the polarity of your elec- trons profoundly," speculated the director. "It can probably alter your brain waves. After all, we're nothing but masses of electrons to begin with...."

Which explains some things. But sometimes, in Japan, there is no explanation save that single four-word mantra, uttered by the visitor in awe and italics:

They are the Japanese.

SWAYAMBHUNATH
THE JEWEL IN THE LOTUS

Whenever I read historical accounts of travel to ancient empires—be they through Mexico, Tibet or Arabia—I'm struck by the spell these cities cast upon their visitors. These were cities where the fire of mythology still burned; places where one might hope to walk along gold-paved avenues, meet a levitating lama, or free a grateful djinn. What places remain, on this guidebook-papered planet, that have maintained that aura of mystery, of possibility? Spend a sunset at Swayambhunath, and that question will be answered. There are still a few places on this Earth where one's breath is taken away, and the presence of live magic permeates the air with a visible, bee-like vibration....

Once upon a time, there was a lake.

The lake was called Nagavasa, and it filled what is now central Nepal. A large body of water ("seven calling distances across," the old texts say) Nagavasa was famed for its sweetness and clarity. Deep within that cool, pure reservoir, a race of noble Snake Gods lived in palatial luxury. These *nagas* were responsible for bringing the crucial monsoon rains, and for safeguarding earth's vast trove of underground treasures.

One day, long before recorded history began, the great saint Bipaswi visited the lake. Bipaswi was the first of all the human buddhas, and he had extraordinary powers. After meditating on one of the high green hills surrounding Nagavasa, Bipaswi took a tiny seed from the folds of his robe, and tossed it into the waters.

Bipaswi's seed bloomed into the most fantastic flower the world had ever seen. It was a thousand-petaled lotus, with pistils of diamond, anthers of blazing ruby, and a stalk of semiprecious stones. From the center of that lotus emerged a beam of brilliant light—an umbra of radiance that illuminated the rippling surface of Nagavasa with a cool fire.

For thousands of years, the lotus and its miraculous flame attracted pilgrims from all corners of Asia. One of these visitors was the famous saint Manjushri, the Buddha of Wisdom. Manjushri realized at once that the lake and the flaming lotus, beautiful as they were, were simply place-markers for the sacred landscape that lay below....

After walking around the surrounding hills three times (and arranging new accommodations for the more or less compliant *nagas*), Manjushri raised his sword and brought it down on the lake's southern ridge. A deep gorge opened, and the waters of Nagavasa rushed out—revealing the lush, emerald bowl of the Kathmandu Valley.

Manjushri's work was nearly done; he had but one last, quick task to perform. With a feat of magic too powerful to be understood, he transformed the marvelous lotus into a perfect little hill. Atop that hill, the radiant beam of light focused, took form, and became a glowing crystal *stupa*—a glimmering dome crowned with a diamond spire.

The stupa was named *Swayambhunath*: Temple of the Self-existent One.

. . .

Halfway up the hill I stopped to catch my breath, leaning against the base of a huge, brightly painted stone buddha.

As much as I love Kathmandu, it felt good to get away from the city center. Swayambhunath, a short bicycle ride from downtown, is a world apart from the noisy roads, pollution and overcrowding that are turning Nepal's unique capital into just another congested Asian city.

Mornings and evenings are by far the best times to visit. I arrived at the base of the hill at sunrise, when the cool mist that often blankets the Kathmandu Valley was just lifting.

The ancient site was alive with activity. Pungent Tibetan incense wafted through the air. Manangi women, wearing heavy beads of turquoise and coral, clutched strings of prayer beads and prostrated themselves on the ground. Monkeys leaped through the trees, dropping down to pilfer discarded mango skins, pick lice from their coats and generally terrorize each other.

Pilgrims from Tibet, clad in lined hats and heavy woolen coats, approached the long stairway with undisguised awe, spinning copper prayer-wheels and muttering the divine mantra *Om Mani Padme Hum*: "O, the jewel in the heart of the lotus!"

The daunting climb up to the temple complex is marked with statues, shrines and stone carvings—some over a thousand years old. But the large orange and yellow buddhas, built by the great-grandfather of Nepal's present king, are the most impressive.

These depict the historical Buddha—Siddhartha Gautama—in the famous posture of "Calling the Earth to Witness." The pose recalls the moment when Siddhartha, after a period of deep meditation, sat on the very brink of enlightenment. At that precise instant Mara, King of the Underworld, arrived on the scene to seduce the would-be Buddha with all kinds of worldly pleasures. Our hero wouldn't budge. At last, in a rage, the bested Mara demanded to know just who had given this individual the right to assume the lofty mantle of buddhahood. Siddhartha, in reply, simply reached down and touched the Earth.

The final approach to the hilltop is a climb of 300 broad stone steps, worn into deep grooves by the feet of countless pilgrims. Ahead and above, the white dome and golden finial of the stupa gleam in invitation. Making the ascent, one passes painted statues of the five divine vehicles—a bird/woman, peacock, horse, elephant and lion—belonging to the five celestial buddhas.

Stopping by one of these impressive guardians, I couldn't help but recall the first "guardian" I'd seen that morning: a dark-eyed girl who'd demanded three rupees in "protection money" for watching my rented bicycle.

. . .

At the top of the stairs, a giant bronze *vajra*—a highly stylized diamond-thunderbolt—rests on a circular plinth. Symbolizing power, clarity and compassion, this is the potent ritual symbol of *vajrayana* (literally, "Diamond Vehicle"): the unusually intense form of Buddhism practiced in Nepal and Tibet.

The vajra's base was surrounded by a group of Nepalese teenagers wearing designer jeans and smoking Yak cigarettes. Just behind them, the stark white dome of Swayambhunath's stupa rose into the sky like an enormous scoop of Clear Void ice cream. Atop the dome, from each face of a gilded, four-sided *harnika*, the eyes of Buddha gazed serenely across the Kathmandu Valley. This *harnika* was crowned with a gleaming, 13-tiered spire, topped by a broad golden parasol. I took a deep breath, swept away by the palpable sense of history—and holiness—that permeates that mythical hilltop.

Stupas are structured a bit like onions; the domes begin small, but expand over time. Those who seek to make improvements simply add more layers. The original Swayambhunath—the radiant, crystalline stupa created by Manjushri—was covered up sometime around the fourth century, in an effort to protect the fragile structure from the oncoming "Age of Confusion." (Which, in case you're wondering, has already arrived.)

In the 14th century, Swayambhunath was completely destroyed by Moslem invaders. It was quickly restored, though, and probably took its present form in the late 1600s. With each successive effort, the builders have been careful to provide "airholes": escape ducts through which the inner stupa's luminous power continues to radiate outwards.

For visual impact alone, the great stupa of Swayambhunath deserves to be ranked among the wonders of the world. But the appearance of this legendary monument, stunning as it may be, is far less important than what it symbolizes.

The great white dome, which may have evolved from the shape of ancient burial mounds, is likened to the womb. Deep inside rest the sacred relics of revered lamas, or the Buddha himself. But like the womb, the stupa is inviolable. There is no access to that secret, innermost chamber.

On top of the dome is the gilded *harnika*, with its four pairs of painted Buddha-eyes facing the cardinal directions. These eyes are unique to Nepali stupas, and there are countless interpretations of their meaning. Some say the eyes represent the sun and moon, and thus serve as a kind of cosmic dividing line. Below Buddha's gaze lies the realm of *samsara*: the human condition, defined by desire and illusion, suffering and stealth: Our Town. Above, the heavenly holds sway.

Between the eyes appears a long, question mark shape. This symbol, representing unity, is actually an *ek*: the number "1" in Nepali.

The harnika is crowned with an immense gleaming spire which rises upward in a series of 13 golden rings. Home to hundreds of pigeons, this multi-tiered finial serves as a reminder that there are 13 obstacles to enlightenment (desire, dishonesty and anger, for example, are the first three).

Avoiding those pitfalls, we at last reach our goal: the gilded parasol, which represents *nirvanah*. Nirvanah is not death; it is the end of sorrow and the realization of Truth. Siddhartha Gautama reached this state at the precocious age of 34. He then traveled around the Indian subcontinent, teaching his method to others, until he passed away some 46 years later.

Around the base of the stupa, on the broad hilltop that is almost a miniature village, life goes on as usual. An endless stream of pilgrims arrive upon the site and perform devotional circuits, walking clockwise around Swayambhunath while spinning the prayer-wheels recessed into its massive plinth. Monkeys leap between the roofs of concession stalls, competing with feral dogs for the choicest scraps. Parents lift up their children, the better to see the images of celestial buddhas occupying dark niches in the stupa's sides.

Long strings of prayer flags descend from the spire, flapping their blessings into a steady wind. From within the adjacent monastery, which houses the largest bronze buddha in Nepal, float the haunting sounds of drums, bells and *kanglings*—trumpets made of human bone.

. . .

The great stupa of Swayambhunath is surrounded by a maze of buildings, temples and shrines. Directly behind the dome sits a two-story temple in typical Nepalese style, with gilt pagoda rooftops (the Nepalese, incidentally, appear to have invented the pagoda). The little temple is always thronged with worshipers, but I never knew what it was until my most recent trip to Nepal —when I learned, to my amazement, that it was the single most important temple on the hill.

During Buddha's time there lived an ogress named Hariti—the goddess of smallpox. Hariti had 500 children and, in order to feed them, routinely kidnaped other children and included them on her menu. The people of the region appealed to Buddha for help, and he complied. One day, while Hariti was out hunting and gathering, Buddha absconded with the ogress's youngest baby and hid him beneath his begging bowl.

Hariti returned home to find her baby gone. Crazed with anguish, she searched the world for him... but in vain. Finally she, too, showed up on Buddha's doorstep, and implored him for help. Buddha immediately returned her child, but took the opportunity to point out that all of Hariti's victims had suffered in just this very same way. Hariti, much abashed, pledged to reform.

Within the week, however, Hariti and her 500 children found themselves starving to death. The ogress accosted Buddha, and demanded that he find a way to feed them—or else. Buddha, ever cooperative, solved this problem by placing Hariti at the head of his entire retinue—thus giving her first pick of the abundant offerings that were continually passed his way.

Today, Hariti is known as Ajima: great-grandmother of the world. She is revered as the goddess of pediatrics, the protectoress of all children. What's more, she still—after all these years—gets first dibs on Buddha's bounty. Before any offering is made at Swayambhunath, or before any renovation is begun, it must first be cleared with grandma Ajima.

. . .

North of the Hariti/Ajima Temple, after crossing a forest of small white votive shrines, you will find Shantipur. This is one of the most mysterious temples in Nepal—if not all Asia.

Remember the *nagas*? When the Snake Gods who control the monsoon were relocated by Manjushri, there was one character who refused to leave. This particular serpent caused so much trouble that he was finally killed... but his stubbornness also won him a great honor. His wide skin was rolled out into a parchment; a quill was fashioned from one of his bones. Using the snake's own blood as ink, a fantastic *mandala*, or sacred painting, was drawn, encoding the priceless formulas for starting the critical summer rains.

The mandala is hidden in a sealed chamber, three levels below the ground. Six other rooms must be passed to reach it; each one is guarded by deadly spells, giant cobras, and a host of other fantastic beasts. At the very lowest level rests Shantikar Archaya, the temple's mythical founder, meditating in utter bliss.

Once every few centuries, when a terrible drought threatens the land, the King of Nepal must purify himself, practice the tantric protection mantras, and make his way into the depths of Shantipur to retrieve the mystical scroll.

During the 17th century, King Pratapa Malla—who built the huge stone stairway, as well as numerous other temples on the site—faced such a drought. In an adventure that makes Indiana Jones look like Captain Kangaroo, Malla descended to the seventh chamber and brought the mandala out. The moment it was touched by the sun, rains deluged the kingdom.

But Pratapa Malla never forgot the intoxicating sense of power he had experienced in Shantipur. Years later, the King surrendered to his obsession and made the odyssey once again—this time for personal gain. When he emerged from the depths a few days later, he was completely insane.

. . .

Another day, another miracle. It was already early evening and the low sun, sinking behind the foothills, illuminated the eastern sky with a sweeping rainbow. Below the bright arc, the capital appeared a mosaic of brick and stucco, punctuated by wisps of smoke. Surveying the bowl-shaped Valley, it was easy to imagine the area containing a lake. Geologic evidence, in fact, indicates that it did— until an earthquake or volcano created a draining rift some 200,000 years ago.

The onset of evening awakened a symphony of sounds: growling dogs, thousands of birds, the screeching of monkeys and children, and muted blasts from conch shell trumpets. Monks prayed in the *gompa*, their anamelodic chants broken by the clatter of bells, cymbals and drums. The butter lamps ringing the stupa were being lit, and the air was laced with their slightly acrid smoke.

I made a final visit to the monastery, and purchased a small candle from a monk. Being a Westerner, candles always make me feel I should make a wish. My only wish was that the unusual sense of calm and delight I had earned at Swayambhunath would last, and ease my return to the griddle of western civilization. I placed the candle on a low table full of flames, below the kind, half-amused regard of the large bronze buddha.

Outside, the half moon hung in the sky like a celestial mirror of the stupa. I rang the heavy bell beside the giant vajra, threw a cracker to the monkeys, and made my reluctant descent back into the world of samsara.

AS THE WHEEL TURNS
BACKSTAGE AT THE BIG SPIN

The first story that I ever published in a San Francisco newspaper was an exhaustive investigation, in 1985, of the now-discredited "Face on Mars." (The evocative formation turned out to be a bunch of weathered dunes, rather than the monumental remains of a vanished Martian civilization.) During the years that followed I became an almost weekly presence in *Image*, the Sunday magazine of the once credible *San Francisco Examiner*. I was crazy about my editors, a trio of savvy women who understood my strengths and sent me out on a vast spectrum of human-interest assignments— from explaining state-of-the-art earthquake prediction to infiltrating New Age "pyramid" schemes.

Of the dozens of stories I wrote for *Image*, this one is far and away my favorite. The entire piece was written in single, six-hour sitting. And though it's set close to home, the phenomenon it recounts seems somehow universal: a bittersweet homage to unbridled human desire.

$6.45 MILLION MEANS never having to say you're sorry.

But Francisco Campos didn't know about the money when he came up to apologize to me across a table littered with powdered donuts.

He was still, as per the micro-biographies distributed by the California State Lottery Commission, a 44-year-old aluminum sign maker from Stockton. His wife, Rosie, worked as a meat packer for Hormel. We were waiting backstage on the Big Spin set, at the Cal Expo in Sacramento. In a matter of moments, Campos would be ushered before the cameras, aligned with various tape-marks on the floor, and presented with a three in 100 chance of winning an obscene amount of money. The Lottery's progressive jackpot, which had started three weeks ago at its usual base of $3 million, had been climbing steadily with every successive miss, and now rested at a giddy altitude indeed.

Campos was dressed in a scarlet shirt, a wide tie, and a sports jacket. He was also wearing a glazed, goofy smile—standard attire for the morning's event.

"I'm sorry I deedn't get a chance to talk to you last night," he said. Even his friends love to imitate his Speedy Gonzales accent. "I was so tired, you know.... We had dinner, and then I tried to sleep."

I noticed that he was fondling something as we talked. It was obviously a totem—the lucky charm he'd bring on-stage when it was his turn to spin the Wheel. He raised it up to eye level: a card-sized picture, hand-colored, of San Martin Caballeros, patron saint of the poor. "My grandmother used to believe in him," Campos explained. "She used to light candles for help from him..." The picture showed the Saint, elegant on horseback, reaching down to assist a fallen man.

"I'll be happy whatever I get," said Campos. He was staring at the picture in a weird, obsessive way, and I realized that he was utterly immersed in it, a character in the background, watching the Saint with awe. "If I get rich," he said, entranced, "I like to buy me a house for my mom... because where she lives now not too nice... all the water goes in the basement... and I don't like to see her like that, you know?

"And if I win a lot of money I like to... to.... " His voice trailed off. Our conversation was cut short by the roar of the audience as they practiced cheering.

. . .

John Schade and I sat in the Beverly Garland's Fillmore Bar, Friday night before the Big Spin. Schade is a Public Affairs man with the Lottery. He had bought the first round; "that way you can't be antagonistic." I paid for the second, third and fourth.

I had dragged Schade to the bar in an effort to ferret out "Lottery People." This weekend's fifteen contestants—along with their respective entourages—were being put up at the Garland in Sacramento.

It seemed a safe bet they'd be drinking; the following morning, each would have a single shot at the California State Lottery's absurd jackpot of $6.055 million (payable in installments over the next 20 years). Everyone who spun the wheel would walk away with at least ten grand; but it was not difficult to hit $50 or $100 thousand, or even a neat million.

One million dollars is a reasonable amount of money; we could live with that. But for most of us the task of managing the Grand Prize—over a quarter million dollars a year, every year for two decades—would be like trying to drive a herd of humpback whales across the deep blue sea. "Don't you feel," I asked Schade, "that those huge sums of money are too much?"

"It's the American Dream, though. Did you ever think about that?"

The American Dream: being bathed in money, swamped by money, more money than the imagination can conceive how to spend. In California! Is the thought delicious? Or is it the equivalent of stuffing one's face with eight hundred chocolate Amaretto truffles?

Schade put on his windbreaker. He reminded me of a high school baseball coach; a subdued, moderately beefy guy who loves to see people win. The California State Lottery's longest-term employee, he was by that evening a veteran of twenty Big Spin shows, and had seen 404 people win nearly one billion dollars in prize money.

A group of Hispanic people came in and sat down near the fireplace. Schade motioned to them with his head. "Lottery people," he said.

"How do you know?"

"Trust me."

Indeed, it was the Campos family. They sat around restlessly for a few minutes, but by the time I approached them they were standing up to leave.

"We're going to have dinner," Francisco said. "But I'll come back here afterwards."

It was getting pretty late. In desperation I began to accost anyone who seemed to fit one of the sparse descriptions on the bio sheet. I found Edith Amos, the seventy year-old woman with ten great-grandchildren. She was at a low round table among her family—displaced Georgians and Okies, surrounded by empty Budweiser cans—listening to everyone else talk.

Edith was confident of the Grand Prize, ready to "fly, travel in all directions."

"But we're not hurtin'!" her husband roared in a gritty voice. "We don't have to have it. But it sure would be nice."

I asked Edith if she had a message to the world from this pinnacle of good fortune. "Happiness is what you make yourself," she said reverently. "Money has nothing to do with it."

Looking from face to face, it seemed they all believed it.

"Those people are the salt of the earth," Schade ejaculated when I returned. He was in his cups, and keeping an eye on the waitress.

It occurred to me to have the front desk page a few contestants whose bios seemed especially interesting. Schade was dubious. His worst fears were realized as the receptionist woke three people in a row, conveying their groggy and irritated refusals verbatim.

By midnight I was on my own, back at the bar, sitting between a middle-aged man and a teenager who was apparently his son. Something about the way they were dressed made me think they'd just come down from the snow. I was surprised to hear they were Lottery People.

"I buy five tickets every Friday night," the man told me. "Along with a pizza and a videotape. Then I go home and we scratch the tickets. It's kind of a ritual." He ordered another Steam beer. "About six, seven weeks ago we scratched the ENTRY ticket. My wife wanted to know if she could spin if we won, so I gave it to her."

"What's her name?"

"Linda McBride."

She was one of the contestants I'd awakened. Her bio had intrigued me—it said that she studied yoga, and dreamed of touring through the Himalaya.

"So what's she doing to manifest victory?"

"My wife does tarot cards—she did a reading for the spin, and it came out good. And she's wearing the colors of the Grand Prize slots— gold and pink. Other than that, just a lot of positive thinking."

I asked if they'd ever watched the Big Spin show on television, and McBride snorted. "Once. It was pretty dumb. A lot of people braying, and making asses of themselves."

"You think you'll manage to avoid that fate?"

"I don't really care!" McBride hollered, startling me. His son burst into nervous laughter. "I'll be the biggest ass in the world for six million dollars!"

Walt, the bartender, gave me a look. After the McBrides had retired he came over to refresh my drink. "They certainly don't tip like winners," he observed, speaking more of the general case than the McBrides in particular.

"You've seen a lot of them?"

He had. "They're recognizable by a kind of goofy look on their faces," Walt said. "Like the cat that just ate the mouse. And they usually get really smashed; more than most people do in a week." The waitress came over to the station, and he went off to deal with her. "But most are very nice, working class people. You don't see a bunch of yuppies going out and buying twenty lottery tickets a week."

. . .

Saturday morning. The contestants and their families assembled in the Fillmore Lounge. An air of repressed mania pervaded the room. There was little cross-conversation between the groups; most were preoccupied with their own thoughts, struggling to anchor the blimps of expectation, trying to remain relentlessly positive while acknowledging the possibility of a mere $10,000 spin.

At seven-thirty the agitated mob was loaded into a huge green bus and driven to the Cal Expo Exhibition Hall #1. A cold, obnoxious rain fell on Sacramento, somehow tightening the threads of anticipation. It was an overwhelming, almost generic tension; these dazed throngs might have been medieval serfs invited to the king's wedding, or prisoners on their way to the gallows. They were silent, humble, obedient.

Arriving at the pavilion, we were fed through a metal detector and ushered toward the back of the cavernous sound stage. I followed the contestants past the Big Spin set, garishly appointed and blindingly lit, to a rear room blocked off by heavy black curtains. Just outside the room was a table laden with black coffee and a dozen varieties of donuts. The spread of caffeine and white sugar was telling— the contestants were being subtly drugged, hyped to the legal limit for their television debuts.

Carole Heiniger, an attractive, athletic woman I'd met briefly on Friday night, bolted from the "briefing room" in a craze.

"I work in military electronics," she confessed, "so I deal with the defense department and all kinds of pressure, all the time. But I have *never* felt this kind of just total.... I'm a wacko!!" she wailed. "I'm a basket case!" She gave me her wrist; it pounded like a dorm party.

"Last night I said to myself, 'Okay, there's no skill—it's not as if you can study or practice. Just get up there and spin the wheel!' So certainly I'll be disappointed if I don't hit the Big One. But I really think I can be happy with the $10,000. It's money dropped out of the sky." She finished her cigarette, threw it absently into her coffee, and drank the whole thing in one gulp.

Kathy Sanchez, the Lottery's vivacious Game Show Coordinator, came into the curtained-off area to soothe and otherwise distract the 15 contestants, whose clamorous families now filled the rows of folding chairs facing the set. It was a scene familiar to anyone who has ever attended kindergarten, or an encounter group: each contestant was asked to stand, and tell the others a little bit about who they were and how they got there.

A theme of incredulity linked the players; few could comprehend the odds they had beaten. Only one lottery card in 2000 conceals an ENTRY ticket—and of those coveted ENTRYs, one in 1250 makes it to the Big Spin. With eerie clarity, the contestants recalled their hopeful scratch-offs in neighborhood 7-11's and Kwik-Marts across the state; they recalled mailing in their tickets, and exactly what they were doing when those miraculous phone calls had arrived, two nerve-wracking weeks earlier, from State Lottery Officials.

The upbeat Ms. Sanchez was followed by a host of less chatty staff. The orientation concluded as a man with a blonde beard began passing out a prodigious load of paperwork. A few of the contestants groaned. "If you win big," the official said dryly, "just make sure the Lottery knows where you are for the next twenty years." He, like all the speakers, was being videotaped by lottery agents; in the event of a lawsuit, no one could complain that he or she hadn't been told the rules.

I skirted in next to Ceslo Lopez, a lean, dark man with a long neck and curly silver hair. Lopez was a retired lightweight boxer, a veteran of bouts in the States and overseas. When I asked after his luck, he proudly told me that he'd never been knocked down. Then we touched on the subject of adrenaline.

"For me, this is the same thing as going into the ring." His voice was calm, almost timid. "I felt good; so I feel good here. I don't feel scared, that is. I'm going to leave it all up to the Lord—see what he says."

· · ·

There was commotion in the audience, and an audible gnashing of teeth. The Wheel itself, Dispenser of Fortunes, had arrived.

Six days a week the Wheel rests in a sealed cage in a patrolled warehouse, guarded by a net of magnetic scanners and hidden cameras that would make the Pentagon eat its heart out. On the morning of the seventh day it is fetched out of hibernation and transported, in an unmarked Volvo truck, to the Cal Expo site. Once in place it is tested for aberrations, and given a few practice spins.

How the officials loved testing that wheel! They thrilled when the ball landed on big money; sighed despondently when it did not.

"The first time I spun it," said Susan Eddy, who had helped design the $20,000 Wheel (which was built by Beitel Displays, in New Jersey), "I hit the $2 million—which was at that time the top prize.

It was so exciting... I just can't imagine what it would be like to hit it for real."

Alas; this was as close as Ms. Eddy would ever get. Lottery employees and their families are prohibited from playing.

During the first practice spin, a silence like unto death had descended on the audience. This modern icon, this circus prop, this transfiguring Wheel, had fixed them in its potent voodoo. But in the middle of the third ersatz spin a shriek of panic pierced the set. *"Is that wheel fixed?? Is that wheel fixed!?"*

Jeff Edwards, Master of Ceremonies of the Big Spin, leaped out of his seat in the sidelines. He paraded to the stage, screaming like a maniac and pointing a crazily shaking finger. *"I just wanna know: is that wheel fixed??"*

I had to admire Edwards; he's good at his job. The tension on the set shattered, and the audience exploded into grateful applause.

· · ·

There was a period of about one hour during which the taping was poised to begin, but paralyzed by a maddening procession of glitches. Time and again Edwards went through the motions of opening the festivities; time and again the frantic audience was obliged to applaud uproariously. Edwards, ever the pro, tried to keep a happy face on things, but the nice, working-class folks on the folding metal chairs were growing discontent.

"How much are *we* gettin' paid for this?" Someone howled from the crowd. Edwards giggled, and loosened his collar. I made my way back to "death row."

Quiet lunacy infused the briefing room. A mischievous lottery official had brought in a few props for safekeeping—like the huge mock "checks" that would be handed to million dollar and Grand Prize winners. The appearance of these had caused visible sweat on a few foreheads.

The food table was nearly empty; not even the powdered donuts, messy pariahs that they were, had been neglected. The coffee urn was licked clean.

One woman seemed close to swooning. "This is torture," I heard another mutter. And, "wish I had a bottle of slug...." Even Melvin Hudspeth, invincibly cool, interrupted his dreams of a 911 Porsche (hooked to the back of a luxury motor home) long enough to pace maniacally around the room. "It's startin' to affect me," he crowed. "It's startin' to affect me."

I found Linda McBride off by herself, clutching a lucky pig and a four-leaf clover. She had forgiven me earlier for phoning her room on Friday night; now she sat in transcendental bliss, the yoga of money lifting her in a single morning to a state that a trained *saddhu* might practice for years to attain.

But it was a fragile achievement. There was a roar from the stands, and Linda looked at me with panic. "I'll have to take a vacation for a year," she admitted breathlessly, "to get back to the state I was in two weeks ago."

. . .

We got off to a slow start. James Fitzgibbons, a twenty-one year-old student from Grass Valley, dumped the ball for a lame ten grand. Carole Heiniger did the same. Castles were crumbling left and right; meanwhile, every miss increased the progressive jackpot by $65,000.

Ceslo Lopez was called forth to account for himself. He left the briefing room wearing a necklace of plastic charms—little hands, bears, and life preservers in hot pinks and purples—and a "Luck o ' the Irish" garter belt around his left biceps. The Champ gave it a good spin, and when he came back into the room he was $50,000 richer.

"Amazing, amazing," he mumbled. "Once in a lifetime." He sank, spent, into a chair.

Now it was Melvin's turn. Mr. Cool turned the wheel for an awe-some one hundred thousand dollars, throwing his fists triumphantly into the air. "We call that the 'Rocky' win," one of the directors whispered to me.

Linda McBride was next. I joined her briefly before the spin. "Were you really serious," I asked, "about taking a trip to the Himalaya?" She muttered something that might have been an affirmative. "Good.

In that case, take this." I thrust a tiny statue of Ganesh—the Hindu god of auspicious travels—into her hand. McBride clenched it, along with the little stuffed pig and four-leafed clover, and made her way to the stage.

I watched from the audience as she spun the wheel and won a million dollars.

Pandemonium broke loose. Lights flashed; bells rang; McBride's husband and son ran, braying, to the stage. In all the commotion Francisco Campos, waiting his turn along with the leftover donuts and San Martin Caballeros, had a glass of water spilled onto him. As he was next in line, this was a minor disaster. The wardrobe people went to work, and hauled the finished product to the stage.

The contestants in the back room watched the proceedings on a monitor. Everyone laughed as Francisco rolled his eyes at Jeff Edwards. Then he grabbed the wheel by the knobs and gave it one hell of a spin.

The little white ball flew around the wheel, dancing across the stops. Campos watched evenly; his family, in the audience, screamed. And then everyone was screaming, because the ball paused on one of the three slots marked GRAND PRIZE, and stayed there.

The forty-four year-old Campos, who had been taking in about $16,000 a year most of his adult life, was suddenly one of the wealthiest men in Sacramento. He was led offstage in a state of abject shock, as if he'd just experienced a horrible accident.

The jackpot was once again down to its base of $3 million, with Campos having cleared the coffers of exactly $6,445,000. Twenty percent of that would be lopped off the top to buy a new space shuttle; but even after that, the man in the bright red shirt could anticipate a check for over a quarter million dollars, every year until 2006.

John Long, an almost gigantic salesman from Bakersfield, took his place under the hot lights. "Third time's the charm," he declared to Edwards. "Let's go!" Less than a minute later he, too, was a multi-millionaire.

The group in the briefing room was rapidly dividing into four distinctive, if unspoken, castes. There were the glassy-eyed Big Winners; the commiserating little winners, also know as "losers"; the frantic and jubilant contestants still awaiting their turns; and the melancholy journalist.

· · ·

The two Grand Prize winners sat in the back of the briefing room, staring into space. Long would gaze at the floor, then explode into fits of laughter. Campos sort of hummed and moaned, occasionally lapsing into silly giggles. I sat between the two, working something out on a small calculator. "Listen to this," I said to Campos. "The way I figure it, it's as if they're paying you $16.72 an hour, in back wages, for every day you've been alive."

But Campos was not listening. *Mister* Campos, that is. He was in another world, shell shocked to the edges of the Twilight Zone. His branch of the family tree, in one immutable instant, had been pruned from a mesquite shrub and grafted onto solid oak. The wildest fantasy he'd had that morning would not even scratch his staggering wealth. His life, as he knew it, had ended.

"Ooooohhh... oooohhh... do something... slap me... pinch me...."

Long was likewise numb. "It won't hit me until tomorrow," he promised himself, and lapsed back into a daze. "Oh, man...." he shook once, all over, like a dog. "It's beautiful."

Campos leaned over toward his comrade, nearly weeping. "It feels good to be over, eh?"

You could see the words slowly sinking in. "Oh yes. Oh, yes. That's the best feeling of all."

· · ·

Eight more contestants spun the Wheel, but there were no more Big Winners. Even Edith Amos, who Schade and I were privately rooting for, had to conceal her disappointment as the unyielding ball awarded her a trifling $10,000.

Low spins move the show along quickly; before we knew it the stage was being broken down, and the families of most of the spinners prepared to leave. McBride, Long and Campos were exceptions.

They stayed on for photographs and a short press conference, and were chauffeured back to a reception at the Beverly Garland in presidential limousines.

I hung around with a few of the security agents as they loaded the Wheel back into the truck. Inevitably, we found ourselves discussing the morning's events, and the almost cruel absurdity of the Grand Prize.

"I'd rather give ten people a million dollars each than give one person ten million dollars," said one of the men, riding the lift with the boxed and cushioned wheel. "Fifty thou'—what the $1 million winners get a year—is manageable. More than that and the money controls you.

"And even if these people can actually comprehend how much money they've won—which they *can't*—then what? A lot of them have all kinds of trouble. Depression; they lose their friends; I wish we could just take all the contestants and say, 'okay—who ever would agree to give up the spin and just take a million dollars, stand up.' We could have 'em sign on the dotted line, and that would be it."

Maybe so—but then where's the horse race? Where's the drama? Where's the ecstasy of victory, the agony of defeat, the vicarious thrill of seeing an aluminum sign maker transfigured? The California Lottery was not designed around a profit-sharing scheme; it sells tickets to a mass public ritual, shamanistic in intensity, during which a lucky few are levitated to flabbergasting heights. Any other purpose the game might serve—funding state education, for example—is, at best, secondary. You could have asked every member of that audience "who won?" and nobody would have answered, "the schools."

I drove back to the East Bay with six dollars and the little statue of Ganesh in my pocket, bent on a single task: to buy my first five lottery tickets, and to do it before sunset. The Palestinian lunch joint was closed; I was reduced to performing the ritual in a 7-11.

Hope springs eternal, even in journalists. I rubbed the graphite off each ticket slowly, lovingly, chanting elaborate ablutions to the Hindu pantheon and San Martin Caballeros. Then I spent my last buck on a cup of coffee.

FIJI: WHAT I CAME FOR

This little sketch, a memento of my single, too-brief visit to Fiji, has never before seen the light of day. It was among the notes written on my way to the Solomon Islands, for a story which appeared in *Islands'* July/August '87 issue. Though I brought very little home (by way of souvenirs) from the Solomons, I did pick up a sack of powdered *kava* in Fiji. Shortly after my return, my friend Joan Walsh and I mixed it with water and drank it together in one marathon sitting. Alas; though its soapy flavor remained intact, the *Mbula* had been lost in transit.

SHORTLY BEFORE DAWN, as we made our approach for a three-day stopover in Fiji, I opened to the appropriate chapter in David Stanley's *South Pacific Handbook*. His praise was so effusive that I became immediately suspicious.

"Fiji is the perfect place to go native... you immediately fall in love with Fiji's vibrant, exuberant people... the smiles are always genuine and hospitality comes from the heart... *Mbula*, welcome to Fiji, everyone's favorite South Pacific country."

"Give me a break." I rolled my eyes, closing the book. Then the plane broke through the clouds, and the main island—Viti Levu—appeared below.

Oh, Mama. Within two seconds my face was flattened against the window like Silly Putty. The voluptuous emerald island undulated below, Mother Earth in a moss teddy. Could such a place be real— or was this merely a jet-lagged illusion? Realizing I would have only three days to find out, I burst into bitter tears.

Having been thus initiated, my next move was to read everything Stanley had written with intense interest. Was there something I could do, in my limited time, that would give me an indelible impression of what Fiji was all about? Apparently, there was. I could somehow get myself invited to an informal *kava* ceremony.

Kava, a drink prepared from the dried root of the pepper plant, is an absolutely essential ingredient of the Fijian's social life. The brew—locally called "grog"—is served informally, but was also an important part of traditional rituals.

As common and all-pervasive as the root tonic was rumored to be, I never seemed to come across anybody drinking it. During my first two and a half days I saw a lot of things—from cannibal forks to spotted moray eels—but not a drop of *kava*.

The evening before my departure for the Solomon Islands, I asked the proprietor of my inn to cash a traveller's check. Lacking suffi- cient funds, she recommended I stroll to the Grand Pacific, a larger hotel down on the beach. This I did, with success.

The Grand Pacific's cashier was a young man named Joe. As he counted out Fijian dollars, I decided to go for broke.

"Excuse me," I asked hesitantly. "Do you know where I might try some kava?"

"Oh, yes." Joe regarded me with an enormous smile. "My home. You come tonight. I invite you."

. . .

An hour later Joe finished work, and we took a cab to his house. It lay about a mile from the Grand Pacific, down the oceanside Queen's Parade. Joe's brother Gregorio was the guest of honor. He was visit- ing from the neighboring island of Vana Levu, and just happened to have brought some of that region's notoriously high-potency kava.

The actual grog ceremony was held at Joe's uncle Dominico's house. Dominico is a semi-professional soccer player, a stocky, square-shouldered man who has a reputation as the clown of the family. Throughout the drinking—which took place on a cane mat fringed with colorful tassels, and included Joe, Gregorio, Dominico, and three peripherally related, highly spunky Fijians—he served as a droll master of ceremonies.

The kava looked and tasted like dirty dishwater. After a cup or two it wasn't bad. The numbing of lips, tongue and mouth was milder than I'd expected, and I hardly noticed any effects of the drug until my fourth cup. By then, of course, I had more or less mastered the ceremonial mores that are a requisite part of the event: the single clap, followed by a shout of "Mbula!" Immediately, there's a cup in your hands. Then, "Mbula vinaka!" as you gulp the stuff down. Finally, on swallowing, three more claps: smart and sharp, palms ringing together.

I was feeling good.

"How come I never see any cats on Fiji," I asked, a propos of nothing.

"Oh, there are lots of cats," Joe replied.

"I have a cat," one of the women said. "A big one, sleeping in the other room." She meant the adjoining room, where Joe's mother was watching a video with a neighbor. "It's name is Blackie."

"Blackie," I repeated absently.

"He's black," Dominico explained.

The evening passed in a mood of extreme conviviality. The locals wanted to know my opinion of Sylvester Stallone; *Rambo* and *Cobra* were making box-office history throughout the South Pacific. They wanted to discuss soccer, drug smuggling, kava, travels. There was no sense of a color barrier, or even of national boundaries. I felt as if I'd been whisked off to another planet where everyone spoke perfect English—just like in all those old science fiction movies. Who could imagine that, a mere 125 years ago, the evening's bonhomie might have ended with my sweetmeats in their stockpot?

As midnight rolled upon us, I became cognizant of the fact that my plane to Honiara would leave in less than six hours. It was a brutal thought, but there was nothing for it. We bade our farewells, slurring, amid vows to keep in touch and promises to meet again—in Fiji or America. I had known these people for only a few hours, but felt as if I were leaving family.

I walked back home along the Queen's Parade, a white man in a white shirt on a balmy bright night, as the ocean clapped against Viti Levu. Above, the Southern Cross burned between the clouds. I was very, very happy. I don't think it was just the kava.

The next morning, a small jet carried me off to the Solomon Islands.

POSTCARD FROM BANGKOK

WHEN I HEARD one could buy magic buddhas in Bangkok—small, sculpted images which, worn around the neck, protect the wearer from harm—my only question was, where? The answer was, Wat.

Wat Mahathat is the site of the Saturday bazaar: the best place to find these amulets. I took a *tuk-tuk* to the Oriental Pier, where the Chao Phraya River Express carried me to Mahathat. After navigating a labyrinth of back alleys (clouds of oily wok-smoke, the ground littered with banana leaves, pressed dried squid stacked in straw baskets), I emerged into the light. All along the sidewalk, tables stood covered with tiny, exquisite buddhas. Shoppers leaned over the displays, examining the wares through loupes. Some were ancient, worth many thousands of *baht*; others, mass produced, might be had for the equivalent of a dollar or two. Traditionally, of course, nobody may buy or sell a magic buddha; any money that changes hands is merely a "donation."

I spent all afternoon at the buddha bazaar, oozing from stall to stall in the hot-tub humidity. Finally I returned home, four bite-sized buddhas in tow. Each amulet, I knew, addressed a specific purpose— but I hadn't a clue what their various powers might be. The cashier at my hotel perused the lot, and eyed me quizzically.

"This one will protect your jackfruit crop from hail," he explained, "and this one will ensure success on your high school equivalency exam. This third one goes around your waist when kick-boxing; it will safeguard your testicles. And this fourth one will make you invulnerable to bullets."

"That might come in handy back in Oakland," I admitted. "But how do I know that it works?"

"You may be sure," the cashier replied, dead serious, "that all these amulets have been very carefully tested."

THE FIGHTING SPIRIT
OF PHUKET ISLAND

Islands, in the late 1980s, did what few other travel magazines would or could: they ran long, impressionistic stories with little or no interference in a writer's rhythm and style. Paul Theroux, Tim Cahill, Frances FitzGerald, Jan Morris and Barry Gifford were fortunate enough to publish in that surprisingly literary magazine, and so was I. Today, this (somewhat abridged) piece on Thailand's most popular tourist destination seems a bit naïve; the boom in world travel and the AIDS epidemic have made Phuket a more frantic—and cautious—place. Still, Thailand is a country with a very skillful sense of development. I doubt that mere tourists will be able to do what generations of other invaders failed to accomplish: break the island's spirit.

"This is the place!" I yell above the wind and the hacking roar of the motorcycle into Charlie's ear. Not that he could miss it; Phuket's Spanhin Stadium is lit up like a power plant, and festooned with gigantic banners in Thai and English:

SUPER THAI BOXING TONIGHT!

Charlie leans into the dirt lot, skidding, and wedges his bike among countless others. Hundreds of men mob the entrance—eating, drinking, comparing notes, tallying the odds for tonight's eight matches.

Smoke rises from stalls roasting spitted chickens; a woman holding a tray of cigarettes and sweets illuminates her goods with a flashlight. The air is scented with hot chiles and pineapple, the familiar stink of sewage, nameless sultry island perfumes.

There's a spontaneous roar, the beat of a drum from somewhere inside. The crowd surges, carrying us toward the doors.

It's not easy to keep your wits in a strange environment; there is an instant of disorientation and panic. But I recall the words of my scuba instructor before my first ocean dive: "Watch the fish, and do the same."

We follow the mob into the arena, out of our element but sure of one thing: on a peculiar Asian island that many consider an ideal refuge from adrenaline, two men are about to beat each other senseless.

. . .

I'd seen the little truck earlier that morning, as I sat at the Marina Cottage hunched over fruit salad and the *Bangkok Post*. It was a billboard truck, the kind that spends its days blaring its message up and down Phuket's city streets and village roads, hawking some newly arrived American shoot-em-up. That morning, though, the *Rambo* ads were down and, in their place, garish pink, black and blue boxing posters bumped along the Kata Beach jeep track.

Thai boxing is a savage sport that developed in central Thailand some 600 years ago as a form of self-defense. The fighters may not wrestle, bite or spit, but that's about as far as the rules go. Kicking, shoving, punching and kneeing are common tactics, and the entire body is fair target. It seemed unlikely—and therefore irresistible— to encounter this ferocious game on tranquil Koh Phuket.

Then again, what did I really know about this "Siamese Serendipity," as the tourist brochures call it? I knew that the island's coral-laced waters are considered the rival of any in Asia; and that the seafood is the best in Thailand (and, for that matter, the world). I'd heard about the nightlife in Patong, where the pleasures are obvious, and for sale. I knew enough, in short, to make any human being want to drop everything, and run slobbering to the island's beaches.

The boxing was a lucky find, because it opened my eyes early on to the deceptive passivity of Phuket. Beyond the beaches and boiled lobsters there's another island, fighting for balance and economic punch as its major industry, tin mining, collapses—and tourism muscles in.

Phuket is a province of Thailand, a tough and independent country adept at staying on its feet in a part of the world where governments routinely hit the mat. But if it is to prevail into the 21st century, Phuket will have to do some pretty fancy dancing—of a sort that the island hasn't seen for a good 200 years.

. . .

History is like the weather; where you sit on the planet, your relationship to geography and currents, helps determine how much or how little of it you get. While upcountry Thais spent over a thousand years fighting the Khmers and Burmese along their central and northern borders, the islanders living further south, off the southern Isthmus of Kra, remained relatively undisturbed.

Sir Francis Light, a captain in the employ of the British East India Company, dropped anchor off Phuket's coastline in the 18th century. Light's intention was to annex the island for Great Britain. Early on, the ease of accomplishing this task fell to doubt. He reported to his superiors a rather sobering historical anecdote:

After losing a battle for Siam, the Malays had taken possession of Phuket, treating the local Siamese as slaves. One night one Thai islander fought bare-handed against an armed Malay and, by Light's account, "beat the Malay to a mummy." This victory was catnip for the locals, who resolved to eject the Malay weaklings without further delay. "As it was necessary to be secret," Light related, "seventy chosen men were assembled in the dead of night. They attacked the Malayan town with fire and sword. The governor, conceiving the whole island was raised against him, fled with his people.... In the morning not a Malay was to be seen. They left their guns, tin, money and merchandise to the islanders, and never dared return."

Light had a good eye for historic color; little did he realize he was destined to become a patch of it himself. It so happened that his arrival on Phuket had coincided with the death of Phraya Pimonkhan, the island's ruler. For Khunying Chan, the ruler's brilliant widow, bad luck came in threes. Her husband was dead, his kingdom left without a head of state, and a colossal foreign power was filing its teeth just offshore.

Khunying devised an elegant strategy. She installed herself as ruler, welcomed Light ashore and introduced the captain to a blindingly beautiful island maiden. Light fell in love, married the woman, and settled in Phuket, where he and his wife became model citizens. Some years later, Light recommended to the British that they annex Penang, in Malaysia, instead.

As Light enjoyed his early retirement, Khunying's adventures were just beginning. In 1785, the Burmese army arrived and tried to capture Phuket. Still acting ruler of the island, Khunying recruited her sister, Khunying Mook. Together, the two women led the island's army into combat. They routed the Burmese—and Rama I, King of Siam, bestowed the highest state honors upon them.

. . .

The back room of Spanhin Stadium reeks of camphor, bringing tears to my eyes. Sweat, urine, and the metallic scent of fear commingle into an olfactory overload that makes me want to jump out of my skin. Coaches crouch behind the fighters, helping them lace up into stainless-steel crotch protectors; the boys pound the cups with their fists for drill. "When they get into the ring," Charlie informs me, "the refs will check the cups for spikes." For many of the boxers, steel is not enough. They tie on waist cords as well, hung with magical amulets: carved coral and wooden phalluses.

Out on the floor, an atmosphere of subdued mania prevails. At ringside a three-piece band—the music sounds Middle Eastern—tunes up. Two boxers already lurk in the corners, their gloved fists fidgety on the ropes. We find seats close to the ring, and sit next to a striking Thai woman and her pale, obese European escort. As soon as we've settled in she leans over, places her hand on Charlie's thigh

and whispers to us. "This man is only my *boyfriend*. My *husband*—
" she smiles conspiratorily, "is back there!" We glance to the rear,
where a tall German glares at us.

"Oh?" Charlie answers dryly. "And what's the difference?" She
giggles, slaps his arm and turns quickly away. At that moment, the
bell rings. An almost electric charge sweeps the arena, tightening
the crowd like a muscle. The band kicks into a bellydance rhythm,
and the boxers pounce upon each other.

. . .

One seldom thinks of tin—humble, pragmatic tin—as the kind of
metal to drive people mad.

In 1979, though, deposits of slag were found on Phuket, sparking
a feverish "tin rush." Nearly 10,000 islanders, from housewives to
civil servants, ravaged the ground like crazed moles, digging up public
roads and private lands in search of riches. Many were arrested; it
took a squad of policemen to control the manic hordes.

Those were the days. The soft, rust-resistant metal was still in
high demand, and Thailand became one of the world's top suppliers.
But things change fast in the industrial world, and by 1984 the tin
market was on the brink of collapse: "beaten to a mummy" by lighter,
stronger aluminum. Today, Phuket's huge tin plants—like old bull
elephants abandoned by their herds—loom uselessly offshore. What
to do? Islanders of any means at all have tied on their gloves and
barreled forward in hot pursuit of the latest prize: tourism.

Big businessmen—like Wichit Na-Ranong, whose grandfather
owned some profitable mines—built big hotels. Wichit's Pearl, in
fact, was the first five-star hotel to open in the town of Phuket. By the
end of the decade the building fever had infected even modest in-
vestors, and clumps of rustic, no-frills bungalows began to spring up
along Phuket's formerly empty beaches.

In the early 1980s, as demand for tin took a nosedive, the casual
pace of Phuket development began to turn. Villagers with a bit of
savvy (and seaside property) became rich overnight. The smart money
began catering to a new brand of tourist: those who preferred ceiling

fans and hot showers to "roughing it." There was money to be made, and out came the stops. An airport was built, and the outside world began to arrive in force. Bungalow wars began in earnest.

Somchai Sillapanont, owner of the Marina Cottages on Karon Beach, is a thin, intellectual-looking man whose tortoise shell glasses magnify his eyes to bug-like prominence. He has a rueful countenance, the sort of look that makes you feel vaguely guilty over some unknown affront.

We sat in his open-air restaurant, practically shouting to be heard over the roar of the ocean, the whine of buzz saws and the whack of hammers nailing palm fronds to corrugated tin. A rival hotel, the Kakata Resort, had bought the beach in front of the Marina Cottages and was erecting an enormous lodge. To add insult to injury—for the lodge completely blocked the Marina's ocean view—the roofers had been instructed to leave the slope facing Somchai's property bare of fronds. Instead of the ocean, Somchai's unlucky visitors now gazed out, ironically, onto a sea of blank tin.

I gazed at the construction in empathetic dismay. "There must be something you can do."

"I think so," he agreed. "The law in Thailand is good, and the community wants to keep the place beautiful. Anyway, I'm not worried. Because, by next November, I will have the best-placed restaurant on all of Phuket Island. You see, over there?" He pointed beyond the new bungalows, directly into their ocean view, where a spectacular promontory shouldered its way into the sea. "I own that rock."

Despite the building craze, the majority of Phuket's beaches remain relatively unspoiled. Most of the demons of development, it seems, are gnawing upon one location in particular, some miles north of Karon. Over the past two years, Patong Beach has become sexual Disneyland, catering to an industry that first flowered in Thailand during the Vietnam War.

"It'd be a great place to shoot a movie," suggested Charlie, who drove his motorcycle to Patong every morning "for some freshly brewed drip coffee." I knew what he meant—especially at night, when colored bulbs race above rows and rows of booth-sized saloons, reflecting off the chrome of a hundred parked motorcycles, and sloe-eyed women lean out over every bar ("Hey, you beautiful man, come here!") while Conan, Godzilla and Bogart flicker across video screens behind their heads. Sometimes an entire flotilla of U. S. Navy ships will anchor at Patong, releasing 1,500 sailors at once into that cinematic wet dream.

"When I go to Patong," Somchai had earlier confessed to me, "I feel sick. But also very proud. Those girls, you see, are from the mainland; no one from Phuket does that."

Whether Somchai's small vanity is true or false, there's no doubt that prostitution remains one of Thailand's biggest draws. Some call it a victimless crime and, on the surface, many of the women appear to enjoy the excitement, attention and money. But an article I read in a local weekly gave me pause. In the middle of this glitzy throwaway—a magazine mainly devoted to thinly veiled ads and stuffed-bikini shots—the editor had included a strangely poignant interview with a "typical" Thai prostitute.

The woman, Kanari, had been married, with an infant daughter, but was abused and abandoned by her husband. To stay afloat, she'd ended up working the high-volume nightclubs of Pattaya, Patong's mainland sister city. "I don't hate my work," Kanari told her interviewer. "And I don't like it, either. It's simply what I do for survival. My only happy moments are when I'm alone, with my little girl."

. . .

"GO! GO! GO!" The boxer from Chon Buri falls against the ropes, and the Phuket favorite pounds his knee once, twice, three times into the walled-in fighter's gut. Every blow is accompanied by a manic shout from the audience. "There's no wrestling allowed," Charlie reminds me. "They've got to punch or kick their way out of trouble." Sure enough, Chon Buri gets a leg up somehow. He punts the local favorite off, and follows up with a flying kick that would have broken my ribs. This isn't stunt work; Chon Buri is going for blood.

We sit two rows from the ropes, sweating in our seats. I feel giddy, my breath catching on every blow, surrounded on all sides by the joyful, lunatic rush that some men feel as they watch other men beat the crap out of each other. The horn, flute and drums intensifies the drug-like effect, winding around the action, the sound as thick a presence as smoke in the air.

After the match, I meet the two young fighters in the warm-up room. They're leafing through a picture magazine, arms draped around each other's shoulders, the picture of guileless brotherhood.

. . .

Calamitous things can happen to islands when they become famous tourist destinations. Already-limited resources are often pushed to the limit by developers—and mercenary fishermen—who do not realize just how fragile the balance of nature really is. Coral, for instance, is more than exotic window dressing; it's a living, growing organism that takes hundreds of years to mature and plays a critical role in the food chain.

As Phuket moves into the big leagues—hosting up to half a million tourists a year—the demand for coral, sea-turtle shells and swimming space skyrockets, with disastrous effect. A dramatic example of this occurred in 1984, when an Italian-Thai company began destroying Patong's coral reef to make a swimming pool for its guests.

"We made them stop," declared Boonlert Phasuk, Director of Phuket's Marine Biology Research Center (MBRC). "But it took a long time. So what we're pushing for now is a new, far-reaching law, to protect all the island's living resources." Like most of the Thais I met, Phasuk had an air of self-deprecating humility. It was impossible to guess that this slouch in a baggy red T-shirt was one of the toughest champions in Phuket's newest battle: conservation.

"For example," he continued, "we hope to make it illegal to use coral for decoration, such as you see around many of the bungalows and in the hotels. Present coral owners will have to tag their coral; those found with untagged coral will be fined."

An assistant served us Chinese tea. We carried our cups into the Research Center's recently-built aquarium, stopping before a huge tank. Several varieties of sea turtle sluiced heavily through the water, regarding us with huge black eyes.

"Ten hours north of Phuket by boat," Phasuk said, "there's a beautiful group of islands called the Similans. For years, this has been a nesting place for sea turtles. But there was no watchguard, and people collected everything: the turtles, the eggs, the corals. Now that the islands are a national park, there is one guard—but the damage is done.

"We've tried to turn that around here at the MBRC," he continued. "Last February we raised about 5,000 baby turtles here. We hatch them at the aquarium, and release them once they can fend for themselves. Fortunately, our Queen is very keen on conservation. She gave us an island, where we're building trenches for the turtles' mating and egg-laying. When it's finished," Phasuk added wistfully, "we'll bring tourists over to watch them go at it."

The most unorthodox scheme adopted by Phasuk is directed not at the big offenders, but at the local fishermen who pump up their income by catching and selling the occasional turtle or spiny lobster to collectors. Under Phasuk's plan, the aquarium has offered to compensate locals for the captured creatures. The animals are then tagged, and thrown back in.

"The fishermen can still get more money on the outside," the biologist admitted, "but we're trying to introduce the idea out of personal responsibility and conservation. We're trying to raise an ecological consciousness." He shrugged dismissively, clearly ill at ease with his own tactics. "For children, the primary thing will be education. But for the older generation—" His hands spoke a universal language as they pantomimed a payoff— "We must first go like this."

· · ·

By the seventh match of the evening, the boxers have transcended brutality. They now move through their rounds in a practiced, intricate dance. Their arms and fists are up, not in front of their faces as in the Western style but to each side, forming an open frame. Within this frame their heads wag from side to side, teasingly, menacingly, like cobras.

Both men are smiling. Their eyes are glazed. Every few moments a series of blows and kicks explodes above the mat, but the violence is illusory. These are mere cues, punctuations in a high-level trance. Earlier in the evening the boxing ring had been a part of Spanhin stadium. No more. It is now a "floating world," like the Japanese *kabuki* stage. It's as if all the hype, all the music, the roasting chickens and roaring crowd, were assembled for one reason only: to give the boxers a springboard off of the Earth.

I'd seen such a trance before. Early one evening, as I rode home from Phuket town through the insect miasma, I encountered a shamanistic ceremony: a drum and tin pan beating out the rhythm while a group of islanders tied fluorescent lights to the trees. Two other men set up a sheet: an impromptu projector screen. Ignored in the midst of the construction activity, a tall young man danced vividly before an altar. Lying on the ground by his feet was an awful mace. Razor-sharp nails emerged on all sides in deadliest sea-urchin fashion. A long handle of woven cord was attached. Someone was actually going to beat himself with this grisly thing. And afterwards—for comic relief?—there would be a movie. The dancing man accidentally kicked the mace with his heel; blood welled from a dozen tiny punctures.

In the late 1880s, during the reign of King Rama V, an estimated 30,000 people from China and Malaysia arrived on Phuket to work the tin mines. These immigrant Chinese brought their own rituals, including mystifying trance rites in which selected participants withstand horrible, self-inflicted tortures to exhibit the depth of their faith. The most elaborate of these rites can still be seen during the annual Vegetarian Festival, a nine-day celebration held in October.

"It constantly amazes me," Wichit Na-Ranong remarked during our lunch at the Pearl Hotel. "I have seen people washing their faces with boiling oil. Or a spirit gets in a person, and suddenly they can speak fluent Chinese. You *know* the person, you've known him since childhood and know he *can't* speak Chinese, but the god is in him and he speaks fluently. I have seen people pierce their cheeks with metal rods and feel no pain. They take out the rod; no scar. And I have seen a friend...." He leaned forward so as not to disgust the other diners before continuing: "I have seen him *cut out his own tongue*, stick it on a spike, parade it around the town for three hours, and stick it back in his mouth. It sounds horrible—but no harm came from it."

Though liberally salted with animism, Phuket, like the rest of Thailand, is predominantly Buddhist. At a few of the larger *wat* (temples), gilded statues of revered monks are as popular with the islanders as likenesses of the Buddha himself. At most, though, a complacent image of the "Awakened One" presides. These images are often invested with strange histories, and uncanny powers. My favorite story revolves around Wat Pratong, a temple some 20 kilometers north of Phuket town.

Many years ago, the legend goes, a young man tending his family's water buffalo decided to take a rest. He tethered the animal to a strange metal spike that was sticking out of the field, lay down under a shade tree, and fell asleep. That same night, the boy felt ill. By morning, he was dead. His family was devastated, and utterly mystified.

Several days later, led by images from a dream, the boy's father brought a group of people to the field. He located the fateful spike, and implored everyone to join him in digging it out. Their efforts unearthed a solid-gold Buddha—the "spike" was actually part of the head-dress. But hard as the party worked, they couldn't extricate the statue; it was entrenched at chest level. At that point, the islanders did the only sensible thing: they left the statue where it was, and built a temple around it.

Years later, during a raid on Phuket, the Burmese also tried to excavate the golden Buddha. Their efforts, too, met with failure. Finally, to put a stop to such annoyances, local villagers disguised the golden statue with a thick coat of plaster. There have been no more attempted robberies—and by now, the unique Thai custom of honoring sacred images by pressing tiny squares of gold leaf onto their surfaces has virtually restored the Pratong Buddha's original gleaming appearance.

The line between Buddhism and animism gets pretty thin in places.

Most Thais, for instance, dilligently built small, sometimes elaborate "spirit houses" outside new homes or businesses. These shrines ostensibly keep the former, mercurial earth spirits from working mischief (and worse) among the new, flesh and blood residents.

By and large, though, I found Phuket's Buddhist population a pragmatic lot. One night at Marina Cottages, after the other guests had sipped the last of their Mai Tais, I questioned the two boys who served as the bungalows' night watchmen. "Do you believe there's some kind of strange power," I asked, "that makes it impossible to dig up the Wat Pratong Buddha?"

They gave me a look, and launched into their own theories. "It's very simple," the older one said. "The Buddha was being cast, and they ran out of gold. They were embarrassed, and didn't want anyone to know. So they made up the story."

"I think the Burmese *did* try to steal it," his brother said."First they cut it in half, because it was too heavy to carry all at once. But we drove them out before they could take the top part."

I found the implications of this second opinion amusing. Might one find, enshrouded by its own legends in the thickest jungles of Burma, a Temple of the Golden Lap?

. . .

A spray of sweat and saliva flies from the Phuket boxer's face as he goes down, another victim of the "TV Champion" from Bangkok. The crowd cheers madly for the underdog, who has held his own for three of the five rounds. In the end, though, there are no surprises. The local boy is peeled off the mat, revived with salts, and plopped onto a stool. The masseurs go to work on him. We make our way out, gagged by the camphor.

"Good fight," says Charlie. He buys a pressed, dried squid from an old man and begins chomping on it.

"How can you stomach squid at two in the morning?"

"Only two? The night is young! This is *Phuket*, man! In fact..." He pulls out his wallet, and leafs through an impressive stash of bills. "I'd be delighted to continue this party at that new disco, near the Club Med. My treat."

Two hours later I lay motionless on a beach chair, feeling the equatorial breezes blow over me. I'd tossed the half-empty pint of Mekong whiskey just out of reach. Considering my state, this is an adequate preventive measure.

It is a huge relief to be away from the disco, away from the blaring music and artificial light, the baby teeth of a newly hatched economic order. Overhead, stars fill the sky like graffiti. An intoxicating perfume blows in off the sea. It is a perfect moment, in a perfect place—until I find myself obsessed by an inane, Plimpton-esque thought: What would've happened, I wondered, if *I* had been forced to jump into the ring? What if I had been compelled—as a matter of life and death—to don my own crotch cup, rub liniment on my shoulders, and slug out a niche among the pros?

Would I pull through in one piece? The most interesting parts of me would be left unrecognizable, and the remaining regions badly bruised....

I settle back into my chair again, glad that I won't have to find out. But at that moment, I feel a powerful empathy for the people of Phuket Island.

KATHMANDU'S FIRST ESCALATOR

Shopping for Buddhas, first released by Harper SanFrancisco in 1990, was republished as part of Lonely Planet's *Journeys* series in 1996. It remains my most popular and successful book. Few people are aware that the story began as a monologue, inspired by Spalding Gray's *Swimming to Cambodia*; it premiered at San Francisco's Intersection for the Arts on the full moon of May, 1988, and had a short run that October at the Julia Morgan Theater in Berkeley. (As luck would have it, the second of three shows conflicted with the World Series—Oakland vs. Los Angeles. I performed for nine people.) The closing night's audience included Mark Salzwedel, an editor with Harper, who asked if I'd like to expand the material. This short chapter, a delight to perform, made a direct transition from the stage to the printed page.

There are many new roads in Kathmandu—the oldest of which is named "New Road."

New Road begins at the Tundhikhel Parade Ground, and plows a broad swath through what has become, such as it is, downtown Kathmandu. I steered my rented clunker—an India-made "Hero" with tassles streaming from the handgrips—through the brightly painted arch, flanked by images of Shiva and Ganesh, and glided to a halt at the first *gundpak* shop on the left. I bought fifteen rupees worth of the sweet, nutty, brown mass. The *sowji* wrapped it, still warm, in yesterday's New York Stock Exchange report.

Then it was off again, past the shimmering displays in the gem and jewelry shops; past Vision Stationary and New Human Fit Tailors; past shops selling soccer balls and tricycles, chutneys and doughnuts, King and Queen commemorative dinner plates and Singer sewing machines; past a crowd of Nepalese massed before a storefront, watching fresh photos spew from the maw of an instant film processing machine; past the steel-shuttered windows of the American Cultural Center, with their dramatic display of Space Shuttle images; past the ancient pipal tree, beneath whose spreading branches lay broad blue tarps covered with alternative newspapers; past Central Drug, Twenty-One Flavors ice cream, Optic Nerve, huge black bulls chewing complacently in the road as traffic swerved obediently around them—and in the windows of the tour agencies I read the brightly lettered signs proclaiming,

VISIT DAKSHINKALI!
LIVE ANIMAL SACRIFICES
EVERY TUESDAY AND SATURDAY!

At the end of New Road is the old royal palace with its towering pagodas and fantastic courtyard populated by gods, goddesses and demons. Not a bad venue for some shopping! But before making that plunge into the giddy world of Buddha buying, I stopped my bicycle and locked it by a telephone pole at the corner of Dharma Path and New Road. And there I gazed up, face to face with the entrance to the city's most grotesque capitalist monument: three tiers of sooty raw concrete, and a hand-lettered sign reading "Super Market." This was Bishal Bazaar, Kathmandu's first mall: only seven years old, but already an ancient ruin.

I'll tell you why I stopped. Some friends had come to town a couple of weeks earlier, and they returned from a stroll one afternoon to inform me that the management of this so-called Super Market had just finished installing an attraction that had proved to be the modern-day equivalent of the Hanging Gardens of Babylon. We're talking about Kathmandu's very first escalator, linking the first and second floors of the gritty enclosed mall.

Now, I'd been by before, hoping to find this marvel of technology in action. As a rule it was broken, covered with an enormous sheet of blue plastic, like a minor work by Christo. Today, though, contrary to any of my expectations, the escalator was running; and this I had to see.

. . .

There were two enormous crowds. One was gathered at the foot of the escalator, where a sneering guard wielding a nightstick pushed the bravest of the brave, one by one, onto the veranda, the no-man's-land at the base of the procession of hypnotic, endlessly ascending steps. A barefoot porter in filthy, tattered rags—some lost refugee from the hills—stood immobilized at the starting line, awed to paralysis by the stream of metal that flowed as if by divine writ from beneath the rubber cowl by his toes. And as I watched, I realized that the man was experiencing a beatific transformation. His knees weakened; and within a moment he was bowing, praying, practically prostrating himself before this divine sight, this holy river of steel issuing miraculously out of the ground, just as the great Ganges flows from the scalp of the great lord Shiva! The guard reached forward, and jerked him rudely aside.

The next victim was a twelve-year-old boy who, poised at the bottom, eyed the rise with all the trepidation of a young show-off who suddenly realizes that, hmmm, the high diving board is really a lot higher than it looks.... He swung his arms and took a few deep breaths before plunging out in his best urban swan dive. Right behind him stood an elderly Moslem lady who took one look and tried frantically to back away; instead she somehow stumbled *onto* the device. At first she kept her eyes closed, heaving a sigh of relief as her senses convinced her that she wasn't moving after all. But as soon as she opened them, her face whitened into a mask of abject horror. She clung desperately to the rubber rail, crouched as if for combat as her sisters, her husband, her sons and grandsons all faded away, lost against the backdrop of blinking advertisements far below.

The second mob waited at the escalator's summit, delighting in the huge joke of relative motion. These sophisticated voyeurs—many of them seasoned escalator veterans themselves—shouted with glee as each of the hapless riders was propelled, panicked and staggering, from the apparently motionless safety of the escalator onto the utterly unexpected menace presented by stable ground.

I ran up and down the stairway parallel to the marvelous escalator, enslaved by the realization that I could not leave—could not bear to leave—before demonstrating my utter command, my consummate prowess with escalators. No; I positively could not continue my search for a perfect peaceful Buddha before leaping onto this escalator like a trapeze artist, and wowing the local yokels with a bit of spontaneous street theater.

So, after mingling patiently with the downstairs mob (who ushered me forward with the kindness and generosity characteristic of all Nepalese) I found myself at the coveted brink. At first I made a show of trying to back away—and then, letting loose an awful howl, mounted the flying stairway in the most histrionic fashion imaginable, a pantomime of sheer terror, flailing and doubling back, slipping down the railing, disappearing from sight, finally rising to my feet only to be propelled like a rag doll into the waiting arms of the electrified upper crowd.

Ah, they roared! They loved it! These people! *My* people! I walked back down the steps, Nepalis slapping me on the back. Whew! Hey! What a riot! That was great! *I* was great!

But then the grin slid off my face like a wet towel, because the crowd was captured by a momentary silence. Down below, making their way through the swinging glass doors, a retinue of Buddhist monks entered the Super Market. They approached in single file, heads shorn, their robes flowing behind them like a flood of fresh-squeezed Florida orange juice.

The crowd melted, parting like a biblical sea to allow them through.

The guard abashedly lowered his nightstick and stepped hastily aside. And the monks, without panic or ceremony, simply mounted the escalator, and

rode it

to the next

level.

THE RAW AND THE COOKED
AUSTRALIA'S COBOURG PENINSULA

I nearly missed my flight to Darwin; the control tower literally turned the "Flying Guppy" around on the Ayers Rock runway to let me climb on board. Once we were airborne, a woman reading a newspaper turned to face me. "You're a Yank?" I nodded an affirmative. "Do you happen to know," she asked, "where Oakland, California, is?"

"*Oakland?*" I was incredulous. "*I'm* from Oakland."

"Well," she said, passing the paper, "your town is on fire."

The front-page photograph—of Oakland's Claremont Hotel surrounded by flames—was the most startling thing I saw during my 1991 trip to Australia. My neighborhood, as it turned out, was spared; some close friends, alas, were not as fortunate.

When I wrote this story for the *San Francisco Examiner*, "eco-tourism" was in its first flush—and I wasn't quite cynical enough to view it as a clever marketing ploy. Reading this today, I find myself wondering if Brian Rooke was right—or if the magical site we visited was finally fenced in, after all.

YOU KNOW YOU'RE in trouble, I told myself, when you're alone on the beach at sunset, and the only sign of civilization is a crocodile trap. An *empty* crocodile trap....

Otherwise, the setting was beautiful. I was at the tip of the Cobourg

Peninsula, a remote finger of bushland jutting from the top end of Australia's sparsely populated Northern Territory, watching a crimson sun sink into the Arafure Sea. Warm waves lapped at the shore, sieving through the labrinthine roots of a mangrove tree. A kookaburra laughed in a nearby tree—warning its fellows, no doubt, of the approach of a huge reptile.

Ironically, I was about a quarter mile from the most populated settlement on the entire Cobourg Peninsula: Seven Spirit Bay. The five-star resort, featuring 24 individual, lavishly appointed "habitats," is a flagship of Australia's somewhat self-conscious eco-tourism movement. Seven Spirit bakes its own bread, draws fresh water from artesian wells, processes its own sewage, and ships all of its empty Vegemite jars off to Darwin, some 150 miles south-by-south-something or other.

The hexagonal habitats themselves, hidden in the woods, feature panorama windows, freshly ground coffee and a bevy of other comforts like blow dryers and ironing boards, which appear vaguely surreal in the wilderness. But this seems to be the direction that "adventure travel" is taking. Tourists would no sooner face the hardships of the Australian outback than they would brave the "natural" conditions of a resort on, say, the Moon. The idea, here as elsewhere, is to provide all the luxuries of home—along with an authentic taste of the bush.

. . .

The question here, however, was whether the bush was going to have a taste of me. It seemed possible. During a brief cruise up a local river with resident naturalist Steve Hughes, we'd seen at least one gigantic croc: a 14-footer, looking extremely territorial and cold-blooded. They were, Hughes assured me, everywhere.

"They don't chew their food," he'd mused, watching the beast sink into the river, ten feet from our dinghy, with barely a ripple. "They just pull you under, stick you in a crevice and let you ripen a while. The bait attracts big fish, which are a crocodile's main diet."

I sighed, watching the sun disappear. Off in the distance I spied

Seven Spirit's yacht, plowing toward home. There had been several activities offered by the resort: sailing, fishing, and a boat trip to the deserted remains of Victoria, a failed attempt at settlement made by the British from 1836 to 1849. Too squeamish to fish, unable to sail, and generally oppressed by the sight of colonial ruins, I'd selected a final option, written in red and blue letters on a dry-erase board in the resort's lobby:

8:30 A.M.: THREE HOUR HIKE THROUGH SWAMP

Needless to say, I was the only participant. I was met by Steve, who waited behind the wheel of an old Toyota Land Cruiser (the vehicle of choice in the Australian bush), and John Williams: a portly, white-haired aboriginal elder who had grown up on the Cobourg Peninsula before being shipped off to school by missionaries.

The idea of a swamp walk appealed to me. This was October, the dry season on Australia's Top End, and what little water had survived the heat and bush fires of winter was confined to small, compact swamps. It was likely we'd find animals—wild pigs, Timor ponies, Indonesia cattle and dingos—around the waterholes. All of these animals, Steve told me, had been brought in by the early settlers and left to fend for themselves after Victoria failed. It was funny; on Kangaroo Island the wild animals had been practically tame, while here on the Cobourg Peninsula, barnyard animals roamed the bush, wild as sin.

We bounced along a narrow dirt track, bush in all directions. I rode in the open back cab. Huge brown termite mounds rose from the forest floor like stalagmites. Every so often Steve would slam on the brakes, raising a cloud of dust which enveloped me instantly. "Buffalo!" he'd holler; but by the time I wiped my lens, the animal would be gone.

After an hour of this Steve pulled over, and we got out to walk. The hike would take us through the bush, around a swamp, and out to a beach called Kennedy Bay; then we'd make our way back to the car. Steve tested his walkie-talkie, handed John a full canteen, and we set off.

As we made our way through the woods, my guides explained the various flora. Steve pointed out the blackened eucalyptus trunks, evolved to withstand bush fires, and the brown tannin stains on the paperbark trees, which indicated how high the swamp water would rise in the wet season. "It'd be suicide to stand here six months from now," he said, ever mindful of crocs.

John, born and bred in the bush, actually peeled the spongey skin from a paperbark and fluffed it out, demonstrating how the aborigines made their bedding. At one point he picked up a huge frond from a kantia palm, and slung it like a surfboard over his shoulder. "My people would make a billy out of this," he said, using the local slang for a water container. "I reckon I'll soak it overnight, and show the tourists how it's done."

It was wonderful to hear John reminisce, as we wandered through the forest, about the days when he and his brother Nelson hunted for "bush tucker" among the trees and tidepools. "My people ate everything," John said, eyeing the trees as if they were rare delicacies. "Palm hearts, sting rays, wallabies, crocodile tails; you name it, we ate it." Local plants and insects were refined to produce a wide variety of medicines, he said. Some of these have been shown to contain the same basic ingredients as modern pharmaceuticals.

We saw a few animals: mostly buffalo and elegant Timor ponies. But I was most fascinated by the termites, who seemed to virtually own the bush. Their condominiums towered beneath some trees and swelled in the branches of others. The "arboreal mounds," as Steve called them, were linked to the ground by mud-walled tunnels. When he scraped away an inch of tunnel, the highly specialized insects instantly emerged to form a defensive line: workers began plastering the walls back into place while soldiers formed a ring around them.

After an hour in the bush I was glad to emerge into the open air of Kennedy Bay. John pointed across the strait, indicating the silver roof of his brother's house. Then he led me across the beach, following the path of a white-tipped reef shark with his thick finger.

"Nelson and I, we'd come here all the time," John recalled. "We'd catch 18, 20 fish in one hour." His eyes glazed over, peering into the past. "I'm deadly with a spear...."

A weird pink slime, like something out of *The Cat in the Hat*, was washing up with the waves, leaving Pepto-Bismol colored arcs on the sand. "My people call that whale vomit," said John, poking at it with a stick.

"Um.... No, no," Steve spoke softly, hesitant to contradict a local elder. "That's coral spawn, John. At certain times it washes up off the corals, and makes its way to shore."

John nodded, deep in thought. "Yes. Mmm hmmmm. I reckon it's whale vomit...."

Apart from the slime the beach was gorgeous, with dramatic cliffs towering over shell-strewn sand. In some places the cliffs were folded into narrow crevasses—illustrating the aboriginal name for the area, which John shyly translated as "Women's Privates." The entire region is sacred land, he explained, worshipped as the arrival point of *Waramurungunji*: an ancient aboriginal goddess who created all the clans, as well as the "wet" foods and sea-dwelling creatures.

. . .

It was afternoon when we arrived back at our vehicle. Sunset was still a few hours away and I wanted to view it, in solitude, over the sea. After some hesitation Steve agreed. He drove me across the narrow peninsula. I hiked down a long mountain bike trail that John had hacked through the bush, finally arriving at a secluded beach.

Oblivious of time, I strolled, wrote and collected shells. But the sun drops fast near the equator, and I was soon faced with an unhappy choice: get back to the resort at once—or risk making a contribution, however modest, to the local food chain.

It's amazing how quickly a night walk can turn terrifying; especially when one begins to consider the many infamous animals— snakes and crocodiles, to name but two—which are nocturnal. That crashing in the bush: was it a python, or a hungry reptile? I tripped over a narrow root, and my yelp was answered with a chorus of howls. Large was my relief when, after 20 minutes of near panic, I spied the lights of the habitats ahead of me.

I took a long, cool shower in my semi-outdoor bathroom, keeping an eye on the trail of green-bottomed honey ants circumnavigating my sink (I was one of the eco-resort's few patrons, the management wryly informed me, who had not requested insect spray). After dressing I hopped on one of the resort's battered mountain bikes, and zoomed to the dining hall.

That morning, before the swamp hike, I'd expressed a single regret to Sue and Basil, my hosts at the resort. Though the Cobourg Peninsula was aboriginal land, the area around Seven Spirit Bay didn't have any examples of their paintings. I'd been hoping, I told them, to see some of those wonderful and mysterious artworks.

Sue and Basil nodded thoughtfully. John William's daughter and son-in-law, they said, ran a small safari company down in Arnhem Land, some 70 miles southeast of Seven Spirit Bay. Within this region lies Umorrduk: a rocky canyon peppered with caves and aboriginal art "galleries." They would make a few calls, Sue promised, and see what could be arranged.

As I sat down to a dinner of tiger prawns and pan-fried barramundi, Basil and Sue joined me. "It's all set up," Basil said with satisfaction. "A small plane will pick you up tomorrow and bring you down to Umorrduk, along with Brian Rooke—John's son-in-law."

This was excellent news. I followed the Habitrail back to my habitat, feeling very much the pampered hamster.

. . .

"You'll like my key." Brian Rooke jammed a screwdriver into the ignition of his Land Rover, and twisted. The engine cleared its throat. Behind us the twin-engine Cherokee pulled off the landing strip, disappearing in a cloud of dust.

Umorrduk lies in the middle of nowhere, on a vast parcel of land some 400 square miles in size. Only some 50 aboriginals live there, and no more than 16 tourists may be on the land at any one time. Permission to visit the area, Brian told me, is available only through Umordduk Aboriginal Safaris: the company started by Brian and his wife, Phyllis Williams.

Brian is a tall, lanky man with small teeth and surprisingly caucasian features. His aboriginal blood, he explained, comes from his grandmother. He leaned over the wheel, a wireless radio by his side and a massive .357 Magnum on his belt ("In case of wild pigs"), and began a bone-jarring jaunt into the bush.

"We're about to see artworks created by local people possibly 15,000 years ago," Brian shouted. "They may be even older. Dating the artworks exactly is impossible, but we know that our people have been here at least 40,000 years. And one of the paintings shows warriors hunting a diprotodon: a huge animal that became extinct about 15,000 years ago, around the same time as the gigantic carnivorous kangaroos."

We emerged from the bush, and Brian killed the motor. I stared in amazement. A range of huge, rocky promontories lay before us, made of billion-year-old sandstone weathered into caves, gullies and fantastic shapes. Inside those caves, Brian said reverently, are thousands of aboriginal art galleries, many still undiscovered. They record legends known and forgotten; tales of goddesses and spirits, mythical animals and religious rites lost to antiquity. "My father-in-law knows better than I what they mean," Brian said. "As the eldest of his tribe, you see, John is the owner of all this land."

Brian and I spent hours exploring the site, awed by the strange designs and vivid colors of the ancient artworks. There were paintings of the Rainbow Serpent, who controls the rains and keeps the law; of Warigag, Waramurungunji's unfaithful husband, who was turned into stone; and of the *mimis*, female spirits who live within the rock and are believed to have made the earliest paintings themselves. There were countless portraits of animals: sea turtles, kangaroos, goanna lizards and fish, often rendered in the mysterious "X-ray" style, where the bones of both the hunted and the hunter are revealed.

It was brutally hot. After a long swig from our canteens Brian and I lay on our backs beneath a painted overhang, enjoying a cool breeze. I gazed up at the parade of crimson, yellow and ocre figures above our heads. Brian had told me that I was the first white person ever to see some of these paintings. I found it incredible that this area should be so undeveloped.

"There'll be a fence around all this 20 years from now," I guessed.

"Never," said Brian. "That's not what this place is about. It'd lose its magic appeal. If this place gets developed for mass tourism," he stated, "I'll be the first to leave."

I could have spent days in Umorrduk, combing the knobby skulls of stone and discovering new caves and paintings. With more planning, that might have been possible; Brian's safari company has a tented camp nearby, complete with a generator and fully equipped kitchen. He and Phyllis hope to pursuade local tour operators to include Umorrduk on their itineraries, along with Seven Spirit and Kakadu National Park. It's bound to happen; Umorrduk's little-known paintings are at least as good as the famous galleries in nearby Kakadu.

The Cherokee was due to return for me in an hour. On our way to the airstrip Brian and I stopped at a local *billabong*: a backwater pool surrounded by trees and boulders. It was exactly the kind of place where, according to Steve Hughes, a person could expect to be devoured by crocodiles. I watched in horror as Brian stripped, waded in and swam to the center. He floated lazily, the picture of bliss, and peered at me with amusement.

"I'd be lying to you if I said there was absolutely no chance of a croc attack," he confessed. "But it hasn't happened yet—and my people have bathed here for many, many years."

I had to laugh. There are, I understood, two very distinct schools of eco-tourism: the raw, and the cooked. Seven Spirit Bay, with its "habitats," hair dryers and chocolate macadamia nut brownies, is one extreme; Umorrduk, with its mimis, Magnums and billabongs, the other. And though I'd spent much of the previous evening terrified of crocodiles, I realized we had at least one thing in common.

I jumped into water, as raw as I could get.

CAMBODIA:
THE TIME TUNNEL

This piece first appeared in the *Washington Post* in 1993, and a few months later in the *San Francisco Examiner*. Though it's mentioned briefly in the story, I'll add this expanded footnote: in November of 1979, a friend and I were touring Thailand when the Cambodian civil war erupted. We left the beaches of Koh Samui and signed up as volunteers at Khao-I-Dang, the largest of the Cambodian refugee camps. The story I wrote about that experience—"Very Alive"—appears earlier in this book, and launched my career in journalism. For that reason, among others, I'd long felt a strong bond with the Khmer people. The opportunity to visit their country, just emerging from Pol Pot's black shadow, meant a great deal to me.

"WE HAVE AN EXPRESSION in Khmer." My *samlor* driver glanced back at me as he peddled up Achar Mean, the main boulevard of Phnom Penh. "*Meuch tauk nung ngous kluon eng*," he recited nasally. "It means, 'to take a shower in your own sweat.' "

Though I'd arrived only a few hours earlier, I was already a living illustration of the proverb. But heat—even this kind of heat, which threatened to melt me like a mocha truffle—seemed a small price to pay for being, at last, in Cambodia.

The flight from Bangkok to Phnom Penh had taken just over an hour—a reminder of the tiny physical distances that separate the capital cities of Southeast Asia. It was a journey I'd dreamed of making since 1979, when I worked with Khmer refugees at a camp on the Thai-Cambodian border. Over the years, my casual interest was sharpened by a growing obsession to see Angkor: the ancient Khmer capital which hovers in an Oz-like nimbus.

But even though Phnom Penh is just 290 miles from Bangkok, for most of the past quarter century it may as well have been in the middle of Mare Imbrium. Secret bombings, civil war and genocide have bedeviled the former Khmer empire since 1970, when Prince Sihanouk was overthrown by Lon Nol, a rightist general backed by the U.S.. Only in 1990 did Cambodia, whose spectacular monuments once drew thousands of international travelers, open its borders to visitors again. How long they will remain open—given the violence that marked the May elections—is anybody's guess.

Odd thoughts arise when one visits another country. One image that kept occuring to me in Cambodia was a silly '60s television show called *Time Tunnel*. The "star" of the show was a time machine: a seemingly endless tunnel, lined with black and white bands (imagine looking down the middle of a half-extended Slinky). At the beginning of each episode the main characters would fire up the tunnel, run into its circular maw, and leap out through one of the pulsing bands. They never knew where—or when—they would end up.

By the end of my first few days in the country I knew that Cambodia, too, was a place where time behaves unpredictably. Instead of flowing steadily forward, it seems broken into fragments: a piece of the past here, a chunk of the future there. I found them scattered, often haphazardly, across the landscape of the present.

. . .

Certain details, rarely in the guidebooks, are immediately striking about a foreign city. Phnom Penh impressed me as a city of iron grilles and lattice gates, spiked fences and high walls; a place where centuries of invasion and decades of stress have created a kind of architectural paranoia. It wasn't readily apparent on the streets, where locals spoon soup at outdoor restaurants and whole families crowd into bicycle rickshaws. After a bit of touring, though, I deduced that Cambodia's capital, despite its broad avenues, lively markets and sweeping views of the Mekong River, is a city of private fortresses.

An amazing number of vehicles-for-hire—specifically, motorscooters and bicycle rickshaws (*samlors*, or "cyclos")—cram the city's streets. Every time I stopped, even for a moment—to check my map, blow my nose or tie my shoes—a dozen such conveyances would surround me, their drivers patting hot vinyl seats to beckon me over.

Together, these first impressions of Phnom Penh gave me an idea of what contemporary Cambodians must see as the basic necessities of life: personal security, and the ability to beat a quick escape.

It's not surprising. Anyone who has read *Sideshow* or seen *The Killing Fields* has an idea of what Cambodia experienced between 1975 and 1979—when the maniacal Khmer Rouge, led by Pol Pot, tried to transform the former French colony into a Maoist farm commune. Over a million Cambodians were killed as part of the "cleansing" process—many for wearing eyeglasses, or speaking a few words of French. So many adults perished during those years that, today, more than half the population of Cambodia is under fifteen.

Phnom Penh still bears the scars of that dark era. Driving through town, looking beyond the rows of flowering plumeria trees, I could see the gutted classrooms of the Technical University; the abandoned School of Fine Arts; the obsolete Olympic stadium. Saddest of all is the empty, eerie hulk of the former French Embassy: an indescribably forlorn shell that looks more like a broken heart than a building. On April 17, 1975, when the Khmer Rouge took Phnom Penh, 600 Cambodians who had sought refuge here were forced to surrender. Torn from their foreign lovers, husbands, wives and co-workers, they were led away to hard labor, torture, or the killing fields of Choeung Ek—just 10 minutes southwest of Phnom Penh.

Parking in the dirt lot and approaching on foot, there seems nothing especially remarkable about Choeung Ek. It is a small, cratered field, marked by a tall memorial pagoda. The pagoda's roof is supported, at each corner, by white marble columns, and between the columns rise high glass walls. Coming closer, one staggers to behold that the high glass vault is packed with human skulls. There are nearly 9,000 of them, exhumed from the mass graves amidst which one is standing.

Choeung Ek is one of many such memorials scattered across the innocent Cambodian countryside. Walking among the excavated graves, upon a surreal landscape littered with torn clothing and human bones, I stopped for a moment to pray—and heard an astonishing sound. Not a hundred yards from this nightmare, in a little school, Cambodian children were gleefully singing the *ka-kha*: the Khmer version of our own "A-B-C."

These were the children and grandchildren, I knew, of the men and women whose bones lay beneath my feet. But the violent deaths of their forebears had won them neither stability nor security. Despite the efforts of the UN, few expect that the recent elections, boycotted by the Khmer Rouge, will bring a lasting peace. It seemed incredible to me that these children could be singing and laughing in the midst of so much uncertainty; and as I stood in the killing fields of Cheoung Ek, head bowed, my only prayer was that they would have the chance, quite simply, to grow up.

While the most compelling sites around Phnom Penh are the grisly reminders of Khmer Rouge atrocities, the city's memory predates that awful regime. As recently as the late 1950s, Phnom Penh was a beautiful and very cosmopolitan capital marked by grand hotels, garden cafes and other signs of long French stewardship. Landmarks of that era remain, and the current lull in hostilities has inspired feverish bouts of restoration and modernization. It's happening fast; every guide to the metropolis is made obsolete long before it's published.

Phnom Penh is a city best explored by slow-moving vehicle. Cyclos are ideal for this purpose. For 4,000 *riel* (about a dollar, although the exchange rate fluctuates hourly) I spent an entire morning being lazily peddled from one destination to another. Aside from lively markets, great french bread and some of the most grotesque theater posters imaginable (e.g., multi-tentacled, drooly-fanged octopus women in hot pursuit of bicycling soldiers) Phnom Penh is known for its elegant Buddhist *wats* (temples). My favorite among these was Wat Phnom, a small shrine perched on a knobby hill near the docks and inhabited by a gold Buddha decorated with wild party lights. Legend says that the hill was once an island, inhabited by a devout but eccentric woman named Dawng Penh. Over time, the waters receded into the Mekong, and Phnom Penh—Ms. Penh's hill—lent its name to the new city.

The Royal Palace, with its elegant architecture and fine art collection, has been closed to the public since Prince Sihanouk returned to Cambodia in 1991 (he actually lives in Beijing). Nearby, though, in the musty, guano-speckled halls of the National Museum, I discovered an unexpected treasure.

It was a sandstone statue of the meditating Buddha, seated on the coils of Muchilinda Naga: the multihooded snake god who protected the young prince during his enlightenment.

Gazing at that serene face, with its half-closed eyes and subtle smile, I remembered what the Buddha was up to at that very instant. Having freshly conquered the illusion of Time, he was viewing the past, present and endless future as a single moment—and recognizing the fact that every human emotion, from joy to utter despair, will finally vanish like smoke.

The image of the meditating Buddha has rested for centuries at the center of all Khmer art and philosophy, and seems to embody the point of view that enables contemporary Cambodians to accept their present circumstances—whatever they may be—with grace and equanimity. It was something I had noticed in the refugee camps as well: few Khmers seem to dwell on the past, nor invest much faith in the future. They seem far more interested in cultivating a stable present within which, moment by moment, they might safely live.

· · ·

Kampuchea Airlines doesn't have the prettiest airplanes in the world, but they do get you to Siem Reap. During the short flight toward that extended village, which lies close to the ruins of Angkor, I gazed out the window at the sparse, flat landscape of Cambodia. Signature sugar palms dotted the terrain, and narrow roads stretched like trip-wire across the ground. Tonlé Sap, Cambodia's large inland lake, mirrored the pagoda-shaped clouds which hung, absolutely still, in the humid air. The placid vista was, I knew, deceptive. Despite the best efforts of UN peacekeeping troops, there were dangerous people down there....

The monuments of ancient Angkor, of which Angkor Wat is the largest and most famous, were built between the 9th and 13th centuries A.D. by a succession of Khmer kings attempting (successfully, one imagines) to impress God. During this epoch the Khmers controlled much of Southeast Asia; their empire reached from South Vietnam northward into China, and westward to the Bay of Bengal. Inevitably, though, the cost of their giddy building sprees sapped the kingdom. In 1431 the invading Thais sacked Angkor, compelling the poorer but wiser Khmers to move their capital eastward.

The spectacular ruins first caught the western eye in the 1860s when Henri Mohout, a French naturalist, described the "lost city of Angkor" in *Le Tour du Monde*. What has since evolved is an icy debate between advocates of reconstruction—who would restore Angkor to an approximation of its former glory—and pure romantics, who feel that the sight of an ancient stone temple overgrown with jungle is poetry itself.

Ignoring complaints from the latter, the French began a concerted effort to clear the jungle (which eats temples like candy) and restore some of the damaged structures. Tossing a bone to the poets, they agreed to leave one temple—Ta Prohm—to nature. Ambitious reconstruction efforts on the other temples continued until the 1970s, when they were halted by the war.

Today several groups, from various countries, are working to restore the major temples. Not all of these teams possess the same expertise, or even the same philosophy. During my visit there was considerable controversy surrounding the team from India, whose wire brush approach to cleaning Angkor Wat's *bas relief* murals has been called careless and even destructive. The fiasco has generated a lot of press, but I was more interested in visiting the group working on Preah Khan: a small but very elegant temple three miles north of Angkor Wat. The project, managed by the World Monuments Fund in New York, is being directed by John Sanday—a reserved, thoughtful architect whose conservation work on the temples of Nepal has been skillful and sensitive.

I left my hotel, crossed the Siem Reap river on a narrow footbridge, and found the local office of the World Monuments Fund. John Sanday was upstairs, rolling out a map. A tall, red-faced man with swept-back hair, he asked about my plans. I assailed him with an elaborate itinerary.

"Okay. This afternoon I'm driving out to the Ruluos temple group. I'll see Preak Ko, Bakong and Lolei. Then, between sunset and dusk, I'll shoot over to Tram Neak, and...."

"Forget it," Sanday said. "I'll tell you what to do. Leave your guidebook at home—and your camera. Just go and see Angkor Wat. Immediately. It'll blow you away."

And I did.

I confess that I was worried at first. I expected swarms of tourists, a carnival atmosphere around the temples. As I approached, though, and beheld the sheer *scale* of the place (you could dock the *QEII* in its moat), I saw that Angkor Wat is a bit like the Himalaya: there's room for everyone.

Over the next two days I'd spend endless hours exploring Angkor Wat, but I'll never forget my first impression. Entering through the huge gateway, I felt a strong adreneline rush; the same dizzy cultural vertigo one feels when first seeing the Pyramids, or the Taj Mahal. Angkor Wat loomed before me like a mirage, legendary and enormous, a shimmering tapestry of history in stone. The wide causeway seemed to stretch on forever. In the distance Angkor Wat's five central towers—modeled after lotus buds—bloomed toward heaven. The temple, created during most of the 1100s, was meant to model Mt. Meru, the mythical center of the Hindu universe. I've never seen Meru, but I can't imagine that Angkor Wat's architects were much off the mark.

In short, it's overwhelming. One detail, though, may serve to convey Angkor Wat's infinite complexity. Just inside the outer wall of the complex, facing the huge central structure itself, are scores of sculpted *apsaras*. These celestial dancers, graceful as swans, appear as spiritual muses in temples throughout Southeast Asia (there are more than 2,000 at Angkor Wat alone). Usually, their lithe figures are just repetitions of a single motif. But as I walked along the sandstone wall at Angkor Wat, visiting one apsara after another, I realized to my amazement that *each one was different*. The shape of their eyes and their breasts; their earrings; the soft, sculpted *sarongs* that flowed down from their hips; all were completely unique. These particular apsaras, I intuited, were not mere mythical beings. They had to be portraits of flesh and blood women who lived over 800 years ago, and danced in the court of Suryavarman II: the great Khmer king who built Angkor Wat.

Leaving the temple and driving north, I penetrated the high south gate marking the entrance to Angkor Thom. This is the site of the Bayon, an amazing monument built 50 years after Angkor Wat. Around the four walls at the Bayon's base are long, intricate bas reliefs depicting the most prosaic details of court life. Chessplayers, people picking lice out of each other's hair, even circus vignettes provide comic relief between endless images of violent battles, replete with severed heads and other gruesome details.

The most magnificent part of the Bayon, though, is its uppermost level: a broad dais from which 172 gigantic heads (depicting Avaloketesvara, the buddha of compassion) smile aloofly into the surrounding jungle.

Back home in San Francisco, I often look out over the city and contemplate how empty and unspoiled that metropolitan landscape must have been only 200 years ago. In Angkor, I found myself doing just the opposite. I sat silently among the massive heads, gazing into the jungle, and tried to imagine Angkor Thom during its heyday, when it was a thriving city of over a million inhabitants. It was difficult; any trace of a human presence has long ago vanished. The

Khmers, consummate masons though they were, built their own homes out of wood—reserving for the gods their immortal palaces of stone.

The next morning I got an early start, and set off to meet Sanday at Preah Khan. Arriving at the western entrance, I understood at once why so many visitors to Angkor call this temple their favorite. It has a seductive *rawness* to it. While some of the structures seem relatively intact, others have been claimed by the jungle. A lush chaos holds sway. Avalanches of carved stones spill through massive beam-and-lintel doorways (Khmer architects had yet to discover the arch); crimson dragonflies perch on the impassive noses of stone deities. Not as wild as Ta Prohm, which is choked with foilage, Preah Khan manages to be mysterious and accessible at the same time.

The World Monuments Fund's real work on Preah Khan started in November 1992, when 80 workers began the arduous process of clearing jungle and bolstering the most precarious structures. As Sanday and I walked toward one of the buildings on the northeast of the compound, I asked him why no one was excavating the area for archeological evidence of the great Khmer empire.

"It's a question, really, of priorities," he replied. "We can leave things that are under the ground for quite a long time; not so with these buildings."

We stopped in front of a large pavillion that stood alone, away from the main temple complex.

"Preah Khan was a huge monastic complex," Sanday said, "built in 1191. This may have been where the "sacred flame" was kept. At any rate, it's a real microcosm of all the problems one finds at Angkor: structural separation, vegetation and foundation settling." He indicated, in turn, a section where the massive masonry wall was leaning away from the roof; the multicolored lichens that were slowly eating away the stones; and a series of chalkmarks which showed how the southern portion of the building was sinking, inexorably, into the earth. Then he pointed, with considerably more enthusiasm, at the wall.

"Look at this. You just don't see it anywhere else. It's all dry stone construction; no mortar at all. The stones are set in place and rubbed. No two are exactly alike; they were all made individually, and jogged into place."

Preah Khan was littered, I noted, with the building blocks of crumbling temples. Did the World Monuments Fund plan to piece the whole complex back together again?

"Not at all." Sanday seemed appalled by the idea. "Our goal is to conserve and present Preah Khan as a partial ruin. We're not trying to falsify its history; history began one second ago. We're preserving the buildings as we found them, and undertaking partial reconstruction in places where buildings are dangerously unstable."

The indomitable jungle (along with art theft, which has led to the presence of armed guards at many of the temples) is one of the most serious problems at Angkor. Lichens, which slowly blur and devour the delicate carvings, are bad enough; but now I spied a giant ficus tree that was wrapped around the southeastern face of Preah Khan's central temple. Trunk and stone were woven together like bone and muscle.

"And what," I asked, "will you do about that?"

"What *can* you do? You can pull it down; but the tree is so deeply imbedded in the structure that the whole place will come down with it." Sanday grinned. "I've taken the romantic point of view, and feel it has every right to be there. What we'll do is to isolate the structure, to prevent the tree from influencing the stonework on either side. Then the tree can carry that section a hundred feet into the air, without bothering anything around it."

Around sunset, as I piloted my rented scooter down the well-maintained road leading to Siem Reap from Angkor, the erotic scents of the jungle broke over me like surf. It was March—the *ruumduel* flower season—and the warm air was filled with their sweet aroma. It was blended with smoke and lemon, incense and chlorophyl, the dense and sultry perfume of inner Cambodia. But scattered through that musky jungle, hidden among the ruins of ancient Buddhist temples, were lethal mines. Rarely in my travels had I encountered a landscape so hypnotic, yet so threatening. Here were flute and cobra, all at once.

. . .

It was a shock to return to Phnom Penh. During my final day in Cambodia I desperately needed an escape—a refuge from the frantic traffic and tireless swarms of *samlors* and scooters that dogged me at every turn. Late in the afternoon, I had an inspiraton to ferry across the Mekong River to Mekong Island: a green and uncrowded slice of land not 10 minutes from Wat Phnom.

The moment I stepped off the ferry, I knew I'd stumbled into that zebra-striped Time Tunnel once again. Mekong Island was peaceful and uncrowded, a luscious throwback to the quieter days of French Indochina. Cattle grazed on broad meadows overlooking the river, children chased hoops, and shirtless men played volleyball. An old woman, seated on a wisteria-draped porch, greeted me in musical French. I joined her for tea.

As we sat on her fragrant porch, the noise and political tension of the mainland seemed light years away. I was again reminded that Cambodia is a place where time plays by its own rules—running together like spilled paint in some places, evaporating entirely in others. Or maybe, as the Buddha said, time is only an illusion; and what we call past, present and future is just a single, elastic moment. In Cambodia, I found this very easy to believe....

I caught the last ferry back to Phnom Penh, paying my five cent fare and taking a place against the wooden rail. On my right, a lean, muscular boy held four ropes, each tethering a massive water buffalo. To my left, a man in a short-sleeved shirt leaned against his Honda scooter, playing Tetris on a handheld computer.

ORIENTAL SUITE

In 1995 Jill Kluge, marketing director for the Mandarin Oriental Hotels, offered me a four-night stay in the Bangkok Oriental's legendary Authors' Wing. There was one catch: I'd have to write a story about the experience. I consented—provided I could write anything I wished. Jill bit her nails, and agreed. I don't think I disgraced her beyond redemption... though you're unlikely to find this article in the hotel's press kit.

At least part of this story is now obsolete. Bangkok's new Sky Train, completed in 2000, has transformed the experience of navigating around the city. It's the most visible improvement to any Asian metropolis since Kathmandu began a solid waste disposal program.

THE FIRST NIGHT in my hotel room, I dreamed of my hotel room.

I dreamed that I was leading all of my friends, one after the other, up to the Noël Coward Suite for a giddy potlatch. I dreamed I was uncorking the bottle of Tattinger champagne that, surrounded by custard apples and gardenias, had attended my arrival. And I dreamed that in the midst of all this I was in Bangkok, just a stone's throw from the city's mirrored temples and snake farms, relaxing in the Oriental Hotel's historic oasis of palm fronds, Thai antiques, and pay-per-view Sharon Stone movies.

And when I awoke that first morning, slightly dizzy after the long, sweet flight from L.A., I discovered that—although my nearest friends were 10,000 miles away, and my complimentary champagne and exotic fruits languished, untouched, in a bath of melted ice—the morning screening of *Basic Instinct* was only 15 minutes away.

But there is a cloud around every silver lining. The great tragedy of my tenure in the Noël Coward Suite was that I was alone, with no one to share it with. Or, more to the point, to show it off to; because there is something about a $1,000-a-night room at the Oriental that calls for shameless display.

The room was sheer opulence, light years beyond anything I'd experienced in 15 years of professional travel. Lapis and emerald wallpaper in vivid Thai motifs scampered up the walls like hallucinatory fungi; a golden antique deer rested atop a teak cupboard holding gleaming crystal flutes. One could spend an entire day in the marble-floored bathroom, frolicking beneath the roar of its Niagaran shower head, swimming laps in the gilt-clawed bathtub, and stocking the bidet with trout. A small but adequate collection of CDs — *Best of Liszt, Richard Clayderman Live in Beijing*, etc.—rested in the stereo well beneath one of the two enormous TVs, ready to drown out the sigh of the air-conditioning at a single remote command. Finally—the ultimate vanity—the handsome rolltop desk was aquitted with a stack of gold-printed stationary:

JEFF GREENWALD, IN RESIDENCE AT THE NOËL COWARD SUITE
THE ORIENTAL, BANGKOK

Thus was my natural humility overcome. Never have I succumbed more shamelessly to peacock-like pretentions than those mornings when I quit my lavish rooms and, clad only in a terry-cloth robe, stood at the head of the carpeted stairs and gazed down into the brightly-lit atrium where travellers, tycoons and other inconspicous guests drank tea and ate small cakes while casting furtive glances at my person—wondering in whispers about whom, what manner of artist or celebrity, might be emerging from one of the four rooms in

that precious wing, whose very entrance stood guarded by a polished
bronze plaque:

AUTHORS' SUITES:
RESIDENTS ONLY

Whom? Why, myself, of course... striding down the stairs with my
head held high, the big brass key and carved wooden pendant swinging
from my bathrobe pocket like a lure. What bliss! What opportunity!

Yet despite this enviable situation, there lurked in my mind an
ironic and cynical prescience. Never, while I abode in that luxurious
den, would I make the acquaintance of a woman of any age, creed or
station. Never, while I had custody of that Tattinger champagne, claw-
footed tub and canopied bed, would the chance arise to display my
plumage. It would inevitably be during my *next* visit to Bangkok, as
I languished in some budget guesthouse with a leaky toilet and khaki
sheets, that I would meet the girl of my dreams—and have no place
to bring her.

. . .

Bangkok's name, incidentally, isn't really Bangkok at all. That
familiar but arcane appellation is a bastardization of Bang Mekok,
which is what the town was called before King Chao Phraya Chakri
(also known as Rama I) moved his nation's capital down the river
and took over the site in 1782. In 1785 the place was renamed *Krung
Thep*: the City of Angels. The river itself would eventually bear Chao
Phraya's name.

The history of the Oriental Hotel mirrors, to a large degree, the
evolution of modern Bangkok. The original structure, which no one
remembers, seems to have burned down in 1865, just ten years after
King Mongkut (aka Rama IV) opened Siam to the West after years of
isolationism. Eleven years later a new Oriental opened, probably on
the same location. It was run by two Danish sea captains named Jarck
and Salje. Eleven years after that, the proprietorship shifted to the
hands of yet another retired Danish captain—H.N. Anderson—who
would ultimately launch the famous East Asiatic Trading Company.

And it was one year later still, in January 1888, that a 30-year-old Polish sea captain named Korzeniowski, about to assume his first command, navigated his ship up the Chao Phraya river and wrote these words: "One morning, early, we crossed the bar, and while the sun was rising splendidly over the flat spaces of land we steamed up the innumerable bends, passed under the shadow of the great gilt pagoda, and reached the outskirts of the town.

"There it was, spread largely on both banks, the Oriental capital which had yet suffered no white conqueror; an expanse of brown houses of bamboo, of mats, of leaves, of a vegetable matter style of architecture, sprung out of the brown soil on the banks of the muddy river."

The seaman stared up at the Oriental's edifice with a mixture of desire and trepidation, certain that a room in the already famous establishment would exhaust his modest means. Anderson, though, was sympathetic toward brother mariners. He took the salior by the arm and led him off to Room 1.

Korzeniowski would eventually change his name to Joseph Conrad—and the fortnight he spent at the hotel, waiting for the iron barque *Otago* to be properly outfitted for its sail to Melbourne, would inaugurate the Oriental's literary history.

During the next 30 years the Oriental became a conduit between the Kingdom of Siam and the cultural tides of the West. Carl Fabergé arrived in 1912, and enlisted the hotel for an exhibition of his jewelry. A Moliére play was staged in 1913, while Siam's first major performance of western ballet—led by Nijinsky himself—took place three years later. W. Somerset Maugham, near the tail end of the Southeast Asia expedition that would result in *A Gentleman in the Parlor*, arrived at the Oriental in January of 1922, and promptly fell ill. The event was worth a mention in the local papers:

"We regret to learn that Mr. W. Somerset Maugham is down with malarial fever, doubtless contracted when coming overland from Mandalay. His temperature this afternoon was 103."

The manageress contemplated evicting the hapless Maugham, terrified that he planned to die in her hotel. The writer survived, however, and his reflections of his tenure in Bangkok seemed deliciously poignant as I read them on the verandah of the Authors' Wing, staring past the flowering orchids to the gleam of sunlight on the nearby river...

"The hotel faced the river. My room was dark, one of a long line, with a verandah on each side of it; the breeze blew through, but it was stifling ...."

"I was weak as a newborn babe and for some days could do nothing but lie on the terrace at the back of the hotel and look at the river. Motor launches bustled to and fro. The sampans were innumerable. Large steamers and sailing vessels came up the river so that it had quite the air of a busy port; and if you have a passion for travel it is impossible to look at the smallest, shabbiest, dirtiest sea-going tramp without a thrill of emotion and a hankering to be on it and on the way to some unknown haven."

. . .

The current Authors' Wing—to the left of the hotel's main entrance, and down a narrow shopping arcade—is the venerable part of the Oriental, dwarfed by the more recently completely Tower and River wings. A spacious atrium with wooden stairways leads up to the old hotel's four famous suites: Michener and Coward on the north side, Conrad and Maugham on the south. Each author has, at one time or another, stayed at the Oriental—as have many other writers and artists. I think of Duke Ellington, Graham Greene and Tennessee Williams; of Paul Theroux, Robert Rauchenberg and Gore Vidal. And I think of Noël Coward, the very writer whose suite I now occupy, and reflect how bizarrely appropriate it is that, of all the illustrious possibilities, I've landed in the only suite named for a notorious cynic....

Michener and Coward, Conrad and Maugham; all have gazed through their high windows over the lushly planted plaza, over the swimming pools, down through the rows of planted orchids sweeping toward the Chao Phraya River. I can't imagine the river has changed much, even in 107 years. As I was sitting on the veranda in broad daylight, a tug rattled by. It towed two barges, each as big and black as a storm cloud. Except for the fact that I was toting a Sony video camera, and had just been inoculated with the new hepatitis vaccine, it might have been 1930. Diesel smoke rose across the water, the air smelled of roast pork and sewage, and as the sun got smudged by the damp rag of a low-lying cloud I took a long pull on my beer and recalled a few words written, over a century ago, by Konrad Korzeniowski:

"Here and there in the distance, above the crowded mob of low, brown roof ridges, towered great piles of masonry, king's palaces, temples, gorgeous and dilapidated, crumbling under the vertical sunlight, tremendous, overpowering, almost palpable, which seemed to enter one's breast with the breath of one's nostrils and soak into one's limbs through every pore of the skin."

It soaked into mine, and through my shirt as well.

. . .

What is it about Bangkok? It's quite easy to love and hate this city simultaneously, to feel the wash of utter glee run through your veins one moment and the gnaw of total disgust the next.

"It is impossible to consider these populous modern cities of the East without a certain malaise," W. Somerset Maugham reflected of Bangkok in *A Gentleman in the Parlor*. "They are all alike, with their straight streets, their arcades, their tramways, their dust, their blinding sun, their teeming Chinese, their dense traffic, their ceaseless din.... They are hard and glittering and as unreal as a backcloth in a musical comedy."

The secret to appreciating Bangkok lies, without a doubt, in learning to appreciate the Thais themselves. The first step is to abandon any notion of personal space. Learn to love being crowded, jostled, bumped into and stepped on. Touch people whenever possible. A hand on a passing shoulder; a pat on the arm. The Thais are an amazingly physical people, a fact witnessed by their love of rough massage and full-contact boxing. The egg-shell armor that surrounds most westerners had better bend in Bangkok, or it'll shatter into a million pieces—and cut you to ribbons.

But the main obstacle to enjoying Bangkok, for most people, is the traffic. The city's traffic, like China's Great Wall, is probably one of the very few man-made phenomena visible from the Moon. A steel and fiberglass torrent that twists with dreamy slowness down canal-wide avenues, it swells with up to 3 million vehicles during the commute hours; a figure growing, as reported in Lonely Planet's *Bangkok City Guide*, by 1,000 cars a day. It's a spiritual and pulmonary nightmare; you don't want to get near it.

Luckily, the places you want to see in Bangkok—the Grand Palace, the floating markets, the Temple of Dawn, the amulet market and the Wat Pho massage school—lie close to the banks of the Chao Phraya, within easy walking distance of express boat stops. For a minuscule fee (six *baht*, less than a quarter) you can board at the Oriental's pier, perch on the rear deck of one of these boats and watch the water slide past, feeling the blow-dryer air in your face while advancing, with negligible risk of heart and lung disease, upon one's destination. After more than a dozen visits to Bangkok, I'd never get around by any other means. In fact, I've totally lost interest in seeing anyplace in Bangkok that *doesn't* lie along the river; the stress that Bangkok traffic puts on my ganglions far outweighs any cultural thrill derived from the experience. (One exception is the Chatuchak Weekend Market; but on Sundays, the best day to visit, traffic congestion is at its lowest.)

. . .

Final night at the hotel. Long-tailed boats and huge barges sluice by on the river, pouring soot into the air and oil into the water. The last of the sun, behind low clouds, colors the river antique brass, while the day's final ferry brushes the Oriental's pier. A tug throbs by, towing four long barges, each filled to the brim with sand. And as the sun disappears the party lights woven between the leaves of the veranda's potted jacaranda trees are turned on, gleaming like constellations against the pastel sky.

How many times have I raced through this city, so eager to get out, to get to Kathmandu or India as quickly as possible? Now I feel

I could stay in Bangkok forever. All I need is a veranda, the river close by, and golden antler to hang my hat on. All I need, in short, is a private suite at the Oriental Hotel.

Stocking up on shoe-mitts, toilet soaps and personalized stationery as Richard Clayderman plays to an audience of adoring communists, I flip open the hotel library's signed first edition of *A Gentleman in the Parlor* and finish reading Maugham's description of the Asian capitals:

"They give you nothing. But when you leave them it is with a feeling that you have missed something and you cannot help feeling that they have some secret they have kept from you. And though you have been a trifle bored you look back upon them wistfully; you are certain that they have after all something to give you which, had you stayed longer or under other conditions, you would have been capable of receiving...."

I know what Maugham meant. Yet, for the moment at least, I quite disagree. My four days at the Oriental, exploring Bangkok from the oasis of Room 103, have left me completely satisfied. If the city had anything else to give me, it could only have been malaria.

THE PARADISE OF WIND ROSES

It has been said, and I believe it's true, that I was the first person to travel around the world while posting live stories on the Internet. From December 1993 to September 1994, while Sally Knight and I circled the globe for *The Size of the World*, I filed a total of 19 dispatches. All appeared on GNN (Global Network Navigator, a now-defunct subsidiary of O'Reilly & Associates). I sent them from everywhere—Mexico, Mauritania, the middle of the Atlantic Ocean. As online connections were so difficult to find in those primitive days, they were sent in various forms: as faxes, teletypes, and trickles of electronic data creeping between molasses modems. This dispatch, the shortest of all, was filed from the *Ursus Delmas*, a cargo ship traveling from Brooklyn to Senegal. It was written on a coding machine, regurgitated as a punched ribbon, and fed into a teletype transmitter. It was then printed out at the Delmas office in New Orleans, and faxed to my visionary cyber-liaison—Allen Noren—at GNN headquarters in Sebastopol, California.

IT'S A LOUSY, stinking cliché, but I'll say it anyway: the sea is like glass.

But what glass! Not the cheap, pathetic panes that screen out rain and mosquitoes and ultraviolet light; not even fine lead crystal, or prism, or quartz. The *Ursus Delmas* is surrounded by an ocean of elemental glass, the deep volcanic runoff of the primordial atmosphere. It is jet black, protean, an ever-changing fluid that seems infinitely dense. Its weight is unimaginable. Seen from the safety of "C" deck it resembles a shifting plane of stone-age obsidian, ready to be chipped and flaked into primitive tools: axes, knives, arrowheads, scrapers for skinning wild animals and working their hides. Sometimes it appears frozen, and for a microcosmic second the entire ocean hangs motionless around us, tipped with razor-sharp blades. At moments like this I want to vault over the rail and walk alone among those amazing formations until the ship is out of sight and the eerie black horizon stretches around me like a priest's collar.

At other times the ocean, which descends more than 2,000 fathoms beneath our hull, appears as clear as a crystal ball, and if I stare unblinking through the surface I can observe its most profound depths: past the domain of the currents; past the point where color dissolves; beyond the realm of light altogether.

I can see down to the unmarked highways where caravans of gigantic blind predators glide by and, after they pass, down further still, into the deepest canyons of the sea: the kingdom of illuminated creatures, sacred snake gods, and steaming sulfur vents twisting cords of vaporized magma into the diamond-dense water. And then, damn it all, I feel the hands gripping my ankles, pulling me back toward reality as I tip dreamily over the rail....

Sally is on the deck behind me, smoking a Benson and Hedges. "The sea is like glass," she remarks.

ACROSS THE PERSIAN GULF

One of the most difficult calls I had to make for *Scratching the Surface* was deciding which excerpts to include from *The Size of the World*—my favorite among my books. Herewith, much reduced, is my escape from Arabia, via the United Arab Emirates—accomplished with the help of a young Pakistani named Shahid. Although I offered him an opulent fee for his services as translator, Shahid replied with the most uplifting words a traveler can hear. "I will help you for friendship," he said. "Not for money."

During the global circuit that gave birth to *Size*, I made it a point to write in (on? at?) my OmniBook at least two hours every day. The discipline kept me sane, providing an oasis of predictability in an otherwise maddening journey. Aboard the *Fateh Al Khair* I wrote almost constantly; there was nothing else to do. It was my best work of the nine-month trip—and every word of it was lost when my laptop was stolen, a week later, on the night coach to Kathmandu. Eight months later, I did my best to dredge up memories of my weird journey from Dubai to Karachi. Not a bad effort; but I'll always wonder how the recollection compares to the original.

A Good Man, and a Good Moslem

THE GENERICALLY-NAMED CANAL slices into the heart of metropolitan
Dubai, jiggling the lights of five-star hotels and churning the sodium
street lamps into golden tea. Sony and Pepsi signs toss jazzy neon
from nearby buildings, lending strolling lovers a Venusian glow. A
broad green park separates the long Canal from the downtown noise
and bustle, but the smells of frying fish and Russian perfume carry.
The heat of the day had receded, and the air was still and warm.
Spilled popcorn lay strewn on the paved pedestrian corniche. Shahid
and I walked slowly, enjoying the oasis of calm. Along the edge of
the Canal, worn wooden ships bobbed against the dock with soft
crunching sounds. Crewmen's laundry hung limply on the rails; from
inside the boats came the glow of battery-powered televisions, or the
crackle of radio static. Late dinners sizzled on a few of the decks, the
sharp smells of cumin and coriander—those eccentric cousins of
the carrot—commingling with drifts of shit and diesel.

Shahid knew the boats well; well enough, at least, to deduce which
of them might be bound for Karachi. I would bide my time on a
bench while Shahid climbed aboard and negotiated with the sailors.
After an hour of this he'd found a possibility: A fishing boat leaving
for Pakistan in about five days. I was grateful, but my enthusiasm
was tempered by the thought of five days in Dubai.

We were hungry and tired, but I urged Shahid to try one more
time. After bypassing half a dozen ramshackle ferries —"No good
for Karachi," he explained—we came to the last one in line. Beyond
it the Canal widened, disappearing into the oil-slicked waters of the
Persian Gulf.

I popped open a Coke while my companion climbed on board.
Fifteen minutes later he reappeared, clutching a slip of paper.

"They will not go to Karachi," Shahid announced. "But a friend
of this captain, he must be going."

"When?"

"Tonight. Unless he has already left..."

A burst of adrenaline zapped my spine. "Already left? Oh, no...."

Which boat? Where?"

"Not here." Shahid squinted at the paper. "The boat is the *Fateh Al Khair*. Captain Hussain. It is docked across the city, at the Jabah Ali port. We must take a car...."

We jogged toward Nassar Square. A ferret-faced oil company executive and his "date"—a Slavic call girl with industrial-sized breasts—fell back in astonishment as I shot between them and into their waiting cab, pulling the gleeful Shahid along with me.

"American way!" he chortled as we roared off. "Indiana Jones! I like it very much."

. . .

The *Fateh Al Khair* had not yet left. Shahid found Hussain—a roly-poly seadog in a soiled yellow *caftan*—wolfing french fries in the dockside greasy spoon and watching, with childlike fascination, a rock video of Henry Rollins performing *I'm a Liar* on MTV. The Captain, as advertised, spoke no English, but with the help of Shahid and a world map I made my intentions clear. There followed a short dialogue between the two Pakistanis.

"He will take you," Shahid announced. "The time is three days, if good weather. They should go at four o'clock." he glanced at his watch. "In four hours. You must meet the Captain here, at this place, and he will tell the customs to stamp your passport. If you are late— even a minute late—he will go without you. You agree?"

I nodded. "How much will I pay for my passage?"

"You will give as you wish," Shahid relayed. "But there is no need to give anything. He will help you because he is a good man. A good man, and a good Moslem." Shahid and the Captain clasped hands. "Four in the morning. The Captain says if you need anything for the trip, you must buy it now."

We got back to town at 1 a.m. After buying Shahid dinner (Dubai never sleeps) and thanking him profusely I shopped like mad, purchasing everything I might need for three days on an open deck: sunscreen, lip balm, a straw hat, a towel, sandalwood soap, mosquito repellent, breath mints, a dozen AA batteries, two cartons of State

Express cigarettes (for the crew), and a case of root beer (for me). At 3 a.m. sharp, I hailed a cab for the ride back to Jabah Ali.

. . .

Captain Hussain was as good as his word. He signed me through emigration and, using the hand gestures which would be our sole means of communication for the entire crossing, directed me to his boat.

The wooden ferries anchored along the Jabah Ali dock lay four deep. The *Fateh Al Khair*, trimmed to sail, was on the outermost edge. It was an athletic effort to wrestle my pack and provisions across the railings, over the cargo and between the sleeping crewmen of the three intermediate boats; a task made no easier by the pitch-darkness or the dozens of cat-sized rats and rat-sized roaches that scurried underfoot. I boarded awash in sweat, gasping for breath and filthy as a junkyard dog.

It was difficult to get a good look at the barge, but its funkiness was beyond dispute. On the wooden deck, some 50' long by 20' wide, a dozen used cars and two new HiAce Super Custom vans were lashed down for transport to Pakistan. Above the aft deck loomed a one-room wheel house, reached by a wooden ladder. The toilet consisted of two naked planks, separated by a narrow gap, jutting from the stern. Hussain's nine-man crew lay strewn like casualties across the planks and in the wheel house, snoring on rough blankets.

The deck was crawling with cockroaches, but the real problem— the only problem—was that there was no place for me to lie down. In a last gasp of lateral thinking I opened the sliding side door of the nearest van, and crawled gratefully inside. There, on cushions of cunningly whipped petroleum, I slept.

Unplugged

It was unimaginable that, beyond the tiny stage of our boat, somewhere over the gunmetal gray waters of the Persian Gulf (or, by Day Two, the Gulf of Oman), the world was still happening. Israel and the PLO were signing a peace pact; Nelson Mandela was about to be sworn in as President of South Africa; graffiti artist Michael Fay was getting his ass whipped in Singapore. By night, as I lay curled in my dormant vehicular nest, Girl Scouts sold cookies in Wisconsin; Mexicans celebrated Cinco de Mayo; Winona Ryder put on her lipstick. Planet Earth rolled through space, circling its sun at 67,000 miles per hour, and it was jam-packed with creatures doing funny, mysterious things.

I spent my mornings and afternoons—all the daylight hours, in fact—propped on cushions in the wheel house, reading books or typing on my miraculous battery-powered OmniBook as Captain Hussain (whose rank, paradoxically, seemed to release him from any shred of responsibility) hibernated noisily upon his bunk. As I finished each of the novels I'd brought (Pynchon, Asimov, Maugham, Le Carré) I would throw it ceremoniously off the stern, watching it bob briefly before sinking into the loam of the Gulf. Pynchon, I thought, would particularly appreciate this burial-at-sea; there was something poetic about *Vineland* dissolving into the notorious waterway, which I can nevermore think of as anything but alphabet soup.

It was upon the *Fateh Al Khair* that I first experienced the infinite delight of the "bucket bath," taken in my tattered red Calvin Kleins behind the leering yellow shade of a secondhand Caterpillar bulldozer. The broad plastic splash-bowls of tepid water were a holy baptism, rinsing off my Arabian week of accumulated sweat, atomized sand, factor 15 sunscreen, 100% DEET insect spray, primal fear, belly button lint, fish oil, machine grease, powdered rust, spilled pineapple juice, mosquito hoofprints, *chapati* flour, toe jam, melted chocolate and loose gray hairs. I took these baths in the heat of the day, making myself scarce as the more devout members of the all-Moslem crew rolled out their woven straw mats for their own call to prayer. Hidden behind my bulldozer, self-consciously semi-naked, I watched their elaborate choreography of devotion. Each fifteen-minute meditation included a ritual of standing, bowing, cupping the hands behind the ears, extending the palms to receive an invisible liquid sacrament and, finally, washing the blessed ether over their dark, pious faces.

There was no mess. The meals, cooked in a wind-screened corner of the deck and served "buffet-style," were hideous, but I ate them with good appetite, chasing away the boldest roaches and swallowing prophylactic doses of Pepto- Bismol afterwards. I took up smoking, limiting my intake to three cigarettes a day: One at ten, one at two, and one just after sunset. And I shat in terror, once every morning at seven, clinging with both hands to the thick but fraying rope that, dangling damply from the ferry's stern, was all that kept me from following my books into the Gulf.

. . .

The language barrier precluded intimacy with the crew, but a quiet cordiality prevailed. I was treated with unflagging courtesy. By our third day at sea I knew most of the sailors by name. There was Salim Mohammed, the Navigator, who looked like a Pakistani version of Neil Young and wandered the decks in black nylon socks; Bahadin Kera Ibrahim, a tall, unsmiling black man who reminded me of a character from a Conrad story; and Ali Abdul Shaktar, Second Mate, whose teeth were stained crimson from years of chewing *pan*. First Mate Yaakov could always be recognized by his signature blue cap, while Ahmed Allah Rakha, the Bosun, chain-smoked and had the laconic round eyes of a frog. The only one who seemed to resent my presence on board was Muhammed Ali, the cook, who found himself with an additional mouth to feed. On the afternoon of our fourth day at sea, when we ran out of food entirely, this ceased to be a problem.

. . .

And it was during the fourth evening of that long, exquisitely dull cruise, sitting on the bridge in the moonless sloshing dark, that I realized, with a start: *We had no radio.*

No radio! No flare! No way to signal for help, to alert even the nearest passer-by if—as has been known to happen on large bodies of water—our luck went savagely awry. If something were to go wrong on the *Fateh* there would be no hope at all of calling upon the forces that be for a safe, speedy rescue. No radio! And, tied to the roof of the wheel house, only a tiny rubber raft which, when I examined it closely, had the words *Not To Be Used As A Life Preserver* emblazoned on its blubbery side.

In droll anguish I turned to the Captain—dozing off to Hindi show tunes on a leather-encased transistor radio—and inquired, with a flurry of sign language, what we would do if there was a problem. Hussain smiled—a beatific, submissive Islamic smile—and simply waved his hands, right over left, horizontally, like cards being shuffled and returned to the deck. Right then and there I realized that, for the very first time on my entire global pilgrimage, I was truly and utterly unwired. There was no stream of radio waves, no electro-magnetic impulse, no vibrating string or even a smoke signal to link us with the World At Large.

Thus I found myself, after 15 years of travel, finally able to answer a question that had stumped me eight months earlier at the Third Annual Book Passage Travel Writers' Conference. This, right here, was "the single most remote spot I had ever been": The blue-trimmed wheel house of the *Fateh Al Khair*, with Mr. Ibrahim at the wheel, morose Salim the Navigator sitting at the foot of his usurped (by me) sleeping platform and the rotund Captain Hussain lounging in one of those vaguely yogic subcontinental postures with a Rothman's filter king dangling between his fingers and a pinch of snuff tucked beneath his lip.

There was nothing around us but water, comic-book blue, unbroken save for the very occasional flying fish or the smoke-like silhouette of a distant tanker. Anything could happen; and if it did we would die, finally and anonymously, having for all intents and purposes (as my friend Pico Iyer might say) "fallen off the map."

. . .

By the late morning of Day Five I knew we were in trouble. We'd left Dubai with enough fuel to last about 100 hours; come noon, we would have been at sea for 104. Land was nowhere in sight.

Ali Abdul Shaktar spied a fishing boat, and we changed course to intercept. It took us over an hour to reach it, but choppy seas forbid an exchange of personnel. Any confidence I still maintained in Salim evaporated as I heard him—and one needed no Pakistani for this—bellowing for directions to Karachi. The half-naked seamen on the fishing skiff pointed in three separate directions, arguing amongst themselves. Bahadin Kera Ibrahim, usually cool as a cucumber, broke into a sweat. The Captain, acting on executive authority, lay down with his arm over his eyes. Salim and the skiff's captain yelled back and forth, establishing something or other, and we hung a left.

Four hours later we accosted another trawler, and, hearkening their unanimous counsel, hove sixty degrees to the right. It was five in the afternoon. We had by now run out of drinking water, and I was rationing root beer to the crew. Hussain snored soundly, the stuffed tiger he had bought for his grandson tucked beneath his head.

The sun set. I sat atop the bulldozer, gazing at the evening star and flicking ashes into the sea. At any moment I expected to hear the death rattle of our engine, swallowing its last gulp of diesel and dooming us to slow extinction. What I heard instead was the voice of Ali Abdul Shaktar—old eagle-eyes himself—hooting victoriously from the wheel. Strung between the inky sea and indigo sky, Karachi glittered on the horizon.

The *Fateh Al Khair* gagged and sputtered as we entered the harbor, stalling twice before reaching a berth. We had been at sea 112 hours—two days longer than the initial estimate. No sooner had we docked than hundreds of mosquitoes descended upon the boat, eager to graze on our sun-ripened limbs. The cockroaches and rats, sensing our evacuation, reappeared in force, boldly scrambling over the empty food stores and into the dry water barrel. Ibrahim, Salim and the other crewmen bagged their gear and, one by one, abandoned ship for the buses and taxis that would take them back to their families.

I put away my computer, retrieved my backpack and bid a less than fond farewell to the HiAce van that had served as my nest. A generous tip for our narcoleptic Captain was folded into my shirt pocket. Every square inch of my skin was itching to get off that boat. Tonight, my first night in Asia, I would go for broke: An air-conditioned taxi, a five-course meal and a first-class hotel with a sauna and spa. Yes! Yes! I grabbed the cook's hands and danced a little jig, unable to believe it was over.

I was about to step over the railing and make my way to shore when the Captain, more animated than I'd ever seen him, ran over and grabbed my arm.

"No, no, no!" he cried.

"No, no, no!" echoed the remaining crewmen.

I looked at them as if they were crazy. It took twenty minutes of charades before I understood: the Pakistani Immigration office was closed for the night. The officers would return at eleven the next morning. Until then I was confined, by letter of law, to the boat.

LIVE FROM THE YAK HOTEL

This final selection from *The Size of the World* was first published in the *San Francisco Examiner*. It won a place in this collection for two reasons. First of all, I think it's a revealing contrast with the previous "Big World" stories, which were far less political. Written in one sitting during a five-hour marathon on my Lhasa hotel porch, printed in the *Medicin Sans Frontieres* office and faxed to Allen Noren at GNN, it was my most passionate—and certainly my riskiest—dispatch. Secondly, the descriptions of our encounter with the 17th *Karmapa* (lit., "man of buddha-activity") at the Tsurpu monastery are now the stuff of history. The teenaged Karmapa made a daring escape from Tibet in 1999, and now lives as a political refugee in India.

To: *Allen Noren, O'Reilly & Associates*
Subject: *Big World: Live from Lhasa*

SITTING ON A WORN green sofa in the courtyard of Lhasa's famous Yak Hotel, my eyes and nose full of smoke from the wood-burning stove that heats the showers. The sky was thick and gray this morning, threatening rain, but by now, noon, it's broken up into pearlescent cumulus clouds. The sun is foundry white here at 12,000 feet, and the air is thin, but after a few days you hardly notice it (unless you try to climb even a few feet higher... then you're wheezing for breath).

Seven years have passed since my last visit to Tibet. Lhasa, still the spiritual and political center of this high plateau, remains an occupied city, and thanks to an ongoing population transfer the Tibetans are rapidly becoming a minority in their own land. Nonetheless, there is still magic and mystery to be found here, and the spirit of the Tibetan people remains an indomitable undercurrent—seething below broad avenues lined with Chinese restaurants, beneath the watchful eyes of the omnipresent police, and under glitzy billboards portraying, in Tomorrowland graphics, the new, industrialized Lhasa envisioned for the year 2000.

Lhasa is a city of hidden worlds, havens of wisdom and compassion tucked beneath and between the fingers of a merciless Chinese grip. It is a city of musty temples painted in van Gogh blues and yellows, prayer-rooms thick with the smell of burning *ghee*, heavy-curtained doorways, the eyes of wrathful deities staring down from beneath gilded crowns, lone monks sitting on worn carpets and reciting thousand-page sutras as they bang rhythmically on broad drums with fiddle-fern drumsticks.

But the social and political mood here in this city of 170,000 is glum, following Bill Clinton's decision to separate human rights concerns from the renewal of China's Most Favored Nation status. The Tibetan people, under the thumb of the Chinese since 1959, had felt that by conducting their campaign for self-determination with honesty, civility and non-violence, they would win support from the most powerful democracy on Earth. They have learned that they were wrong; that the economic perks to be gained from kowtowing to China outweigh all other concerns.

Chinese response to the White House decision was instant and severe. Less than 24 hours after Tibetan VOA (Voice of America) broadcast the news, Chinese party officials called meetings of local Tibetan work groups and informed the citizenry that the days of leniency were over. Subsidized medical care was suspended, and taxes on Tibetan shopkeepers were doubled. "There's no point in complaining," the officials said. "No one's going to help you anymore." In response the merchants closed their shops and staged a strike, massing in front of the regional tax offices. It was a long and nasty afternoon; 17 people were beaten, and seven of them were hospitalized. Five of the organizers are now languishing in prison.

"There's no doubt," a well-informed expatriate journalist told me, "that the Chinese were acting very cautiously while the U.S. kept an eye on them. Incidents of torture had plummeted, and the Tibetans adamantly believed it was thanks to American pressure. Amnesty International and Asia Watch had a hand as well, but they themselves can *do* nothing. What everyone is concerned about now, with the human rights agenda removed from MFN status, is that the incidents of torture are going to go right back up to where they were before. There are already signs that this is the case. Since the announcement, demonstrators are being publicly beaten, stomped and dragged off to prison. We don't know what's going on *inside* the prisons, but we do know this: The police do what they're told. If they're warned not to be unneccesarily rough, they're not. If they're told otherwise, they beat the hell out of everybody.

"China," he continued, "is very smart. They always say, *No pressure! China will never submit to meddling in its internal affairs!* They maintain a very hard line, and they're experts at bluffing. But if the United States had any sense, any spine, it would have realized that there are infinite shades of gray. You *can* push China. You *must*. You absolutely must prove to China that you are not a nation that will capitulate just because China demands that you capitulate. Once you've done that, you're finished. You are never, ever again considered strong or credible by China again.

"I'll tell you what's happening right now; China is gloating. The very night the announcement came through—all night long and all through the next day—there were meetings on every level, from work groups to party officials, discussing how China had beaten America and deciding how local policy was going to be reformulated in that light. And the very night the MFN decision was announced, the staff of Drapchi Prison—the official penitentiary here, with 260 prisoners—threw a party! They feasted, they sang, and they made drunken speeches about how America had been defeated by China."

. . .

Outside on the streets one sees few signs of tension. Lhasa is a strange, gagged city where every new setback is met, superficially, with equanimity; where Drolma, returning to her restaurant from a meeting in which she learned that her taxes would be doubled, greeted my worried glance with a forced smile. "Good news today, very good news!" There is no sign of trouble despite rumours of recent arrests in the monasteries; no sign of social unrest even though, one week ago, a Tibetan man whose pregnant wife had died on the doorstep on the local hospital—he couldn't raise the 1,000 yuan "deposit" now required for her admission—returned with a pistol, killing two of the hospital staff before shooting himself.

To the unschooled eye, life proceeds unchanged. Tourists are hauled in mini-buses up the rear ramp of the Potala Palace—the Dalai Lama's former residence, now converted into a museum—and shown around by Chinese guides. How many realize that their tour of the Potala, conducted *counterclockwise* through the altar rooms, is a snickering insult to the exiled leader? The spectacular monastery, stripped of its treasures, has become a cash cow. Chinese tourists pose on its roof in Tibetan clothes for souvenir photographs. Meanwhile, a few miles west, the Norbu Lingka—the Dalai Lama's Summer Palace—has been converted into, of all things, a zoo.

The ultimate irony, though, is found on the *barkhor*, the circular flea market surrounding the sacred Jokhang cathedral. There, browsing among felt hats and mass-produced prayer wheels, naïve foreigners purchase colorful woven wristbands, never suspecting that these coveted emblems of political solidarity with the Tibetans are now manufactured and marketed by the occupying Chinese.

. . .

But I haven't spent much time in the city. Most of my visit has involved day-long excursions to the spectacular monasteries and valleys lying several hours by road from the capital.

Yesterday's trip to Tsurphu was a case in point. I made the expedition with Holly Wissler (an old friend from Kathmandu) and Bill Thompson, an ex-*National Geographic* photographer who, having spent years shooting ads for Marlboro, came to Tibet to re-examine his priorities and spiritual path.

We woke up at 5:30 and hit the road an hour later, the sky still bright with hanger-on stars, the barely waxed moon beaming so bright that you could pick out Tranquility Base with the naked eye.

Leaving Lhasa, we motored across a rugged landscape that was once an ocean floor, now uplifted into sharp reefs of stone. Velvet meadows stretched to the bases of gray hills that rose vertically toward the sky. Smoke plumed from distant villages, their salt-white houses festooned with prayer flags. The moon was sinking toward the jagged precipices, appearing fragile as a soap bubble, and we stopped the Land Cruiser to view the sphere through binoculars.

Standing on the roadside, watching Earth's moon disappear behind the gem-colored meadows of central Tibet, I found it impossible to believe that anything so perfect as this planet of ours could actually exist. This tiny marble, this vapor-shrouded ball-bearing rolling around a middle-aged star on the barren hip of curved space, seemed so unbearably beautiful that I found myself in tears. Who the hell are we, anyway? What are we doing here? What's the motive, the meaning, the cause? Is it all, as the Tibetans maintain, an illusion, a completely subjective manifestation of our five gross senses? If so it is a magnificent one, peerless in imagination, staggering in its variety. There can be no question of our deserving it or not. It is ours completely, and we belong to it absolutely. Our fates are eternally and inextricably interwined.

We turned from the main highway up into the Tsurphu Valley. Now we had entered Paradise. Fields of mustard, neon yellow, covered either side of the rough dirt track, and simple carts pulled by donkeys hove aside to let our Montero lumber past. We were closer to the villages now, and climbing. Yaks grazed in the meadows, and the smells of tea, grass and burning dung comingled with the dust.

Anyone who has seen a rice paddy in season, or walked through a Himalayan meadow at 12,000', knows that something completely indescribable can happen to chlorophyll. Under certain conditions, it reacts to sunlight the way a cat reacts to catnip.

Continuing up the valley, we followed a river that churned gray stones and branched out into ingenious irrigation schemes that had filled the landscape with rich crops. Bill forced the vehicle to a stop every five or ten minutes, leaping from the car to take slide after slide of villagers, landscapes, yaks. "This place is a landscape photographer's dream," he muttered reverently, holding an 18% gray card in front of his Olympus lens. "Just incredible."

Our destination was the home of the 17th *Karmapa*: The 10-year-old reincarnation of the 16th Karmapa, who died of cancer in Chicago. I'd seen pictures of this new Karmapa everywhere. He has a round face, flat nose and vastly intelligent black eyes. He had better be intelligent; the young lama has been chosen (by dubious means, some claim) to head a religious sect worth somewhere between 500 million and 1.2 billion dollars (making him the only 10-year-old in the world worth more than Macauley Culkin).

It was our collective goal to visit the boy, and collect blessings from him. For while the Dalai Lama is the political and temporal leader of the Tibetan Buddhist religion, the Karmapa sits at its highest spiritual apex. Far older than the Kagyu sect (over which the Dalai Lamas hold sway), the Karma lineage combines ancient teachings and profound magical powers. The Karmapa's most potent spiritual ally is a black hat, made from the hairs of 1,000 fairies, which he wears during specific rituals. I was present when the 16th Karmapa performed the Black Hat ceremony in Santa Barbara in 1981, four years before his death. During the entire event he kept his hand firmly planted on the huge hat's crown. When I questioned one of the attendants afterwards, he told me why. "His Holiness holds the hat," the monk said, "so it will not fly away."

The monastery was a sprawling complex of chalk-white and maroon buildings, destroyed during the Cultural Revolution but completely rebuilt since 1990. We parked in a broad dirt lot alongside half a dozen other mini-buses and jeeps. The Karmapa's daily blessing, we were told, would occur promptly at one; this would give us just enough time to complete the kora, or devotional circuit, along the towering cliffs behind the monastery grounds.

Following the directions in Gary McCue's *Tibet Guidebook* we set off to the north, passing high walls covered with intricately carved *mani*-stones. Sheep, goat and yak skulls were piled on cairns, engraved with the mantra of Chenrezig: *Om mani padme huun.* By the river, white nomad tents with blue Tibetan motifs billowed in the breeze.

The kora was an arduous walk, climbing steeply to over 15,000 feet. Prayer flags fluttered from high crags, delivering blessings to the incessant wind. Caves used by past Karmapas and itinerant saints, cut into the cliff walls centuries ago, were now enshrined within whitewashed *lakhangs* (hermitages), and within their protective walls I spied monks and nuns brewing butter tea. Bits of hair and yak wool clung to the branches of wild rose bushes, which perfumed the air with an alpine ambrosia I've come to associate, now and forever, with Tibet. Far below, the monastic complex spread out in a series of interlinked roofs. Scores of pilgrims were already massing in the parking lot.

Holly and I stopped for a water break, eating waxy Chinese chocolate bars and feeling deleriously happy. For an individual who makes his living complaining, I found it a highly threatening situation.

Five minutes later Bill Thompson caught up with us, enraptured by an encounter he'd just had. About 500 meters down the trail, he had been invitied into a small lakhang by a group of monks. They had poured him a cup of butter tea and, reaching over, sprinkled a fine powder into the cup. When Bill looked closely, holding the cup to the light, he saw that the powder was pure gold.

This was obviously a fabulous blessing, and I was keen to have a cup of this auspicious tea myself. I ran back down the kora, searching high and low for the lakhang he had described. Finally I located what might have been the place—but it was inhabited only by a young ani who poured me some watery tea and wanted to charge me half a *yuan* for it. It wasn't until I'd wasted 20 minutes running up and down the trail like a madman that I realized the truth: This had been a blessing for Bill and Bill alone. Nothing that happens in Tibet—nothing of importance— can ever be duplicated; and not every miracle is for everybody.

. . .

At 20 minutes before one, at a signal we failed to recognize, all of the Tibetan pilgrims in the parking area made a beeline for the monastery doors. Bill, Holly and I joined the back of the line, clutching our silk *kata* scarves. We crept up the stairs, arriving finally in a foyer where the Tibetans were relieved of their knives.

The gesture was not for show. There has been some controvery over this 10-year-old's appointment, and there is reason to fear for his life. Not from the Chinese; the occupying powers are pleased to have the new Karmapa in Tibet, where he can be carefully monitored. No, the threat to this black-eyed boy comes from a rival Karma sect in India who claim that they, too, have discovered a new, more legitimate Karmapa. Aside from the giddy assets involved, the future of the Tibetan people may be at stake. The Geluk sect—of which the Dalai Lama is titular head—wrested power from the Karma sect during the Mongol invasions of the 15th century, and some people think that the death of the 14th Dalai Lama might provide a golden opportunity for a reversal of the Karma school's historical fortunes. Deadly intrigue fires the Tibetan sects; one is reminded of the struggle for power within the Christian papacy.

After relinquishing my camera to a poker-faced monk, I entered a very obedient line winding into the *sanctum sanctorum* of the reincarnated lama.

Having seen so many impressive photographs of his young eminence, I was a touch disappointed. The 17th Karmapa sat on his throne with a vaguely bored expression, picking his nose. The *kata* scarf I'd brought was plucked away by an attendent, who motioned me forward. A cloth amulet, suspended from a hook, hung in front of my face. It was connected to the Karmapa's hand by a string. I was directed to touch my head to the amulet. It was, I deduced, a spiritual version of a tin-can telephone; the boy's blessing would travel through the string (I couldn't help but wonder if string had been discovered to be the best conductor for this purpose) and pass from the amulet into my skull. Waiting to feel something, I tarried too long. An attendant hustled me onward, and a third handed me a piece of red yarn to tie around my neck. This was the official Karmapa blessing, certified evidence of my pilgrimage to Tsurphu.

I tied the yarn in place, recalling the words of a gruff Australian man I met last night. "It can't hurt," he'd said of his own red cord, "and I'm not afraid of it."

. . .

Afterwards we picnicked on the banks of the river, smearing sunblock on our necks and talking about the future of Tibet.

"Ten years from now," Bill bemoaned, "this whole place might be under water. The Chinese have plans to dam every valley in Tibet in order to power their development schemes."

He was probably wrong, but I took his point. There is definitely something about visiting remote places these days that feels, somehow, like waiting for the end of the world. During 15 years of travel writing I've seen places develop so rapidly that I simply can't bear to visit them again. And the most drastic changes, it seems, have occurred within the past decade. The number of globe-hoppers is increasing exponentially, while the information revolution is bringing the tools of communication—and, by association, capitalism—to every corner of the globe. There are very few human beings who wouldn't jump at the chance to have a television or telephone in their homes; soon enough, the list will include computer links and Internet access.

One dares not complain about this. It's the most obnoxious brand of reverse cultural imperialism to decry the desire of indigenous peoples to possess the tools of "progress" that we find so indispensable. Unfortunately, the introduction of these new tools— and the power sources they require—is usually followed by a shift away from traditional values and appropriate technology. It's heart-breaking to imagine how the process might effect Tsurphu. The road up the valley will be paved, inviting unbridled sightseeing traffic; countless restaurants and snack stalls will open, creating a major litter and human waste disposal problem; the simple wooden carts that ply the present dirt road will be elbowed aside by tourist buses and Land Cruisers, driving out local farmers and filling the pristine valley with smoke and spilled oil.

We had already seen one such harbinger of Tsurphu's future that morning, on our drive up from Lhasa. A mother was working in the fields, spraying her crops with a new Chinese insecticide. The breeze carried the vapors back toward the woman, wafting them past her head and over the infant tied upon her back.

. . .

Late in the afternoon, we walked to the outskirts of Tsurphu and climbed a low hill used for "sky burials": a Tibetan funeral tradition in which one's physical body, having served its purpose, is offered as a gift to the Earth.

The method is always the same. The bodies, set in foetal position, are carried up the hill in rough burlap sacks. They are laid out flat, face down, on slabs of stone. The vultures arrive at this point, but at a word from one of the *tomdens*—yogin-butchers— they scatter to overlooking crags.

First, the soles of the feet are flayed. The corpses are then split lengthwise, down the back, arms and legs. With practiced motions the tomden slices the flesh away, tossing it onto the ground. When he has removed as much meat as he can, the monk steps away and shouts.

"*Shey, shey!!*" Eat!! The vultures descend in droves, tearing at the corpse until it is reduced to a skeleton. Then, at a word, they scatter off again. Now, using mallets and saws, the tomden smashes the skeleton to pieces. He throws the bones into a pit and, adding tsampa flour, grinds the cranium and femurs and teeth, the hips and pelvis and vertabrae, into a fine mash. The vultures are called in again. When they depart, the slab has been picked clean.

The tomdens and birds of prey had, of course, missed a few pieces here and there. Wandering around the hillside, Holly and I found a lower jaw with four molars intact; the ball-joint of a hip socket; scattered ribs and bits of random bone. Empty burlap sacks clung to the bases of stone cairns, and an entire tree was covered with long tresses of white and gray hair. Pieces of clothing, eaten through by the elements, were everywhere.

Standing on that hillside under the naked sun, walking on a landcape littered with human bones, I was reminded of the last place I'd seen such a macabre sight. But I could think of no greater contrast, at least on a spiritual level, than the one between the sky burial site of Tsurphu Valley—where the bodies of the dead are offered back to the earth in a spirit of gratitude and generosity—and the heart-wrenching killing fields I'd seen in Cambodia.

. . .

The mustard was brilliant in the late evening light, a psychedelic yellow that swept up the valley like a spotlight. A crucible sun illuminated the peaceful villages scattered beneath curls of smoke and oscillating prayer-flags. This was It: A Big World of earthly delights, set higher than the crest of Mount Rainier. We knew just how lucky, how blessed and lucky, we were to be there.

My only hope was that the prayers of this occupied nation would finally be answered, so that the people who actually belonged here— the generous, courageous Tibetans—might feel as blessed and lucky themselves.

BALI: THE RUNNING
OF THE TOURISTS

Another odd snippet from the files, originally intended for
Equator magazine. To be fair, my most vivid memory of Bali is
not the pandemonium described in this short vignette; it is of
waking up one lovely dawn in my rustic Ubud cottage, completely covered with ants.

CAFÉS IN THE BALINESE hill town of Ubud—famed for its wood carv-
ers, traditional painters and bootleg cassette tape emporiums—
buzzed with news of an upcoming cremation, to be hosted by an
affluent family in a nearby village.

This would be the Genuine Item, those in the know whispered to
each other over coconut milkshakes and chicken *satay*; not one of
those dime-a-dozen productions staged for package tourists. There
would be a *real body*. For this was the real Bali! Authentic! Exotic!
Don't miss it!

"Thanks! Golly! I sure won't!"

The middle Indonesian isles, once purely animistic, have over
the centuries absorbed the influences of Hinduism, Buddhism and
Islam. But as one travels further east along the archipelago, those
more recent stratas thin out. Arriving on Bali, you find the ancient

spirits still in control....

Indeed, the phenomenon of a traditional Balinese cremation promised a once-in-a-lifetime feast of images. Little did I suspect that the
most contemporary of influences would turn this sacred event into a
rampant real-time manifestation of The Worst That Can Happen.
Don't get me wrong. I meant to be "capturing" the ceremony with
the best of them, but found myself disqualified by virtue of stupidity.
Back at the hotel I'd accidentally loaded my camera with high-speed
film, more appropriate for shooting Midnight Mass in yuletime Kodiak
than a midsummer afternoon's cremation in the tropics. But though I
was prevented, through default, from making a consummate nuisance
of myself, I cannot deny that I was present. I was still a face in the
crowd, doing my small share to promote global homogeneity and cultural disintegration.

The begrieved Balinese family took its time, meticulously decorating their ritual floats as a mob of agitated travellers raised dust in
the village streets. The sun was fierce; tempers flared. What was
taking so long? An old man hobbled by, selling orange Fanta at a
high markup. After another hour, the scene threatened to become
ugly. "I don't see why they have to make it perfect," a British woman
pouted. "They're burning the bloody thing, aren't they?"

"They're making fools of us," a Frenchman hissed.

Just when it seemed a riot was about to erupt, there was a flare of
horns; the funeral procession began. The multi-tiered palanquins
were paraded out of a tall bamboo "hanger," followed by a gigantic
black crêpe bull, trimmed in gold and red cloth. Each float was hoisted
upon the shoulders of 20 shouting men, all wrapped in batik *longis*.
These sweating pallbearers raced their cargo down the avenue at
breakneck speed, careening madly from side to side and shaking the
floats violently to rid the pyre-borne soul of any tenacious spirit that
might still be clinging to its form.

Tourists ran down the packed dirt road, these juggernauts hot on
their heels. The bravest of them would gain a good head start, drop
into a crouch, spin around to snap a pictures of the onrushing menace, then dive headlong into the sidelines. The melee paused for a

moment to water the dazed pallbearers, who immediately heaved onward with a collective roar.

The smart money had waited at the cremation site itself—a lush and fragrant hollow within a circle of palms. The insect gleam of polished lenses and titanium camera bodies clicked and hovered everywhere, recording the next event: the deceased's cloth-wrapped body was taken out of its coffin (atop one of the palanquins), and transferred into a compartment within the giant bull. The moment this was accomplished the crowd surged forward, shoving the priest aside to better photograph the corpse. Like army ants on the march, the voracious shutterbugs clambered over the bulls and pallanquins, knocking heads in pursuit of the most authentic shots.

I remained on the ground, surrounded by gleeful young Balinese. *Fuck You, Sixty Minutes!* screamed an orange T-shirt. The message baffled me until I learned that the news program had recently run a segment trashing the island's burgeoning commercialism, aggression and greed. These shirts, apparently, were a local strategem for denying the charges.

My own camera was an albatross around my neck. I stomped in frustration, unable to dispose of the ungainly thing. Here, I realized, was a foretaste of Hell: to be girdled with an impotent Nikon, and locked into a *Far Side* panel: "The Running of the Tourists in Ubud."

There was a scramble for power atop the bull, and the dead person's family somehow prevailed. A semblance of order was restored. The priest, remarkably nonchalant amidst the chaos, resumed his position over the body and intoned some prayers. The crowd seethed, lighting cigarettes, waiting for the "religious crap" to end. Meanwhile, the nasal calls of innumerable hawkers —"Cold drink!" "Hello, T-shirt!"— mingled with impatient cries of "When will they *burn* it already?"

A gamelan orchestra played in a dell, and the air filled with pungent incense. A mango popsicle lay in the dirt. Into this timeless moment crept a palpable tension, a microcosmic pause. Three Swiss women comparing the length of their zoom lenses cautiously cocked their shutters. Atop the bull, a lid creaked into place. The priest leaped down from the high black back, and lit the crematory fires.

In less than a minute the elaborate sculpture of paper, crêpe and tinsel was consumed, revealing the bull's wooden armature and the oblong casket within. The crackling of lumber was drowned out by the clicking of countless shutters. Motor drives wheezed with satisfaction as tourists knocked each other down in their zeal to shoot the flames. I was reminded of a scene I'd once witnessed in Egypt: one press photographer kneeing another in the groin, as a mob of cameramen rushed for their positions at the Peace Talks.

Miraculously untouched above the flaming chassis, the bull's proud head, still virtually unscarred, gazed impassively into the lenses of the squinting crowd. I watched as it broke from the collapsing framework, and toppled onto the pyre. By this time the entire event seemed like a circus; there was no recognizable trace of spirituality. I grieved for the departed soul. What a way to go—cremated before the viewfinders of 3,000 western tourists, as your children and relatives hop at the fringes for a peek.

One Hour on Bali is Worth 60 Minutes, cried a red T-shirt.

I turned to go. A local boy tugged at my arm, peddling a charred human tooth.

HOLLYWOOD SHAMBALA
IN WHICH A TRAVEL WRITER DISCOVERS THAT THE SAFEST PLACE ON EARTH IS THE SOUND STAGE OF AN NBC SITCOM

It took a lot of persistence, and a few transparent exaggerations, to convince my old friend Don George—who had by then left the *San Francisco Examiner* and was now the travel editor at *Salon*—that this was a travel piece. I only half-believed it myself. But hey; Hollywood is one of America's most famous tourist destinations, no? Don solved the problem neatly by renaming the piece "The Hollywood Tourists Never See." In fact (as the careful reader will deduce) the soundstage audience was full of tourists, but both Don and I managed to overlook that obvious travel hook.

IN THE OLD DAYS, a phone call could change everything. These days, the medium of apocalypse is email.

The message is so bizarre that I don't quite know how to react. The sender, a young woman named Bonnie Zane, has read one of my travel books—*The Size of the World*—and felt compelled to contact me.

"What you wrote about your brother's death was so moving," she writes. "A few days before I left on a trip to Africa, actor Phil Hartman was murdered. The funeral was such a public affair.... In some way, your book helped me deal with my grief."

The connection with Hartman baffles me, until I read on. Bonnie,

I learn, is a Hollywood casting director. She has cast shows for *Mad About You* and *The Larry Sanders Show*. Now, heading her own company, she's involved with two primetime sitcoms: *Sports Night*, and *NewsRadio*, which was Hartman's main vehicle until his death last summer.

Bonnie is smart and funny, and our correspondence soon becomes an almost daily event. She learns quickly that I've always dreamed of acting, and claims that she can get me work as an extra on either of her shows. The problem, she admits, is that I'll be bored senseless. Extra work involves whole afternoons of dead time, waiting endless hours for the privilege of being a nobody. Despite my infatuation with the stage, she manages to make this option sound sufficiently humiliating; I never call in the favor.

. . .

On the first of October, I return from lunch to find a message from Bonnie. The unthinkable has occurred. Julie Bean—*NewsRadio*'s co-producer, who oversees all the talent on the show—had to rush her dog to the vet, and missed the afternoon casting session. "We're giving you free reign," she told Bonnie. "Cast whoever you want." My cyber-friend thus finds herself in possession of a rare prize: an actual speaking role, hers to assign at will.

"Get down here today," her message tells me, "and the part is yours."

. . .

Despite the vast breadth of this country, American history hasn't spawned a lot of mythic destinations—kingdoms like Eldorado or Xanadu or Colchis, where a wild fantasy might explode into reality. New York and Las Vegas are close contenders, but they're easily deconstructed; spend a few months in either, and you'll pretty much know where you stand.

Not so Hollywood. The town hovers within a nimbus of unreality, where anything is possible at any time. Since 1911, its back lots and stages have been a looking glass, a portal through which a select few are invited to pass. From the busboys at Johnny Rocket's to the cashier at the Gap, everybody looks their best: no one knows where, or for whom, that gateway is going to open.

Hollywood is the greatest myth-making machine in human history, and millions of visitors pack its studio tours and souvenir shops each year. But the inner sanctum of the film industry—the sound stage itself—is a guarded and mysterious world, off-limits to the prying eye. Within its sea of cranes, cables and monitors lies an island, more remote than Rakahanga: the tiny oasis of land beneath the spotlights, behind the clapboard, in the shimmering eye of the Panavision cameras.

It is this place, more than any other, which is the Mecca of the American psyche—the place toward which endless shifts of waiters have aspired in vain.

During 1996 and 1997, I spent many hours in the back lots of Paramount Pictures, observing the filming of *Star Trek: First Contact* while researching a book about *Star Trek* in global culture. But nothing in that experience prepared me for the visceral thrill of being on camera—no more than watching a space shuttle lift-off prepares you for orbit.

. . .

Bonnie drops me off at Ren Mar Studios at eleven, well before noon rehearsal. Ren Mar is a private studio, unaffiliated with the networks. *Golden Girls* was shot here, as was—until recently—*Ally McBeal*. The exterior of the studio was used as the location for *Who Framed Roger Rabbit*.

Entering the sound stage, I feel like I did my first day of school: the twittering in the stomach; the dread of one's peers; the overarching desire to avoid disgrace. Bonnie has warned me not to flaunt my "special connection" with her. As far as the other players are concerned, I'm just a lucky dog who'd landed the role after a garden variety audition. I know immediately that I won't be able to pull this off; I don't have enough Hollywood agent horror stories to invent a credible alternate life.

Slowly, the sound stage fills with cast and crew: Dave Foley, *NewsRadio*'s male lead, a Canadian-born actor who looks like Beaver Cleaver come-of-age; Stephen Root, who so convincingly played Mission Control chief Chris Kraft in Tom Hank's *From the Earth to the Moon*; Maura Tierney, whose work I've seen in *Liar Liar* and *Primal Fear*. Andy Dick, the radio station's resident imbecile, is already in character; he's swooning off a desk onto a pile of padded gym mats, yelling at everyone to look at him. I'm also introduced to Langdon Bensing, another guest actor who will play an FBI agent. Bensing has twice my number of lines: two.

Root, Foley and Dick are friendly enough. Tierney and the other female lead—the flame-haired Vicki Lewis—keep to themselves. The actresses, I've been warned, are aloof; it's best not to chat them up. So I gravitate toward Bensing, a struggling actor who's been chasing walk-ons and cameos for years. His biggest break was a scene in *Seinfeld*, but recent months have been lean. After five minutes he's heard my story—the real one—and offers a reality check.

"I had six callbacks for a tiny part on *NYPD Blue*," he says. "But they finally decided to go with someone else. After this happened a couple more times, I told my agent not to send me over there any more. The stress and heartbreak were just too much.

"You have no idea how tough it is," he concludes. "This town is packed with actors who'd give their left nut for your part."

Mike Risner, the second assistant director, approaches us with an affable smile. "Before you get started," he says, "there are a few forms we'd like you to sign."

I've expected as much; acting is probably a lot like the writing business. They'll want me to sign my life away. "In the event you are caught or killed, your editor will disavow any knowledge of your assignment."

The first form is your standard list of medical questions. I check "no" to everything, sign, and move on to the next. After five minutes I hand the papers back to Risner. "So what did I just sign?"

"The first form was insurance. You've now got total medical coverage—until midnight tonight. The tax and talent forms were your contract. You'll get $576.00 for the afternoon's work."

"Whoa! I'm getting six hundred bucks for this?"

Risner shrugs. "Only if the show doesn't go into reruns. If it does, you get another $576. That's followed by what we call 'residuals:' a percentage of all future broadcasts, in any country, until the eventual heat-death of the sun." He clears his throat. "Shall I show you to your dressing room?"

I've barely had time to digest this offer when Jason Saville, the first assistant director, hands me a stack of revised script pages. They're printed on yellow paper, to contrast with the white of the original. I thumb through them eagerly. "Anything I should know about?"

A grim nod. "We cut your line." I reel and stagger, feeling sick. Jason steadies me, grinning devilishly. "Only kidding."

Rehearsals begin shortly after noon. As make-up is not until three, everyone's in their street clothes. My appearance—in Act Two, scene M—includes the episode's semi-famous guest star: the hulking Patrick Warburton, who played Elaine's deadbeat boyfriend "Puddy" in *Seinfeld*.

NewsRadio—a somewhat under-rated comedy with occasional moments of brilliance—was created by 33-year-old wunderkind Paul Simms, formerly the co-executive producer of *The Larry Sanders Show*. Most of the action takes place in the mock offices of WNYX, a Manhattan radio station. In this episode (the first of a three-part story) the station manager (Stephen Root) is hauled off to prison. The reason for this incarceration, we learn, is related to a shady connection with vanished bank robber D. B. Cooper. As soon as this happens, Patrick Warburton's character—"Johnny Johnson"—appears out of nowhere and takes control of WNYX. Despite his transparent charm, Johnson's take-over is unsolicited, unexpected, and totally unwelcome.

Here's a synopsis of scene M: The station's news director (Dave Foley) brings in two security guards to throw Johnny Johnson out. The guards cross the set to the station manager's office, enter it, and shut the door behind them. A moment later the office door opens again and the two guards exit, "laughing convivially" as Johnny Johnson slaps them on their backs.

I play one of the security guards. My single line is spoken as we stride across the set, toward the office: "This won't take a second."

. . .

To the outside world the films and shows released by Hollywood appear as seamless narrative, with one scene following another and characters behaving in sensible, predictable ways. In actual fact, a film or TV episode is a montage of bits and pieces. Scenes are filmed any number of times, in any order, from a variety of camera angles. The best "takes" are edited together to give an illusion of continuity. It is astonishing how long this takes. Scene after scene is flubbed as the actors stumble over words, forget their lines, bump into each other or explode into fits of laughter.

The paradoxical upshot of this—made clear in rehearsal—is that it's nearly impossible to screw up. I walk through my scene several times, under the eye of director Tom Cherones and a cadre of grips, cameramen and crew. My ears are cocked; I half expect to hear Cherones yell from the sidelines: "Who the hell is *that* guy?" But I'm flattering myself. Visible as I may feel, my part is too small to be obtrusive.

When rehearsal ends, I find myself with something I haven't had all day: an appetite. No one has to direct me to the catering table; when I first entered the sound stage I walked past a wall of food, the opulence of which I hadn't seen since my last Indian wedding. Sliced turkey and prime rib, five cheeses, three salads, grapes and kiwis, pound cakes and bagels, candy bars and melon balls; coolers full of fruit juice and designer waters, urns filled with steaming coffee, whole-grain breads and spreads, chips and dips, an avalanche of giddy abundance—think Big Rock Candy Mountain, or your Jr. High School fantasy of becoming Student Council president and filling the drinking fountains with Coke.

But I'm being fattened for the kill. No sooner have I tossed my empty plate than Kent Zbornak, *NewsRadio*'s unflappable line producer, puts his hand on my shoulder. "Time for your haircut," he says.

This is my mortal terror. My hair falls to my shoulders, as it has for years. Okay; it isn't exactly the "security guard" look. But what will they do to me? Images of jug-headed Marines parade through my head; my sister disowning me, my lover in tears.

But my Samson-like terrors are assuaged in makeup, as Mary Guerrero—hairdresser to the stars—ties my bib. "I know a few tricks," she chuckles. Indeed, with a minimum of hacking and a mountain of mousse, this consummate professional—this person who has actually *cut Johnny Carson's hair*—creates a helmet-like coiffure that looks three times shorter than it is. When she's done I move across the room, where her daughter, Jennifer, applies a light palette of make-up to my face. Afterwards, she hands me a mirror. My reaction—like any red-blooded American male—is to wonder if I could get away with wearing makeup in real life.

. . .

Nothing happens for three hours, and then it's dinner time. Everyone eats together: stars and extras, director and crew. The meal takes place in the studio's dining room, a short walk from the stage.

After loading my tray I peer around for a place to sit. And here, good reader, is where my first-day-of-school trepidations come to a head. Who am I to sit with? Bensing is nowhere in sight, and everyone else is buddied up. The only table with an available seat is the one where svelte Julie Bean, executive producer Josh Lieb and— yikes—actress Maura Tierney sit immersed in conversation. A red light goes on in my head: *off limits.* So I sit alone on the edge of a Triffid-sized flowerpot, picking dejectedly at my Singapore noodles.

Not a minute goes by before Julie calls me: "Hey! Why don't you come sit with us?" I lift my tray, sheepishly, and take the seat next to Maura's.

Josh looks up from his julienned carrots and scrutinizes me. "Hey, aren't you... aren't you that travel writer who Bonnie got onto the show?"

I choke on a shitake mushroom. "That's right."

"Neat!" he says.

"Wow—A *real* writer!" Julie echoes.

"Not just a writer. A *travel* writer!" Maura croons.

Incredibly, they are sincere. They want to know where I've been, what I've seen, who I've met. They want to know where they can find my books—and if I'll sign them. Most of all, they want to hear about the world—the mythical "real" world, that lies somewhere beyond West Hollywood. It's a disconcerting turn of events; like visiting rural China, and having amazed locals pull at your arm hairs.

When dinner ends, I make my way to wardrobe and try on my security guard outfit. The entire uniform—from black socks to V-neck T-shirt—fits like a glove. Most amazing of all are the shoes. I'd just spent three weeks combing the Bay Area, without success, for a comfortable pair of sneakers. These industrial clunkers are like second feet; I could run a marathon in them.

NewsRadio is filmed before a live audience. Just before seven the crowd filters in, moving into tiered chairs above the set. The theater seats about 150; enough to provide a good foundation for the inevitable laugh track. The track will be "sweetened," of course; but it's good to know that we will be giving an actual performance, with all the electricity that implies.

Once the audience has settled in, the energy on the set is palpable. An air of informality maintains, but there's an edge. This is where it gets fun; this is where the stakes get raised. Even the stars feel it. I'm charged with a giddy thrill, the same rush I'd feel before diving into unexplored waters, or sneaking into a forbidden tribal rite. This adventure, of course, will have a few more viewers—what we do here tonight will appear on primetime TV.

Since the show is filmed live, the script is performed in chronological order. It's a good one, and the audience laughs. They laugh the first time a scene is filmed; they laugh the second time. Amazingly—repetition being the soul of wit—they laugh during the third, fourth and fifth takes as well.

As my moment under the spotlights approaches, I find myself entering a zone of calm. I realize, quite suddenly, that I am completely at ease in these surroundings, among this extended family of actors and crew. And I feel totally, almost dreamily safe; no possible harm can befall me.

There's a pause between takes. Risner signals to me, and I move into the mock "elevator hallway" that opens onto the WNYX office suite. My partner, a nonspeaking security guard—played by a Korean extra—is already there. As I await our scene, I spy an unfamiliar man of my own height and build, leaning against the wall. He smiles at me, then affects a serious mien. "This won't take a second," he pronounces. I raise an eyebrow.

"So you memorized my line, huh? Impressive."

"I had to." He shrugs. "I'm your understudy."

"My *understudy*? For one line?"

"Something could happen to you. And the show must go on."

"What could happen?" I scan him for weapons.

"I don't know. Anything," he says hopefully. "You might have a sudden heart attack; a beam could fall on your head; you might choke on a melon ball...."

"Ready on the set!"

Dave Foley joins us in the wings, wearing a dumb grin; he's right in character. The Panavision cameras move into position, and the film begins to roll. From out of sight, I hear the clarion call: "Action!"

Foley starts to walk. I follow him onto the stage as if moving through a tunnel, my peripheral vision blinded by the lights. My exhilaration is extreme. On my right, the audience seems to writhe with anticipation. To my left stands the entire WNYX staff, watching my progress with dubious hope.

Dave points: "You'll find him in that office, right over there."

I nod soberly. "This won't take a minute."

I open the office door and enter. The second guard follows, closing it behind us. Patrick Warburton—aka Johnny Johnson—claps a hand on my shoulder, puts a finger to his lips, and bends by the partition wall listening for his cue. A beat after it comes, he jerks open the door and addresses us with glee: "Great to see you guys again!"

We leave the room in a jovial pack, exiting by the same route we entered. Just like that, it's over. I walk, in a postcoital daze, toward the crew. Kent Zbornak is standing by a bank of monitors.

"I flubbed my line," I mutter with shame. "I was supposed to say 'second'—not 'minute.' One line, and I botched it!"

Kent grins. "You *improvised*," he says. "It was great."

It's past eleven when the actors finish their work, and the audience clears out. I return the uniform, remove the perfect shoes, and bid farewell to the players and crew. Huge is my regret as I slink from the sound stage, pausing under the dormant red light that signals "On the Air."

There is a scene, halfway through *Lawrence of Arabia*, when T. E. Lawrence is forced to execute a feuding Arab. Afterwards, Lawrence finds himself trembling uncontrollably: not from guilt, but because he *enjoyed* it. The revelation is earth-shattering; his life will never be the same.

Standing at that threshhold, I feel much the same way. My brief career as an actor, as a citizen of Planet Hollywood, has been devastating. I can't let go.

The angel and devil of good sense and stage fever perch on my shoulders, sketching out my future in a parallel universe. I could leave the viper's den of freelancing behind. I'd sublet my flat, and relocate to L.A. Money? Johnny Rocket's is out of the question... but I could work up from bussing tables at Pinot Hollywood. It wouldn't be for long, of course; just a few months, until a high-powered agent recognized me from my *NewsRadio* cameo. Why not? I may not be the next Schwarzenegger, but people do say I look a bit like Jeff Goldblum....

I turn at the door, facing the cavernous sound stage one last time. "I'll be back," I whisper.

LIVE FROM THE (OTHER) BIG APPLE

In the summer of 1995, when the manuscript for *The Size of the World* was finished, I returned to Asia to edit the galleys in Kathmandu. As a sidetrip, I journeyed to the former Soviet Republic of Kazakhstan, where my friends Rick Gaynor and Nancy Lindborg (who appear in *Shopping for Buddhas*) were working on various projects. While staying at their flat in Alma Ata (and making excursions, with Nancy, to the Uzbeki cities of Samarkand and Bukhara), I filed two stories. One was an essay, for HotWired's *WorldBeat*, on "The New Silk Road." The other was this final "Big World" installment—written for Allen Noren, the brilliant webslinger who had fielded the many dispatches I'd written during my 1994 journey. It originally appeared on GNN.com, the Global Network Navigator.

Dear Allen,

At the moment it's 11 a.m. in Alma Ata (which means, literally, "Father of all Apples"), the surprisingly green capital of Kazakhstan. I'm sitting at the head of a rectangular dining table in Rick and Nancy's elegant apartment near the corner of Tulebay and Kurmangazy Streets. At the moment, both friends are off at work. Nancy is involved with a number of assistance projects in this former

Soviet republic, including the conversion of a chemical weapons plant into a pharmaceutical factory; Rick, an attorney, is helping the no-longer communist government develop tenant and real estate law. I'm planted in a chair in a V-neck T-shirt, listening to *Thelonious Alone in San Francisco* and the birds squeaking in the trees—what's left of them, anyway. Two days ago a furious dust storm swept through this city, howling down the Soviet-era avenues and snapping old-growth branches like twigs. A timely reminder of where we are: on the edge of the steppes of Central Asia, hard against the feet of the towering Tien Shan Mountains.

And so, on this sand-blasted Kazakstani perch, 'twixt the minarets of Samarkand and the towering Vostoks of the Baikonur Cosmodrome, it gives me great pleasure to send a new installment in my continuing saga of complaint and inspiration; my latest dispatch from the far corners of this Big World, coming to you live—from the other "Big Apple."

. . .

There are a total of 880 questions on the Kazakhstani driver's test. They are arranged on 88 cards, with 10 questions on each. In order to pass, you have to score at least 90%—a maximum of one wrong answer per card.

The driver's test is typical of the attitude toward information in the former Soviet republics: High on demand, low on supply. This trend became clear the moment I landed in Alma Ata after a three-hour flight from New Delhi. The airplane (a Kazakhstan Airways jet with busted seats, torn-up carpeting and hopelessly tangled seat belts; the poverty of the infrastructure is revealed at a glance) landed heavily, taxied down the runway, pulled into its little niche, killed its engines and simply sat, motionless, for 90 minutes.

"What's happening?" I inquired of Kunda, an Indian foreign service employee sitting on my right.

"Who can say?" He shrugged. "Perhaps we left Delhi with ten beer bottles, and only nine are accounted for. Perhaps the shuttle bus driver went to the bazaar to do a bit of shopping. Or the pilot may be napping. There is a tradition in Russia, you know. Until the pilot leaves the cockpit, no one is permitted to leave their seat."

Five hundred meters away in the terminal, Nancy—who had skipped work to meet my flight—turned to an airport employee standing beside her and asked, in good Russian, what the problem was. He ignored her utterly. When she pressed her point, he spoke to her with blunt condescension.

"Please remember," he declared, "that you are no longer in your own country."

"I'm well aware of that," responded Nancy, who has lived in Alma Ata for more than two years. "But I still believe that a question deserves the courtesy of an answer."

He looked at her gamely. "Better you go have lunch."

Hours later—as the passengers, fresh from the nightmare of immigration, watched helplessly from behind a locked glass door as our luggage was dumped off a cart and hurled across a small room by a pair of ape-like goons—Nancy cast me a wry glance. "You can take it as a given," she counseled, "that everything in the former Soviet republics is set up expressly to confound the consumer."

. . .

It was not always thus. The Republic of Kazakhstan became independent in 1991. During the 70 years prior it was, as one local put it, "a very small part of a very large country." But long before that— from 200 A.D. to the end of the 16th century—the site upon which Alma Ata would eventually stand was part of an 8,000-mile network of thriving, interconnected cities. Linking the remote silk factories of Xi'an and Peking with the spice, incense, gold, and gem markets of Arabia, India and Constantinople, the network was known as the Silk Road. More than a conduit for sapphires and saffron, the Silk Road ferried fresh ideas and doctrines across the breadth of Asia— carrying the mysteries of Buddhism, Islam, astronomy, oenology, tile-glazing, bronze-casting, printing, paper-making and silk production (it was a full six centuries before Europeans realized the stuff came from worms) between cities as efficiently (though at a billionth the speed) of a garden-variety modem.

The Silk Road was, in short, the planet's first Information Super-
highway. One week ago, after driving past the soot-gray ammunition
factories of Chimkent, over the Kazakhstani border and into the neighboring Republic of Uzbekistan, I explored some of its circuits for
myself.

. . .

The towers of that era still stand. In Samarkand and Bukhara—
two of the Silk Road's legendary oases—one can still find monuments to the grand and brutal days of analog information transfer. In
downtown Samarkand, surrounded by taxi stands and power poles,
the leaning minarets and blue tiled domes of 500-year-old Islamic
madrasas (seminaries) tower above the Registan: the "Place of Sand,"
a central square cunningly designed to absorb the free-flowing blood
of the city's frequent beheadings. Some 150 miles way, in Bukhara,
stands the 155' tall Kalyan Minaret. The tower was originally built
in 1127, to serve as a lighthouse for caravans crossing the Kizyl-
Kum desert. It gained greater fame, however, as the "Tower of Death,"
from which criminals and adulterous wives were hurled by Genghis
Khan and Tamerlane.

(But I must digress a moment, lest I give the impression that the
old emirs and sultans were good for nothing but executions. In the
markets of Samarkand and Bukhara—all over Uzbekistan —one finds
a brilliant fabric called *ikot* silk. It's a glorious weave of prismatic
colors, as vivid and bold as a fractal screen saver. When I asked Nancy
how the wild pattern originated, she told me a story. Many years ago, a
visiting prince wanted to marry the daughter of Bukhara's ruler. The
sultan agreed, but on one condition: the prince had to invent a new
fabric design more beautiful than any ever seen before. For months
the prince sat before his drawing board, trying in vain to come up with
something. One evening, despairing, he went walking in the rain. He
reached the bank of a reservoir, and there waited out the storm. When
the rain finally stopped, the sun emerged—and a huge rainbow arced
across the sky. The prince saw the reflection of the rainbow in the

rippling water, and leaped to his feet. His inspiration—the famous "broken rainbow" pattern that characterizes ikot silk—was perhaps the world's first practical application of chaos theory.)

The monuments may remain, but little else of the great informational legacy of these once legendary cities has survived. For nearly three centuries—from the inept Astrakhanid Dynasty through the blundering years of Soviet rule—the cities of the silk route shriveled up like snails, salted by tyrants and swept into obsolescence by the discovery of easier sea routes and the unwrapping of China's long-hidden silk secrets. Even today, four years after the breakup of the Soviet Union, Uzbekistan's right-wing president stifles freedom of speech. It is only in the shaded *choyhonas*—traditional outdoor tea cafes—that whispers of politics and envious reflections on nearby Kazakhstan's newfound wealth are heard above the click of dominoes and the shuffle of wooden pawns.

Still, the ancient oases of the Silk Road may be in for a well-earned revival. A very different kind of information highway, knit with more threads than the finest ikot robe, now links the most remote outposts of the globe. Cities like Samarkand and Bukhara, once the central nodes of a vast relay serviced by camels and caravansarai, are not about to be left in the cold. Even as I key in this dispatch, two members of the new breed of Peace Corps volunteers— a husband and wife team, specializing in applied business technology—are journeying across Uzbekistan, building a new "caravan" of interconnected computers and Internet sites. The domain name for the Central Asian node, appropriately, is "silk"—and its hardware and phone lines are being financed, in the best Silk Road tradition, by the barter and sale of 2,000 tons of surplus USDA butter.

· · ·

So what does it all mean? What does all this new information, all this sudden potential, portend?

The Russians, virtual readers, have a tradition called the *banya*. It's basically a hellishly intense steam bath. One goes in and out of the banya at least three times. Beginning with the second round, you lean over, buck naked and sweating like a bridegroom, while a comrade whips your body with the long branches of an herbal branch called *veniki*. Then you run outside and, mustering your courage, leap under a gushing cascade of icy glacial water. It's "healthy."

Early one evening, kneeling on the floor of a rustic banya in the mountains above Alma Ata as Rick whipped the shit out of me with a bristly broom of veniki, I realized that the process is a wonderful metaphor for 20th century Russian history. Since 1900 these people have been sweating bullets, then getting the sap beaten out of them. Now— as the millennium draws to a close—they've been turned out into the cold, and tossed into the icy deluge of free-market capitalism.

Is it "healthy?" Perhaps. But—as was made abundantly clear on my arrival at the Alma Ata airport—there's an awful lot to be unlearned.

BURNING BRYTE

This story was composed in Nepal and published on *Salon* in 1998, less than a week after the events it describes. It has the signature style of all the pieces I wrote for Wanderlust: it's a short, anecdotal feature, appended with real-time reflections about my life in Kathmandu. This, I think, is the truly miraculous thing about writing for online magazines: it allows you to combine the immediacy of news reporting with the flavor of adventure travel writing.

I'M LICKING MY WOUNDS, and scratching a constellation of mysterious bites. Just returned from a few days in Chitwan, a huge wildlife park in the Terai: Nepal's steamy southern zone. I reached the place via a combination of vehicles, the most interesting of which was a rubber raft. Spent about four hours going down the rain-swollen Trisuli river, navigating about a dozen rapids (most of them embarrassingly tame) and swallowing several gallons of amoeba-infested river water in the process.

I made the trip to check out Temple Tiger, one of just two resort/ lodges within the boundaries of the national park itself. Over the years I've visited Chitwan three or four times, but this was the prettiest part of the jungle I'd seen. There was a kind of sweetness there, an Impressionist softness to the air and the light. The elephant grass had been cut low by the local Tharu villagers, making it relatively easy to spot the one-horned rhinos who grazed, snorting, by the waterholes. I spent each morning and evening riding through the jungle on elephant back, accompanied by a local guide and naturalist named Jitu.

Jitu grew up in Sauraha, on the border of the national park. He is a small, muscular man, 34 years old, with the perfectly chiseled features of a Tharu Omar Sharif. Jitu's encounters with the local wildlife are legendary, and I have no doubt they are true. Once—on a jungle walk, on foot, with a group of hapless Dutch tourists—he stumbled upon a tiger in dalliance with its mate. The female rose, and immediately charged. Jitu didn't panic; he knew that running would be fatal. He simply stood his ground, smacked his walking stick against a bush, and shouted at the top of his lungs. The tiger screeched to a halt, growling, and Jitu backed the group away. On another occasion, while walking alone to his previous lodge, Jitu realized that a female Bengal—along with her cub—was stalking him. The cats followed the lone Jitu for 45 minutes, sometimes alongside, sometimes creeping behind. "If I'd run, or tried to climb a tree, they would have attacked immediately," he stated. "So I just kept walking, while whistling and talking to myself." Eventually the tigers moved on—as the unperturbed naturalist knew they would.

"Humans are not the tiger's prey," Jitu said with conviction. "They will not attack unless threatened—or unless they have lost the ability to hunt their usual prey."

The problem is, this has happened. About ten years ago, Jitu recalled, the only other lodge within Chitwan's limits—Tiger Tops—made a practice of baiting tigers with live animals. A juvenile buffalo or goat would be tethered in a clearing, and one of the local tigers would saunter in for the kill. Tourists watched from a blind. This practice was ultimately abandoned—not out of compassion for the prey, but because tigers fed this way would gain weight and loose their prowess. Finally, the only animals within their range were domestic cattle... and humans. One of the tigers fed on baited game actually became a man-eater, and introduced her cub to the taste of human flesh. The two animals were responsible for a number of killings in the area. The tiger cub was eventually captured, and transferred to a Kathmandu Zoo. The other cat may still be at large—a fact which Jitu must have repressed while he was being stalked.

Jitu never sat with me in the wooden *howdah*. He stood behind, upright, balanced on the elephant's haunches. We rocked and swayed and crunched through the jungle, stopping every now and then as our pachyderm paused to uproot a stray banana tree (which he ate whole, minus the bananas) or drink a stream dry. It was blissful, in that jungle-fever way: lush and hot, an ecstastic buzz of chlorophyll and pheromones. The orchids were beginning to bloom, and the air smelled of jasmine, chlorodendron and musk. Peacocks screamed from the treetops, sounding like plaintive Siamese cats. There are 450 species of birds in Chitwan National Park; every expedition is accompanied by their *Jungle Book* soundtrack. The colors were fleeting, but intense. Kingfishers sat on the tree branches, looking like turquoise fruit. Chestnut-headed bee eaters swooped above our heads, iridescent gold and green. Our first morning, Jitu and I spied a troupe of white-haired, black-faced langur monkeys climbing through a red-leafed honey tree; a spotted deer, unfazed by our presence, grazed below. It was a scene out of Gauguin. I imagined (inanely) that one of the park's elusive tigers might walk into the scene without raising a stir.

This is the big problem, of course: actually *seeing* a tiger. Like most visitors, I desperately wanted to do so. But it's a tough goal. At last census, only 66 Royal Bengal Tigers were counted within the entire, 500 square kilometer Chitwan preserve. There are perhaps four or five adult tigers within Temple Tiger's 60-70 square kilometers of jungle. They're notoriously reclusive, and masters of stealth and camouflage. It had been four or five days, Jitu told me, since the last spotting.

. . .

My second day in the park, Jitu and I set off at dawn. The sun rose like a squashed persimmon over the jungle mists. Aside from the hooting of invisible Indian cuckoos, the only sound was the pulping of leaves beneath the elephant's feet. It was one of those mornings when almost nothing seemed to be awake. I saw no deer, no monkeys, no wild boar or mugger crocodiles; just the inevitable rhinos, grazing dumbly in the high grass. We were following the foot trail back to camp when Jitu, perched on the rear haunches of the pachyderm, quietly signaled the driver to stop. Jitu jumped off the elephant and squinted at the sandy path, reading a pattern in what was—to me—unintelligible sandy soil. But Jitu recognized the paw prints of a tiger, along with the telltale drag marks of freshly killed prey. He climbed back on our mount, and we hung a right into the jungle.

What followed was the most amazing example of tracking I have ever seen. Using his sight, smell and hearing—and a sixth sense developed during a lifetime in the Terai—Jitu traced the predator's retreat into the bush. He pored through the foliage like a bloodhound, sniffing here, examining a branch there, exploring false leads and doubling back again. After 15 minutes of this, Jitu climbed back onto the elephant. An instant later we rounded a corner—and found the cat's victim. A young deer lay dead in a small clearing, its hindquarters shredded.

"From the paw prints, and the size of the kill," Jitu whispered, "I can say it is a male, of adolescent age. But we're too late; he went into the grass when he heard us coming."

We moved away slowly, hoping the tiger had not wandered too far from its breakfast. Again, the crunching footfalls of the elephant drowned out all but the most strident bird calls. After two minutes, though, Jitu raised his palm.

"I hear chewing," he said.

Jitu sniffed the air, testing for the musky, milky scent peculiar to tigers. Then he turned the elephant silently around, heading back into the stand of grass where we'd seen the deer.

There was a blood-curdling roar, and the tiger leaped at us from the thicket. Our elephant—a monster among the local pachyderms—staggered back, but continued forward at the mahout's command.

"Jitu...." I drew my legs into the howdah, suddenly aware of how close they were to the ground. "Do tigers ever, uh, leap up onto the elephants' backs?"

"Sometimes." He shrugged. "Not often."

The tiger crouched, snarling, and charged us a second time. It leaped forward, claws out. Our pachyderm trumpeted: a single, ear-splitting note, like Dizzy Gillespie on steroids. I clung to the how-dah, my ears ringing. Our little safari seemed about as clever as free-climbing into a live volcano.

But a cat is no match for an elephant; the fact is ingrained into every feline brain. The tiger retreated again, this time for good. For a few minutes Jitu engaged in a tense game of cat-and-mouse, trying without success to flush him back out. It's astonishing how quickly these jungle animals vanish. You'd think a tiger's vivid black-and-orange bands would stand out in the dry grass like a Chanel ski jacket—in fact, the animal seemed to become invisible at will. Though we continued to catch glimpses of his head or tail, we never again saw the whole animal at once.

Nonetheless, our brief encounter with one of Chitwan's endan-gered tigers was unforgettable. The beauty and ferocity of the animal was totally breathtaking. His roar had evoked the same response as an earthquake; it made the ground tremble, and awoke a primal ter-ror that made my mouth dry and my heart race. The oddest thing, though, was how *addictive* the experience was. Sighting tigers is a lot like snorting cocaine; the most compelling effect is to make you de-sire more of the same.

. . .

Home at last, to a jungle of another sort. Actually, it's more like a monkey house. Here in Kathmandu, in the dry and dusty season be-tween the last frosts and the monsoon deluge, I sense an emerging current of defeated self-parody. It's as if Nepal has reached a turning point; a juncture where the local intelligentsia is finally so fed up with the rampant corruption and choking pollution that it has decided to pull out the stops, and begin mocking the establishment in earnest.

The vanguard of this trend has been the capital's best daily newspaper: the *Kathmandu Post*. Over the past few days, the *Post* has run a series of photographs and editorials that have had the locals roaring with glee. On March 30, for example, the lead story was illustrated by a shot of Prime Minister S. B. Thapa. The picture—captioned "Shh. . . . Don't Disturb"—showed the PM napping through a meeting on government corruption. The same day, the editorial page carried a hilarious article about public urination. (The practice will never be stopped, the Op-Ed piece claimed, by the current practice of posting "Do Not Urinate Here" signs; such signs only indicate that the spot in question—e.g., the side of a school building—is a "traditional" public urinal, and therefore a venerable and cherished peeing site.) But the master stroke appeared on April 1, when the front-page photo showed one of Kathmandu's dubious water trucks (used to provide *kani pani*, or pure drinking water, to private homes and hotels) with its hose extended, sucking water directly from the Kodku Khola: one of the city's filthiest urban creeks. Believe me: it was no April Fool's prank.

A far less amusing example of modern-day values came to my attention last night, over drinks with an expatriate anthropologist named Charles Ramble. Ramble has just returned from his own brief trip to the Terai, where he and photographer Thomas Kelly covered a much-heralded event: the public immolation, by Chitwan authorities, of a mountain of confiscated jungle contraband: leopard skins, endangered wild antelope wool (known as *chartoush*), tiger penis and rhinoceros horn (the last two are considered powerful aphrodisiacs by the Chinese, who pay huge sums for the stuff). Tons of this booty was stacked into an enormous pile, doused with fuel, and ignited. The local papers (working, no doubt, from official press releases) heralded the conflagration as a watershed event: a bold signal that Nepal will not tolerate the poaching of protected species, or permit any trade in illegal animal products.

But Ramble and Kelly, on assignment for *Asia Week*, crept close enough to the bonfire to realize that something was wrong. What the authorities were actually burning, they discovered, was garbage: moldy old hides, fake rhino horns, water buffalo skins painted with stripes, ersatz tiger bones. When Ramble confronted Nepal's Minister of Forests about this, he was quickly set to rights. The point of the conflagration was simply to clear out the rangers' warehouses, which were overstocked with junk. Who had suggested otherwise?

So what about the good stuff? It is being held in reserve: a king's ransom of top-quality horns and hides, spirited away behind a well-publicized smokescreen. The current government line: If an agreement with CITES (the Convention on International Trade in Endangered Species) can be reached, the contraband will be sold off legally, and the profits used to fund museums and educational programs.

If you believe that, I've got some pure drinking water to sell you.

GETTING WET
A VISIT TO SOUTHERN THAILAND

In 1992, the *San Francisco Examiner* sent me to Southeast Asia on one of those dream assignments: a pair of stories to be called, "Thailand, Wet and Dry." The wet half, below, included a return to the Phuket region, which I'd visited seven years earlier for *Islands* (see "The Fighting Spirit of Phuket Island"). The dry part—an account of a rather smoky trip to the Thai/Burmese border during the slash-and-burn season—was originally going to appear here instead; but at the eleventh hour I decided that this one was more fun (I also wanted to include a few words about scuba diving, one of the great loves of this traveler's life). If you're interested, you can read the companion story in O'Reilly and Habegger's *Travelers' Tales Thailand*.

IT WAS THE TIME of year when, about to run out of those little soaps they give you in big hotels, I realized I was due for another trip. Indeed; no sooner had the final sliver of "Jardin des Figues" disappeared down the drain than the telephone rang, bearing an invitation to visit the Kingdom of Thailand.

Two weeks later, I was peering out the window of a Thai Airways jet—watching the surface of Phuket Island resolve from a hazy green mass into a welcoming landscape of palm trees and preparing, by way of the ocean, to get enviably clean.

This was my second visit to Phuket. Memories of deserted beaches, Technicolor sunsets and bath-warm waters beguiled me as I collected my luggage at Phuket International. The island had seen some changes, naturally, over the years; the huge new airport, with its 15 incoming flights a day, was certainly one of them. The others, I hoped, would be rather less obvious.

Arriving at my hotel, a wave of déjà vu assailed me. Seven years ago I'd stood on this very same beach, watching a crimson sunset over Koh Poo, a pretty offshore island. Back then, the locals were jumpy. Club Med had just announced plans to build a resort on the unspoiled crescent of beach. "I wonder," my photographer had remarked, "what this place will look like in ten years?"

Now I know. Four huge luxury hotels have shouldered their way between the trees, and the beach is lined with chaise lounges and umbrellas. The Club Med, ironically, is the most tasteful resort of the lot: nestled into the southern corner of the beach, it's the only one that has made a bow to traditional architecture. It looks utterly out of place.

Fortunately, Karon Beach will be only a base. What has brought me here, to the edge of the Andaman Sea, is the desire to immerse myself in Phuket's bath-warm waters. True, the region holds infinite diversions: An endless profusion of shops, bars, video arcades and boutiques line the Kata/Karon corniche, and the availability of short- or long-term "girlfriends" in this part of Thailand is both legendary and notorious. But I want to spend my week developing an intimate relationship with the ocean; and Phuket features some of the world's best water sports. It takes most of my first day on the island just to narrow the field.

Swimming, for example, will probably not be much of an adventure; Phuket has few sharks. And I happen to be among those who believe that all jet skis should be gathered into a pile, doused with gasoline, and burned. Parasailing, or whatever it's called, where they haul you into the air behind a boat, does not qualify as a water sport, since direct contact with the water's surface generally means that your ride, or your life, is over.

There remains, as far as I make out, only two viable possibilities: sea canoeing in Phang Nga Bay, and scuba diving among the Similan Islands.

• • •

"We're an expedition company that takes guests," John Gray, director of Phuket Sea Canoe Center, warns as he greets me at the dock at Pho Bay. "We don't do white sand beaches."

Gray, 47, stands six-feet two in sandals and salmon-pink shorts. His long hair, reddish-blond and streaked with gray, is harnessed into a ponytail. Preparing for our trip he is assisted by Wanda: a large, bald, tattooed and completely intimidating fellow who looks like Mr. Clean, but dirtier.

"He's a beautiful guy," John assures me. "He's done all kinds of stuff. Even been in films; he played the heavy in *Sheena, Queen of the Jungle*."

Gray has his own story. He formerly lived in Hawaii, where he worked as the communications director for a cancer research center. "The great thing about working in Hawaii," he confides, "was that I didn't have to wear a tie."

Ten years ago, he threw out his shirts as well. Gray started his Sea Canoe company on Oahu in 1983, established a branch in Polynesia, and is now gaining steam in Thailand and Vietnam. The thrust of the operation is different in each venue. In Thailand, he delights in taking his hi-tech rubber canoes into *hongs*: open-air chambers (*hong* literally means "room" in Thai) hidden deep within the small islands of Phang Nga Bay.

"The definition of a hong," John said, "is that you're surrounded, 360 degrees, by solid rock." Created by erosion and other natural forces, these hongs are accessible only through narrow, cave-like passageways which open and close with the tides, often in a matter of minutes.

Phang Nga Bay is one of the most beautiful spots in Thailand. Located in a crook of the Malay Peninsula some 60 miles northeast of Phuket, the Bay contains more than 150 rocky *koh*, or islands, that jut from the Andaman Sea. Some are 10 feet high; some are two hundred. Imagine those famous Chinese landscape paintings of Guilin, with their knobby, mist-ringed hills—and transplant that scenery onto the surface of the ocean. It's an astonishing sight.

By late morning we've arrived in Phang Nga, and anchored our mother boat—the *Ol' Lady*—near the cliffs of Koh Panak. After a miraculous lunch of spicy prawn soup, grilled fish, ginger vegetables and Thai-style noodles with chili and chicken—all prepared, some-how, on the boat's single burner stove—John supervises the lower-ing of the canoes. I'd expected that I would paddle my own; but the difficulty and danger of rowing into the hongs is a job for experts. I clamber into my bright yellow canoe, joined by a young Thai oars-man named Sadik.

As we approach Koh Panak, the island's architecture amazes me. It is a huge knob of limestone, freckled with trees and shrubs. The base—where island meets sea—is naped, like the back of a neck, and the overhang is draped with bizarre, drippy rock formations. I see no entrance until Sadik turns the canoe, and steers it directly toward an impossibly low cavern. "You'd better duck," he advises. I lay straight back, hands clasped over my chest like a mummy in an Egyptian barque. The ceiling of the cavern—covered with razor-sharp, calcified oyster shells—passes inches above my nose. And then I clamp my eyes shut, for the sun is suddenly overhead.

We have emerged into The Land Beyond Time: a dreamy, otherworldly environment where the only sounds are the distant squeak of birds and the sloshing of our oars in the warm water. The sun ricochets off the emerald water, throwing Laserium patterns on the sheer stone walls. Mangrove trees rise from the hong's sandy floor, their roots tangled above the waterline like wooden webs. Sadik lifts the oars, and the silence was total—until I hear a low, beating sound to my right. It is a butterfly in flight.

An hour later, back on the *Ol' Lady*, the mood is subdued rever-ence. We sit at the dining table and listen, over terrible coffee, to Gray's philosophy of life. "Here's my lifelong question," he says.

"How do you improve the standard of living in developing countries—while maintaining ecological and cultural integrity?"

For Gray, of course, the answer is Sea Canoe: an environmentally savvy company that will ultimately be handed over to local owners. "I own only 20% of Sea Canoe," he says. "And I get out-voted at meetings all the time." When I ask for an example, he points to my cup. "Nescafé," he apologizes. "I wanted drip coffee, but the locals vetoed me."

At first, Gray recalls, Thai businessmen thought he was nuts. The tried-and-true market was for jet ski rentals, or organized tours of the Bay. (One of Phang Nga's little koh is featured as a solar collector in *The Man with the Golden Gun*, and tourists throng to see this "James Bond Island.") But Sea Canoe proves that a small, ecologically sound company can succeed—and Gray believes the trend will catch on.

"I'd love to see the day," he grins, "when Bangkok businessmen want to build sea canoes instead of a jet ski factory."

During the next two days we explore a dozen more hongs, carefully monitoring the tides. Each hong has its own window: a moment in time when the water level is low enough to admit a canoe, but high enough to avoid the jagged rims of scalpel-like stones and fossilized shells.

The hongs themselves differ in subtle ways. Some are nearly empty, like wells; others teem with bushes, mangrove trees, hanging vines, butterflies, and blue lizards that scamper across the virgin sand bars like wind-up toys. My favorite hong is more like a canyon than a single room; we navigate a long, winding river through a deep gorge, as brilliant kingfishers flit between the vertiginous walls.

For the climax of our expedition, John organizes a night trip into one of the hongs. It is nearly midnight before the tides are right; then we creep into our canoes and paddle, with powerful flashlights, through the womb-like passage into the preternatural stillness of the hong. Above our heads, a circle of stars glimmers in the blackness. The water sparkles with phosphorescent plankton. It is perfectly, absolutely quiet.

The hairs on my neck prickle as I perceive a low, snarling sound.

It grows in intensity, becoming a growl and, suddenly, a terrible roar. It stops for just a moment... then it starts again, echoing off the walls of the hong.

John Gray lays sprawled in his sea canoe like a beached seal, snoring at the top of his lungs.

. . .

The morning before my departure to the Similan Islands I visit Wat Chalong, a newly renovated Buddhist temple about eight miles from Karon Beach. Thai Buddhism is unlike the variety you'll find in Tibet or Nepal; it follows the Theraveda school, a path of austere adherence to the Buddha's basic teaching of simplicity, charity and individual enlightenment.

Entering a wat, or Thai temple, one purchases a sort of "blessing kit" called a *wai*. This consists of a yellow candle, three sticks of incense, and a small, nearly weightless square of gold leaf. One lights the candle and incense, and presses rubs the gold leaf onto the image of Buddha. A stout woman with a wide smile and a bottle of spray glue follows behind, making sure it sticks. Still, a good deal of this gold feathering escapes. I spent nearly 15 minutes hypnotized by a little tornado of gold squares, caught in a wind vortex, spinning outside the temple door.

Our dive boat—the *Sai Mai II*—departs from Chalong Bay, not far from the temple, at sunset. The captain is one Matthew Hendrick, a transplanted American who moved to Phuket from Miami in 1986 and founded the Siam Diving Center.

The Similans are a group of nine islands, declared a National Park in 1982. They lie about one hundred miles up the Isthmus of Kra: the narrow channel of land where Burma, Thailand and Malaysia funnel into each other. In 1985, during my last visit, the Similans were a diver's wet dream: remote and uninhabited, they were seldom visited. Today, at least half a dozen dive companies run trips to the islands, while the Jet Cat—a high-speed catamaran—brings hundreds of snorkelers each day.

The *Sai Mai II* is a beautiful boat, designed to carry eight guests and crew in almost unreasonable comfort. Matthew's wife—a Thai woman named Jimm—is the chef, and the rare moments we spend above sea level are passed in the dining room, gobbling an array of exotic Thai dishes prepared in a kitchen only slightly larger than a phone booth.

Among the divers on the *Sai Mai II* is Ashley Boyd, an underwater photographer whose popular picture book, *Thailand: The Kingdom Beneath the Sea*, has made him a national celebrity. Droll, fit and fifty-something, Boyd has visited the Similans at least 18 times. His considered opinion is that the diving has actually improved. "There's more care about anchoring," he says. "So as not to harm the corals. But this past year the Jet Cat has started its day trips, which are threatening the equilibrium again."

The Similans are ranked among the best dive sites in the world—except for three weeks a year, when the plankton spawn. Those familiar with my journeys will have already guessed that my visit coincides exactly with this period. Still, visibility is fair, and the plankton—slimy green nuisance though it is—increases the possibility of seeing larger fish.

What is it about diving? Being beneath the sea produces a kind of meditative trance. It seems, for the time being, that all my cares exist in a remote, alien world. Scuba diving on coral reefs—and the Similans have some of the most beautiful reefs in the world—is especially wonderful because, everywhere one looks, there is life: simple, uncomplicated life, going about its business without a single thought of upgrading its software.

Rainbow-colored parrotfish gnaw at the corals, their very excreta the raw material of white sand beaches. White-tipped reef sharks glide past, adding a thrill of conditioned terror. Willowy feather worms blink shut with lightning speed as I flipper by; it seems the rocks themselves are winking at me. All around are hundreds of fish, in every shape and color, each one minutely adapted to its own fishy habits. And then there are the corals: ancient labyrinths of meticulously sculpted skeletons, covered with an almost microscopic veneer of living, breathing tissue.

"Almost everything you see underwater," Hendrick reminds us, "is an animal. Touching anything under there is like touching a dog, or cat, or squirrel. My policy, and the policy on this boat, is: leave the animals alone, and they'll leave you alone."

Ten fathoms below, I find it incredible how few aggressive or belligerent animals exist under the sea. True, there are dangers: stonefish with their deadly spines, lion fish, coral snakes, sharp-toothed moray eels, spiky sea urchins, fire coral, sting rays. But nothing seems even vaguely interested in harming me. Getting hurt would require extreme clumsiness, panic, or sheer stupidity. People prone to these traits seem, almost instinctively, to avoid scuba diving.

Over dinner, Hendrick peers from the helm at the other dive boats moored in the snug harbor of Breakfast Bay. As the sun goes down, a dozen squid-fishing boats turn on their racks of water-facing floodlights, designed to lure the hapless cephalopods toward the surface. The glare is tremendous; it's as though we've sailed into a forest of hyperactive Christmas trees.

"Thailand's Parks Department has to decide," Hendrick sighs, "whether they're going to preserve this place, or make it totally accessible. It's definitely unique; the best coral environment that Thailand has. You can see whale sharks, turtles, manta rays, and loads of fish. But they need to start enforcing the rules. You're not supposed to fish here, but there's no way to enforce it. No patrol boats; nothing."

"Unfortunately," Boyd adds, spearing a fried banana, "there's too much vested interest by big business. There's a ban on *collecting* coral, of course—but not on selling it! Nor is it illegal to collect shells, another big business."

"Diving itself isn't a threat," Hendrick rejoins, "if tourism is controlled, and divers know what they're doing. The biggest offenders are the Thai fishermen themselves. They figure it's their ocean, and they'll do what they like with it."

The conversation returns me, too quickly, to the foibles and follies of life at sea level. Going to bed with a belly full of shellfish and chili peppers, I dream of growing gills, and taking my chances among the turtles and trumpet-fish.

. . .

The next afternoon, the *Sai Mai II* drops me off at the ladder of the infamous Jet Cat. My flight for the hill country departs the next day; I must hurry back to Phuket, even as my fellow divers continue their exploration of the Similans. I don't begrudge going; but finding myself on a jumbo jet-sized hydrofoil, with 300 chain-smoking Thai tourists and *Gross Anatomy* blaring on half a dozen screens, seems a bit of a jolt. I am much relieved when, after only two hours, I'm handed the traditional Wet n' Dri, signaling that our ride nears its end.

It is a long, congested drive to the Karon Beach Resort, where a three-piece band plays "Teach Your Children" in the lobby. I shower, change, and forage through the hotel bathroom, loading my toiletry case with neatly wrapped soaps.

YOU ARE HERE:
SIX VIEWS OF SAN FRANCISCO

I had a terrific time with this unconventional story: a meditation on historical maps of San Francisco, from 1775 to the Space Age. The story was assigned by travel writer Tracy Johnston (author of *Shooting the Boh*), guest editing San Francisco's (now defunct) *Focus*. It was written in collaboration with the magazine's art department, which illustrated each of the six mini-essays with the specific map I'd used. Kindred spirits might hear the influence of Italo Calvino; certainly, his *Invisible Cities* inspired these pieces.

Included are current resources for each of these maps. Most of them, or maps very similar to the ones I saw, are available for online viewing—not quite the case when I first published this story, all of six years ago!

"You are here."

There is a private joy in finding oneself on a map. For a moment all confusion ceases, giving way to a wonderful sense of calm.

Such a moment might arrive in Macy's, somewhere between accessories and bedding; it might come on the open sea, with the coast of Africa looming on the horizon, or deep within a Szechuan tunnel.

It doesn't much matter where we are; there is pleasure in the simple fact that our particular location fits, somehow, into the greater scheme of things.

Since the dawn of time, we humans have sought out one thing after another. The hunts of our ancestors continue still; only the quarry has changed. Long ago, we stalked the trails of bison and rabbit. Today we try to find a good Vietnamese restaurant. Once upon a time we sought the Holy Grail; now we drive around in search of an open tennis court. Our quests are many, and the road is long, but we have an advantage over our forebears. Whatever we seek, we shall find— and maps shall lead us there.

Our love affair with maps, perhaps, is a statement about the human condition. Where else can we look for a reflection of our actual progress? How often are we permitted to measure, in inches or centimeters, the distance to our goal?

Modern maps boast an impressive degree of reliability—but there is a limit to their claim. Though we can follow them to the far corners of the world, they can never reveal our ultimate destination. For as our own Saint Francis once declared: "What you are looking for is who is looking."

I. The City's First Graphic Artist

"Plano del Puerto de San Francisco." So reads the formal penmanship, now over two centuries old....

On August 5, 1775, Juan Manuel de Ayala, captain of the *San Carlos*, anchored his ship outside the Golden Gate. His pilot and artist, José de Cañizares, sailed into the Bay on a launch, along with ten shipmates. During the next two months, as the *San Carlos* lay anchored off Angel Island (named by Cañizares), the pilot became the first person ever to map the spiny curves of our peninsula.

The following year, Cañizares returned. This time he surveyed the Bay Area in detail, leading soldiers through old redwood groves and Ohlone villages. He added dunes and marshes to his map, and explored the delta area and its rivers. Weights were tied to ropes and dropped into the coastal waters, sounding depth. The rocky points along San Francisco's crest were drawn as spiky promontories, biting into the Bay like teeth.

As a pilot, Cañizares' mapping task was straightforward. With his work the Golden Gate would be wedged open, and Spanish conquest of the territory assured. As an artist, though, he was beholden to more subtle goals. His map, he realized, was the very first; it had to contain everything that one needs to know at the bare beginning of things. Dividing and conquering, building and damming, sawing and dredging; these would come later.

What is the most important information at the moment of entry? What do we require from our simplest maps? Angles of approach, of course. A sense of size, certainly. An arrow pointing north, to place us among the stars. But even more essential, we need to share the explorer's vision. We must sense the land itself, sniff its air, hear the rustle of its leaves.

So Cañizares the artist painted his map with earthy hues, peppered it with icons of vegetation, and named the islands after the birds and angels that visited him as he drew. While anticipating the future, he was still able to see the land as a whole: unsullied, as yet, by the industry of Man.

Studying this map, we sense a kind of poised admiration. It reminds us of the way a cat will study a bird before pouncing; or of how we admire a carefully arranged salad, before tossing it into the air with tongs.

(To view this map, visit www.lib.berkeley.edu/EART/digital/sf-1766.gif)

II. Wild in the City

The soft blues, tans and greens used by Cañizares have all but vanished from San Francisco's maps, replaced by an ever-expanding grid of street names, buslines and piers.

Now those calm, earthy colors appear again, as a window on the past. *Wild In the City*, a map by Berkeley artist Nancy Morita, recreates the San Francisco known by the Miwoks and Ohlones—in the long centuries before even the Spanish arrived.

This was a peninsula laced with rivers, covered with shifting dunes, quilted with grasslands grazed by elk and deer. Ohlone children ran naked through the Mission, splashing in the small waterfall on what is now the corner of 18th and Valencia streets. Bald eagles cast their slow shadows over Potrero Hill, hunting dusky-footed woodrats hiding in groves of yellow monkey flower. The eastern shore of the peninsula was an amorphous network of marshes and lagoons: a vast sanctuary for migratory birds.

Wild In the City is actually a double map; for alongside her idyllic image, Morita has drawn its modern counterpart: San Francisco today. Here the salt water marshes have been filled, the sand dunes leveled and irrigated. El Polin Creek lies somewhere beneath the Exploratorium, its brackish estuary now a duck-filled lagoon. The rough northern and eastern shorelines of the peninsula have been spackled with landfill, and jigsawed into geometric piers. The skyscrapers of the Financial District stand on the site of Ohlone sweat lodges, and fishing streams have disappeared below a filigree of roads....

Our gaze jumps between the two maps, unsure which one to trust. For a moment we are seized by a terrible nostalgia—for something lost forever. But the feeling passes quickly. The real San Francisco, we realize at last, is the one on the left: that watercolor world of gooseberries and fur seals, kingfishers and ferns, herrings and mint. This is the City in its eternal form. That maze of boulevards, bridges and sushi bars to the right is nothing more than a thumbnail sketch, useful for a mere decade or two.

We have settled ourselves on our cluttered new map, spread it like a picnic blanket over the rough textures of a once wild land. Someday, though, the wind will shift; the sky will threaten rain. The blanket that we rest on will be rolled up. The long grasses will unbend, streams will trickle in, and steam will pour from the sweat lodges again.

(Map source: "Wild in the City," available from Nancy Morita, © 1992. Morita can be reached at 415-459-6915.)

III. *Trying to Find Chinatown*

The railroad lines were nearly completed, and the days of *ku li*—bitter toil—were drawing to a close. But still harder times were ahead; and in the huge rectangle bounded by Stockton and Kearney, California and Broadway, the City's already large Chinese community dug itself in.

One hundred years ago, Chinatown was a world apart. Thousands of immigrants, scorned by white society, had built their western Canton over 12 city blocks. Now, lives and livelihoods threatened, the community fragmented into warring *tongs*, which sustained themselves with the dark trades of old China: prostitution, extortion and drugs.

To the Board of Supervisors, Chinatown must have seemed an ugly and maddening puzzle: a dingy realm of narrow alleys and unmarked doorways, unfathomable signs, suspicious glances. Ducks and pigs ran through the crowded streets, chased by children and dogs. The smell of drying fish overpowered the pungent aroma of temple incense, and the air was laced with sweet breaths of opium that escaped through the cracks in closed shutters.

It was, in short, an alien world. Without a map, the authorities could never hope to uncover the district's unsavory secrets.

No one knows how the information was gathered, or with what degree of accuracy; but in July of 1885 a band of cartographers, working under special orders, finally managed to learn—or guess—the hidden truth about every address in Chinatown. In a color-coded map, they shared their intelligence with the Board.

Salmon pink revealed the gambling houses hidden behind cigar stores, groceries and jewelry shops. Sky blue and jade green exposed the 38 white and 57 Chinese brothels—two dozen on the 800 block of Sacramento Street alone. Red showed the location of Chinatown's dozen Joss temples, where ancient idols accepted donations and dispensed fortunes. Bright yellow betrayed the musty kitchens and lounges—16 in all—of the district's opium trade.

When the "Official Map of Chinatown" appeared in the San Fran-

cisco Daily Report, druglords and pimps found their darkest secrets
exposed: revealed to rival gangs, gawking tourists and lawmen. Perhaps it reminded them of the fierce tropical storms that visit South
China's coast, peeling the rooftops off of buildings and laying entire
neighborhoods bare.

*(This rare Chinatown map is available only from the Main Library Map
Room, University of California, Berkeley. The map's call number in the library is F869
S3 1885 B7; the map room number is 510-642-4940. Last I checked it was not online.)*

IV. *Axonometry*

Just as there are different kinds of maps, there are different kinds
of eyes.

Cool eyes prefer to see the city objectively: as an art form in its
own right, composed of smooth planes, pleasing angles and neatly
drawn streets. Plato had such eyes; their greatest pleasure comes
from seeing straight lines, the elegant skeletons of the ideal.

I am looking at a map of central San Francisco, published by the
Picture Map Company in 1976. It is an axonometric drawing: also
called a "bird's eye view." Rendered in stark black ink on a field of
white, it must be a favorite of architects. It makes me imagine how
San Francisco might appear after a great snowfall, or an invasion of
gigantic seagulls.

The buildings rise from this map in cool relief, towering over the
barren intersections like components on a printed circuit board. There
are no taxis on the streets, no saxophone players outside of Macy's,
no couples lounging on the grass in Levi Plaza. All motion has vanished. Our city seems complete and frozen, like a completed cross-
word puzzle.

Hot eyes narrow suspiciously at this cool, objective approach.
They feast on the hubs of humanity, the lights of arcades, the sting of
sunscreen and seaspray. Hot-eyed people carry maps drawn with
bulbous lines and painted with circus colors—as if San Francisco
were a giant theme park.

While cool eyes want to see the City as a Mondrian painting, hot eyes seek Rousseau. Their maps boil over like the Sunday comics, full of exclamation points and glee. Fisherman's Wharf; Ghirardelli Square; Coit Tower and the Golden Gate Bridge; the City's most vivid attractions leap from these maps like carnival barkers, hawking memories, sourdough, picture postcard views.

We can envy the hot eyes, who would consume the City with a single sensual glance; we can admire the cool eyes, who worship an ethereal urban ideal. But most of us fall somewhere in between, content with the dog-eared road maps that lie, clumsily folded, in our glove compartments.

(You can view axonometric maps of San Francisco at www.mapposter.com, and at www.maps.com)

V. *Instrument Flight Rules*

At 18,000 feet, familiar landmarks all but vanish. The ground becomes a brush-stroke painting, glimpsed through the windows of Boeing jets as we land and ascend, bound for other well-drawn destinations. The Bay Area is reduced to its barest essentials: the geometric notch of Golden Gate Park; the tic-tac-toe of airport runways; the wire of Highway 101, snaking up the peninsula.

Guiding jets at this giddy altitude, pilots use maps that float in the sky like gossamer webs: charts of the vast, linear airways that form a nebulous matrix of bulls-eyes and arrows, dots and dashes, far above our heads.

These demarcations are as invisible to the eye as the lines of latitude and longitude, but they are equally important. Without them jets would tussle in the sky, circling in confusion before dropping into the Bay like wounded dragonflies.

The men and women who keep these airships aloft have long ago traded the imperfect sense of sight for the more precise language of numbers, symbols and radio codes. While our pedestrian maps sag beneath a riot of landmarks and roadways, theirs hover in a rarefied atmosphere of pure data. Everything they need to know has been boiled and filtered, distilled into a subtle liqueur of digits and acronyms. They have learned to navigate like bats, guiding their aircraft by the beeps and pulses that mark entire cities.

(To view an Enroute Low Altitude map of San Francisco, try this link: www.aeroplanner.com/notams/airspace.cfm?apt=sfo)

VI. The Class of 1996

Even from space, the outline of San Francisco is unmistakable: a long and muscular thumb, poised above the continent's spine.

With a single glance the eye drinks in the Bay: a gourd-shaped puddle, striped with a current of eggplant blue. Bridges, fine as hairs, stretch across its breadth; ferries and their wakes sparkle like grains of polished rice. Beyond the slender neck of the Golden Gate looms the vast Pacific, covering half the world.

The shapes on this map are familiar, but the colors are wild and strange. Gone are the subtle, earthy hues of Cañizares; in their place we find psychedelic reds, sodium yellows, emerald greens. To see the City this way, we would have to get high—438 miles high, to be exact—and view the City through the lens of Landsat's infrared scanner.

Seen from this end of the spectrum, life—living things—look hot. The coastal mountains, covered with trees, glow like lava. Vivid yellows indicate pockets of range grasses, nourished by early rains. Green, usually a sign of growth, is now the signature of dry, drought-parched hillsides; while the City itself is an expanse of glacial turquoise, punctuated with little red islands.

Somewhere, in the scarlet rectangle of Golden Gate Park, tourists in the Tea Garden are about to crack open their fortune cookies. There are bicyclists frozen in mid-peddle on the Great Highway; forks arrested in mid-air; half-formed thoughts on the monitors of downtown offices. Crimson cats are stalled in mid-leap, suspended above alleys; airplanes hang above their runways, perched on plumes of smoke.

Am I that microdot of pink, holding a bag of fresh peaches? Are you that crimson pinprick, weeding in the yard?

On July 21, 1996—a sunny Sunday afternoon—a passing satellite winked, and captured a moment in time. The result was not merely a map, but a candid portrait. Each of us might be found within it, if we only knew where to look.

(San Francisco from Space maps are visible on the Spaceshots website: www.spaceshots.com, catalogue #1382)

LETTER FROM LAOS

    I'm the sort of traveler who is never happy unless I'm *doing* something. I must have a purpose. River trips, beach cabanas, frosty drinks with bright umbrellas; these hold no appeal for me, unless they fit into the context of a story. God bless *Salon*. For about three years, I savored the luxury of knowing that, wherever on Earth I might go, the website's Wanderlust editor—the unsinkable Don George—would gleefully publish my dispatches from the field. This testy travelogue was actually written in Kathmandu, a week or so after the trip. To be fair, nearly everyone else I've spoken to has enjoyed Laos enormously – and they didn't even get free T-shirts.

STEPPING OFF THE PLANE in Vientiane, I was greeted with the sort of reception usually reserved for blue-haired package tourists at Waikiki Beach.

    Prepubescent girls in native costume rushed up with leis. A troupe of Lao dancers swayed on the tarmac, dancing to musical accompaniment that sounded like a rhapsody composed on a planet inhabited by medieval cats. Press photographers snapped photos as we accepted free T-shirts, handed out by smiling adolescent boys lining the red carpet that led to the arrivals lounge.

    "This gives fresh meaning," I quipped to my companion, "to the phrase 'accidental tourist.' "

The date was January 1, 1999. My friend Diane and I, along with a load of other unsuspecting travelers, had arrived from Bangkok on the maiden flight of "Visit Laos Year 1999-2000."

This "Visit [your country's name here] Year" business is an honor doled out by ASEAN—the Association of Southeast Asia Nations—to its member nations. Last year was Thailand's turn; this year, for the first time, Laos (which joined ASEAN in 1997) received the mantel. The hope of this poor and landlocked country, naturally, is to cash in on the millions of dollars in foreign exchange—much of it from tourist revenue—that has flowed for decades into Thailand and, more recently, into Cambodia and Vietnam.

Long-restricted Laos dropped most of its travel restrictions in 1994. They now offer a visa on arrival at the airport. They have launched "Visit Laos Year 1999-2000" on the wings of a tender slogan, a phrase they clearly hoped would root in the hearts and minds of the waddling westerners whose shirts and blouses had been permanently stained by the potent botanical oils in their pesky leis: "Laos: My New Love."

. . .

Vientiane is almost cosmopolitan; there's an English-language newspaper, a district of tailors, and countless lanes lined with shops selling silver tins and carved wooden boxes, cheap jewelry, counterfeit antiques, and ethnic minority dolls. French colonial dwellings—some converted to guesthouses—squat in the shadow of gleaming office buildings, and the menus of the French and Italian restaurants around Nam Phu Square list their prices in dollars, not *kip*.

We spent our single Vientiane sunset at Wat Sisikhet, with its long corridors lined with gesturing Buddhas. Also impressive was Wat Phra Keo, whose signature image—an Emerald Buddha, presented to Laos by the King of Ceylon—was looted by the Thais in 1827, just before they razed the place (the image is now in Bangkok's own Wat Phra Keo, in the Royal Palace compound). Still, there are some very evocative Buddhas at the rebuilt temple: one of them looks a bit like Groucho Marx, and another like Mr. Spock.

We did not tarry long in the capital. Our destination was Luang Prabang: a monastic center and former French colonial settlement, situated along the Mekong River.

Diane, a writer and producer who has written for National Geographic and worked on films like *Seven Years in Tibet*, lives permanently in Nepal. Kathmandu's expatriates are always looking for escape valves—places where they can breathe without a particle filter. High in the hills, Luang Prabang had recently acquired a reputation as a retreat of choice. From initial reports, we expected something between Shangri-la and classical Indochina: a sylvan enclave where hornbills nest, the mist rises through bamboo groves, and the gentle peal of temple bells signals the dawn.

. . .

We wound up at the Villa Xiengmouane by accident, after our first choice of hotels—the well-known Calao Auberge—proved a noisy bust. At the Xiengmouane (pronounced sheng'mwan, but let's just call it the "X") we took a suite of rooms facing on one side a handsome wat (from which the guesthouse takes its name) and on the other a large, quiet garden. Laundry hung brightly on the line, and the umbrellas of a riverside restaurant were visible down a nearby lane. In the distance, toward the setting sun, motorboats plied the Mekong.

Despite our luck with lodgings, we were a little let down by the town. It was far from what we'd expected. Wandering the streets, Diane and I recalled the paeons of praise that our friends had heaped upon this rustic peninsula at the confluence of the Mekong and Khan rivers. For all its anti-hype, Luang Prabhan—"LP" for short—is already a typical tourist discovery, a place that was undoubtedly far more charming two years, or even two months, ago. Alternative travel has become a lot like the stock market: by the time you get wind of something, it's over.

A day's stroll was all it took to see where LP is heading. The streets were abuzz with new Honda motorscooters; a few years ago, Luang Prabang was filled with bicycles. A CNN report on Clinton's impeachment trial issued from a coffee house. Above the Scandanavian Bakery, an enterprising Lao had opened a cyber-café. There was construction everywhere, a steady soundtrack of powertools and the steady percusssion of hammers. Observing the new architecture, we had to laugh at the irony. After declaring the old part of Luang Prabang a World Heritage Site, UNESCO proclaimed that all new structures must be of traditional design. But "traditional," in the case of Luang Prabang, means French Colonial. It struck us as odd that, though they'd been oppressed by the French, the Lao would now imitate their style of architecture—as if Cape Town were declared a World Heritage Site, and decided to rebuild in the Boer style.

But LP was not without some purely Lao charms. We passed the afternoon at the town's most fascinating temple: Wat Xieng Thong (pronounced "Washington" by some fellow travelers). Walking into the compound is like stepping into a fairy tale: there is a sense of magic which, once upon a time, must have saturated all of Luang Prabang. Built in 1560, the temple complex is named for its venerable *thong*, or bodhi tree. The ficus—like most of its companions at temples throughout Asia—was probably grown from a cutting taken off the original bodhi tree in Bodhgaya, India, beneath which the Buddha gained enlightenment.

Some of the wats at Xieng Thong are inlaid with mosaics made of colored mirror. The style, showing cartoonish figures on a red background (some with their heads getting cut off), reminded me of "naive" American art. Others are decorated with bas reliefs of carved wood, thickly layered with gold leaf. (The most beautiful building of all, emblazoned with golden panels depicting erotic scenes from the *Ramayana* epic, is actually a car park for the royal funeral chariot.) As the low sun struck the wats, the air seemed to fill with colored sparks; it was like sitting in the middle of a giant jewel box. We caught our breath, looking beyond the temple gates to the shimmering cord of the Mekong River. Only one element compromised the scene. A teenaged monk sat on the steps of the main temples, smoking a Marlboro Light and tapping his Nikes restlessly on the steps.

Enlightenment, I thought to myself. *Just Do It.*

. . .

The full moon rose over Mount Phousi (which I vulgarly mispronounced), casting the wat on its crest into spooky silhouette. Diane and I wandered the old town, searching for a restaurant serving crepes and fruit salad. When we finally found one—after a long walk in circles through the old quarter—I decided to go local, ordering a Lao specialty known as *laap*. Made of minced fish ground in a mortar with spices, garlic and green onion, the savory brown paste was a dead ringer for canned cat food.

It felt good to return to the villa, to put Segovia on our portable CD player and nest in our little suite of rooms. Outside the window, Wat Xiengmouane lay in shadow. I could make out the spires of the small *vihara* shrines and, to their right, the temple's ritual drum: a huge cylinder with two leather heads, suspended from ropes within an elegant gazebo.

I climbed into bed at nine, three days of international travel finally catching up with me. Diane was equally spent. She was fighting off a cold, and the physical memory of four stressful months of work in Nepal. Right away, we ran into trouble. The bed squeaked like a cave full of bats, screaming at every adjustment of an arm or a leg. Tired as we were, we burst out laughing. Earplugs muted most of these high-register sounds, and I drifted off to sleep.

I was shaken out of bed—literally—at 4 a.m. Twenty feet below, the monastery drum had begun to beat: thunderous thumps that shook the room by the neck, punctuated by a cacophony of cymbals and bells. The charming cultural racket continued, unabetted, for fifteen minutes. I tried to pretend I was back in my old Santa Barbara apartment, right next to the railroad tracks. I'd gotten used to that, hadn't I? The clamorous thumping of the freight train, rolling past my window at four each morning? Yes, I had; it had taken two years.

In the strange clarity that accompanies premature awakening, I formulated a cunning plan. Years of travel have taught me the value of preparation, and I carry a few items that most travelers never dream of packing. My noise-addled brain imagined with satisfaction the bewilderment and confusion of the monks as they arrived for their next wee-hour *puja*, only to find their mammoth drum webbed behind the bright yellow tape I'd snatched from an Oakland patrol car:

POLICE LINE: DO NOT CROSS

. . .

Much of what is now Laos was previously a gift horse. The territory was ceded to the French (along with part of Cambodia) around 1895 by the King of Siam in an effort to keep other, more belligerent powers at bay.

But there was never much for the French in Laos. The land was too steep for cultivation, the Mekong River unnavigable, the cheese inferior. So the French set up an administrative outpost in little Luang Prabang, leaving the locals more or less alone and amusing themselves with assorted debaucheries: local consorts, long drinks on the banks on the Mekong, and the opium trade. They built lovely homes, the French; some of the more popular guesthouses, the Villa X among them, are restored mansions.

I thought about the fate of Laos in Luang Prabang's Palace Museum, a compound of white pavillions with mirrored murals and the long, fingernail-like eaves that one sees everywhere in Thailand.

It's a strange and lonely place. The would-be King—Sisavang Vatthana— vanished in 1977, two years after the Pathet Lao communists liberated the country. Rumor has it he was sent to northern Laos for "re-education"; always a dubious fate. He's simply not talked about, and the question of whether he and his family are alive or dead remains a mystery.

The Palace is now a tourist attraction, so sterile and institutionalized that it's hard to believe it was ever really lived in. One particularly depressing room displays a collection of gifts presented by foreign leaders to the former Lao royalty. Far from demonstrating Laotian importance, the stingy presents betray the almost contemptuous disregard in which the country was typically held. There are replicas of second-rate statuary from India; a handful of lapel pins from the former Soviet Union; an absurd vase decorated with mosaic conquistadors; a boomerang from Australia. One case displayed the keys to various American cities, including San Francisco, Los Angeles and Washington, D.C. The biggest key in the collection, oddly, was from Knoxville, whereas the smallest—smaller than an actual house key—granted gracious entrance into the hearts and souls of the citizens of Phoenix.

On the shelf above these momentos, I spied a tiny Lao flag that flew to the moon and back with the crew of Apollo 11. Such flags, mounted on generic brass plaques ("We went to the Moon, and here's a little something for you"), were presented to the leaders of all nations recognized by the UN in 1969, when the first manned lunar landing occurred. Beside the flag, sealed into a glass marble the size of a radish, sat another, more recent gift: a bit of moonrock, retrieved by the astronauts of Apollo 17. Yet another plaque proclaimed that this bit of cosmic rubble was presented to Laos by President Richard M. Nixon in 1973 as "a symbol of the unity of human endeavor, and ... the hope of the American peoples for a world of peace."

What the plaque fails to mention is that 1973 also marked Nixon's reluctant cessation of the "Special War": an undeclared and illegal action during which more than 600,000 sorties, flown during a nine-year period, heaped upon northern Laos more bombs than were rained upon Europe, by all sides combined, during the Second World War.

. . .

No one raises their voice in Luang Prabang; the Lao seem as docile as rabbits. One of the most startling things about walking through LP is that, unlike in any other Asian town, nobody uses their horn. Cars yield to pedestrians; trucks brake courteously, allowing motor scooters to pass.

Bargaining, for goods or for transport, is devoid of any mercenary streak. There's a tiny range between the highest and lowest bids; Laos agree to the offered price with a shrug. They simply don't nickle and dime you. In the endless conversions between Lao *kip* and American dollars, Thai *bhat* and kip, bhat and dollars, they're happy to let you do the math—even if your ignorance of current exchange rates lowers their profit by thousands of kip.

The money itself is strange. For one thing, there are no coins in Laos. All transactions are in currency, with the largest notes worth 5,000 kip. There are nearly 4,500 kip to the dollar, and it is quite possible to find street food that costs 100 or 200 kip. One afternoon, after crossing the Mekong to a village on the other side, I ran into a situation where I felt I was being "cheated." The boatman had charged Lao passengers 200 kip for the ride; he demanded 500 kip from me. I strutted and fretted, howled and growled, and wasted about ten minutes before realizing that I was arguing over seven cents.

Time in LP moves slowly. There is very nearly nothing to do, except for visiting the wats—and there is nothing to do at the wats. So placid are the Lao that the French overseers coined a phrase about their Indochine colonies: "The Vietnamese plant the rice, the Cambodians watch it grow, and the Laotians listen to it grow."

. . .

One morning, restless for an excursion, Diane and I negotiated for a boat and motored up the Mekong to the Phak Ou caves, a shrine by the mouth of the Nam Ou tributary.

It was a long ride, in surprising chilly weather. There were a few small rapids, but nothing threatening. Cement pylons rose from outcroppings of limestone, their red-painted tips showing the river's perilous high-water mark. Diane and I huddled on a hard bench near the front of the long, narrow boat. The jungle along the banks of the Mekong appeared pristine, storybook exotic. Tall stands of bamboo leaned over the water, looking as green and soft as sea fern. Deeper in the forest I spotted tall palms, purple flowers, and strange Jurassic foliage that once sheltered the dinosaurs so popular on Lao postage stamps.

The Mekong is not a lovely river, but it does have personality. Small plots of cultivated land glow on the banks. Still, I was surprised by the lack of wildlife. On the entire trip—which took all day—we saw only two water buffalo. And what I'd romantically imagined to be the cries of exotic langurs, emanating from within the forest, turned out to be the squeak of our rudder. Nor were there any birds. We could never figure out why. A few people insisted it was because they had been hunted to extinction, but this was hard to believe. Laos is the most scarcely populated country in Asia, with a paltry 17 people per square kilometer. A few villagers with primitive rifles can't really decimate an entire avian population... or can they?

The Phak Ou caves were a fascinating stop, filled with thousands of Buddhas in every imaginable media, at every stage of antiquity and decay. Many stood in the uniquely Lao "Calling for Rain" posture. Their long arms descended straight down their sides, giving their forms a rocket-like countenance. Some were so worn that their wooden bodies had all but rotted away, leaving the merest hint of a gesture, or an omniscient smile.

Diane offered candles and incense, but the sacred ambiance of the caves was routinely shattered by the deafening roar of express speedboats—a new feature on the river. Each one zoomed by like an F-16, spiriting a dozen crash-helmeted passengers to the Thai border in a percussive six-hour journey.

· · ·

The following morning we rented a motorcycle, and drove 20 miles south along a dusty, corrugated road. We passed many small villages, the simple homes perched on poles above the ground. There were loads of children. The girls walked by in groups, doe-eyed, arms slung over each others' shoulders; the boys stretched out their palms, hoping to slap me five as I passed along the road. There was none of the begging, none of the mercenary mania that I've come to expect in Nepalese villages.

After an hour, we reached our destination: Kuangsi Falls. The waterfall was surprisingly lovely, a sculpted travertine cascade framed by lush foilage and an unlikely riot of poinsettas. The torrent fanned out over weird, cone-shaped ledges that looked like the hats worn by the Seven Dwarfs, dropping into steel-blue pools. The landscaping was simple and inviting, and there was not a mote of litter. The courteous Lao, evidentally, took to heart the cautionary signs: "Thank Slot, You Do Not Drop Garbage."

We dined that night at a restaurant along the Mekong. The scene was picture perfect. Longboats crossed and recrossed the river, and a grenadine sun sank behind a tree-shrouded hill. I watched the scene through a glass of Beer Lao, realizing that, somehow, our visit had been remarkable after all. Even if the trip hadn't been the romantic interlude we had intended, we'd encountered a society unique in our experience of Asia. It was inconceivable that France and America had spent so many years, and so many lives, trying to destroy these people.

Equally bizarre was the notion that westerners were now flocking to Laos: ordering chocolate soufflé, checking their email, and keeping an eye out for unexploded bombs. And as the expansion of Luang Prabang continues, Laos is poised to become another communist parody: a place where hard-won liberation has been co-opted by Honda, Nike and Microsoft.

. . .

Ever since arriving in Luang Prabang, Diane and I had tried to come up with a more accurate slogan for Visit Laos Year 1999-2000; a truth-in-advertising improvement on ASEAN's "Laos: My New Love." Our efforts had been futile; nothing we imagined did justice to the strange paradox of this industriously emerging backwater.

The next morning—on our way to the airport—we passed another "traditional" guesthouse, rising noisily along Luang Prabang's main drag. Diane straightened suddenly in her seat. "I've got it," she announced. "I've got the new slogan."

"Okay," I replied dubiously. "Let's hear it."

"*Laos,*" she recited. "*Listen to it Grow.*"

POSTCARD FROM TOKYO

EVERYONE WHO MAKES a stopover in Tokyo is confined, for a period of time roughly equal to purgatory, to the Narita Airport transit terminal.

This is a circular building, from which departure gates emanate like spokes. Within, a circular promenade surrounds an overpriced concession vending beer, sweets and seaweed crackers. During my first layover at Narita I tried to escape this drab area, walking briskly. Thirty minutes later I realized that I had merely orbited the central snack bar 17 times.

My most recent visit found the place seething with an odd assortment of humanity. Beside the usual hoardes of tourists, clusters of punked-out Melrose types lounged on their soft luggage, babbling cannily. The air, to use the word loosely, was heavy with cigarette smoke and the sour odor of nervous anticipation.

A series of well-practiced maneuvers brought me out of that dizzying hell-realm and towards a cluster of duty-free shops. There, I oggled the latest in convenience items: televisions the size of a cocktail olive; watches that convert baseball scores into calories; edible ballpoint pen and pencil sets. Even this brief diversion, though, meant I must pass through security again: 20 minutes on line, followed by a sonic scanning so sensitive that an ugly tattoo will set off the bells. The only place with tighter security than Narita is Disneyland—and that's one place I *never* step out of line.

Arriving back at my gate, I realized I'd missed something momentous. The place was abuzz with restless motion, and the black leather T-shirt set was pink with excitement. I approached a bespectacled Japanese businessman, and politely inquired what had happened.

"Madonna," he said. "She got on the plane to Los Angeles."
"Madonna? No kidding? Wow.... How did she look?"

He paused to consider. "She was blonde," he replied.

BUZZ ALDRIN: TO INFINITY AND BEYOND

Casting about for a way to commemorate the 30th anniversary of the first moonwalk, I lit upon the idea of interviewing Edwin "Buzz" Aldrin. This involved jumping through a few hoops—most astronauts are notoriously private—but at length the doors of Aldrin's Wilshire Boulevard penthouse were thrown open to me. Meeting the Apollo 11 lunar module pilot was an exhilarating experience, almost mesmerizing. I was quickly drawn into Aldrin's orbit—so much so that, as this article was going to "press" (i.e., appearing on *Salon.com*) I was drafted to co-write (along with Aldrin's long-time collaborator Wyn Wachhorst) the landmark speech given by the former astronaut at the National Press Club on June 24, 1999.

THERE ARE SOME THINGS you don't ask Buzz Aldrin—questions he's heard so many times they set his teeth on edge. Chief among them: How did it feel to walk on the Moon?

"I try to answer," he admits wearily. "I say, 'It felt terrific. Tremendously satisfying. The mission was going well, and our training had prepared us perfectly.'

"But then people say, 'No... how did it *feel*? How did it *really feel*?'" Aldrin bristles. "For Christ's sake, I don't know. I don't *know* how it 'felt.' I have been frustrated since the day I left the Moon by that question." He shakes his head. "Some things just can't be described. And stepping onto the Moon was one of them."

July 20th, 1999, marks the 30th anniversary of the day that Aldrin, along with Apollo 11 crewmates Neil Armstrong and Michael Collins, became the three most famous men on Earth. Six hundred million people watched their 35-story-tall *Saturn V* blast off from Cape Kennedy on July 16. At least that many tuned in four days later, via radio and television, to hear the first words uttered from another world. Armstrong's "One small step for a man, one giant leap for Mankind" appears on the commemorative coins. But it was Aldrin who provided the more poetic reflection: "Magnificent desolation."

"Desolation" accurately describes Aldrin's life in the years following Apollo. While many of his colleagues entered business, he returned to the military —but no one knew quite what to do with him. In 1971, Aldrin was made Commander of the test pilot school at Edwards Air Force Base. "A highly prestigious position," he says dryly, "if you were a test pilot. I wasn't."

Buzz had always enjoyed his scotch, but he now began drinking heavily. A series of accidents at the school were blamed on "supervisor error." Aldrin felt squeezed. He began to lose control. Depression and alcoholism beset him, and his license to fly was revoked: a staggering blow to the lunar module pilot of Apollo 11. After hitting rock bottom—at one point putting a pistol to his head—Aldrin pulled himself together and sought counseling.

People hearing this are rarely surprised. Life after a moon landing, they assume, must be anticlimactic (how else to explain the fact that a third of the moonwalkers have become artists, spiritualists and Christian evangelists?). Not so, says Aldrin. He's been sober now for 20 years and claims to be at his best: "I'm thrilled, I'm challenged, I'm *with* life more now." Much of his enthusiasm comes from a quasi-spiritual cause of his own: the development and commercialization of civilian space travel.

Aldrin now works out of a Beverly Hills apartment which he shares with his second wife, Lois. The telephone rings continually. "Buzz is an enormous business," Lois says, harried. She's an impish firebrand in a black sweatshirt and loud tights. "He works as if he were still on assignment for NASA: trying to develop better rockets, a better space station. He's been working 15 years on a way to get to Mars. "He's found his niche," she concedes. "Which is space."

. . .

The Aldrin's home is a tasteful blend of oriental decor and astronaut kitsch. A human foot stands on the coffee table: a life-sized, silver replica of Aldrin's bare foot, poised on a bronze moonscape. Paintings and posters of his lunar stroll decorate the walls; mementos and honors from the space program line the shelves. A bust of Aldrin's head rests above the television, sporting a West Point full-dress hat.

The front doors open and Aldrin himself walks in, his hand in a sack of baked tortilla chips. He's wearing faded jeans, and a neon-blue golf shirt. But Aldrin hasn't been golfing; he's been auditioning for a Saab commercial.

Pushing 70, with smoke-white hair and vivid, visionary eyes, Aldrin looks like a cross between Ken Kesey and the Wizard of Oz. The similarities transcend appearance. To his admirers, Aldrin is the ultimate Captain Trips: a brilliant intellect with the energy and expertise to lead us to the stars. To his detractors he's a tiresome showman, using fancy props to buttress an empty promise.

His aura of otherwordly celebrity is palpable. I'll be with Aldrin for hours, but I will never forget who I'm talking to. Let's face it: Everest is tough, but with enough time, money and willpower you can climb it. Circling the world in a balloon is dangerous and wacky, but primarily expensive. You can sneak into Mecca, dive the wreck of the *Titanic*, and dog-sled to the South Pole.

But no amount of time, money or ambition will get you to the Moon. In all of history, only twelve human beings have walked there. Tom Wolfe, Michael Jordan, even Madonna will someday be forgotten—but Aldrin and Armstrong will not. They were the chosen, Earth's emissaries, at the dawn of the Space Age.

Still, a small but vocal cadre of critics—including some former astronauts—are cynical about Aldrin's big plans and Wizard-like bluster. He's drawing too much attention to himself. He has something to *sell*. The fact that what he's selling is the future of space-flight—citizen explorers, orbiting hotels and sightseeing trips to the Moon—matters not. Flyboys, no matter how they milk their fame (and even the taciturn Armstrong isn't above an occasional TV pitch), are expected to be discrete. To keep a low profile. To maintain a facade of humility. *Aw, shucks—it was nothin'. That big ol' bird practically landed itself.* The Right Stuff.

Asked about Armstrong, Aldrin shies from the question. There's a chronic ache there, controlled by loyalty and discretion. It's well known that Aldrin badly wanted to take that first step on the Moon. There was even a precedent for it. On the Gemini and Apollo missions, he reminds me, it was always the second-in-command who performed the EVA, the "extra-vehicular activity" outside the space capsule.

But the issue cuts much deeper. It concerns the mantle of heroism. Aldrin, stumping around the globe in support of space travel, is sick of being asked how it feels to be the "second man on the Moon." The question is especially galling since Armstrong, NASA's banner boy, doesn't seem compelled to promote space exploration. Neil's an airplane buff, not a rocket man. He doesn't share the sense of debt, or the evangelical spirit, that drives Aldrin.

But Aldrin's frequent cameos (he's appeared on everything from Letterman to *The Simpsons*) can be taken as grandstanding, an impression not diminished when he takes the stage in a packed auditorium, holds aloft a *Toy Story* action figure, and declares, "*I am* Buzz Lightyear!"

The joke, as ever, has a ring of truth. Like Lightyear—an All-American superhero who discovers he can't really fly—Aldrin is a complex character, a man who has known the heights and depths at their most extreme. A West Point alumnus and Air Force fighter pilot, he shot down two MiGs in dogfights over Korea. When the war ended he enrolled at MIT, where he earned a Ph.D. in orbital rendezvous theory. Aldrin joined the astronaut corps in 1963, and in 1966 performed the longest spacewalk of the Gemini program: five-and-a-half hours, dangling outside the capsule. Three years later, he and civilian test pilot Neil Armstrong were handed the Holy Grail of the space program: Apollo 11. Aldrin was 39 years old.

One of Aldrin's most vivid recollections of the events of 1969 comes not from the surface of the Moon, but from the *U.S.S. Hornet*: the ship which recovered the Apollo 11 command module at sea. Placed into a quarantine trailer, the astronauts were asked if they wanted to watch the taped TV coverage of their mission.

"And as we watched," Aldrin says quietly, "I remember turning to Neil and saying: *'Look: we missed the whole thing.'*

"Why? Because we didn't see it live on television. We didn't share in the electrifying moment leading to touchdown. Hell, we were right there. We *did* it! But that's not the important thing. We missed the reaction, the emotion embodied by the sight of Walter Cronkite wiping away his tears. That sense of participation, shared by millions of people around the world—people who had their lives affected, touched, changed.

"Why do I think their lives were affected? Because they want me to know where they were when we landed on the Moon. When they see me, they get reminded—and they remember exactly where they were that moment. They know exactly what they were doing. It's crystal-clear in their minds."

. . .

The allure of spaceflight hasn't diminished for Aldrin. He bemoans America's lack of an ambitious space agenda, and scorns the political reluctance to establish a human presence on the Moon and Mars.

"Let's jump ahead 50 years," he posits. "Can you imagine looking back on a nation that got people to the Moon—six times!—and then had such a big gap? It's the epitome of short-term thinking. People ask me, what do we do next? Go back to the moon? To Mars? Neither! We're not ready to do either, because we don't have the launch vehicle system!"

Over a Cobb salad by the pool of a nearby hotel, Aldrin outlines his plan for the conquest (or, in 1999-speak, the "development and commercialization") of outer space. It's achingly attractive—particularly since the goal, the centerpiece of the entire plan, echoes my own obsession: adventure travel.

"Travel and tourism now form the world's largest industry, with a gross annual output approaching $3.5 trillion dollars a year. Space tourism," he claims, "is a logical outgrowth of the adventure tourist market."

Building up space tourism must begin, he insists, with rethinking the Space Shuttle. Designed 25 years ago, our current shuttle rides piggy-back on solid-fuel boosters. It's an outdated technology, with a dangerous drawback: solid rockets can't be turned off after lift-off. The sensible alternative, Aldrin says, is to develop a *liquid*-fuel, "fly-back" booster (LFBB). Such boosters (close cousins of the rockets that powered the Gemini and Apollo missions) would lift a second stage—a space shuttle or satellite—into near orbit. The shuttle or satellite engine then takes over, while the booster flies back to Earth—automatically—and lands on a runway for refueling.

Why hasn't anyone built such a booster? NASA hasn't, because its flight rate isn't high enough. Commercial launch companies haven't, because it's cheaper—in the short term—to use throw-away rockets. "Nobody has the incentive to design a reusable booster," observes Aldrin, "unless they find new, long-range applications."

The application Aldrin envisions is, of course, is space tourism. Before that can begin, though, both government and business have to be sold on LFBB technology. Anticipating this, his company—Starcraft—has patented a small reusable rocket called *StarBooster*. It uses replaceable liquid fuel "cartridges," much like modern fountain pens. The booster itself—which will be about the size of a 737—is still on the drawing board. Aldrin shows me a model, the size and shape of a silver-dipped biscotti.

Aldrin's hope is that "demonstrator" rockets like *StarBooster* will convince NASA and private industry that reusable boosters are good business—leading to ever bigger boosters, and an eventual redesign of the shuttle.

To spur this process, he says, we must start sending private citizens into space. These "Citizen Explorers" could be chosen through a corporate sweepstakes (sponsored by, say, Tang or Saturn), and given seats on the current shuttle. The contests will be so wildly popular that private industry will leap onto the bandwagon. With reusable boosters and a ready market, we'll soon see a fleet of shuttles dedicated to space tourism—built by Boeing/Lockheed, operated by the major airlines, and booked through companies like Space Adventures, Geographic Expeditions and Club Med.

. . .

"Very nice," you sigh. "But what about *me*? With seats priced around $100,000 (headphones and cocktails extra), what chance do I have of watching *Alien XII* in orbit?"

"Chance" is the operant word here. Aldrin proposes a national lottery, overseen by his non-profit ShareSpace Foundation. As the space tourism market grows—i.e., as the spaceships get bigger—so does the number of prizes.

Proceeds will pay for the seats. They'll also be reinvested into education, and into aerospace research that mainstream companies (which were dragged kicking and screaming into the space tourism business to begin with) won't touch. Further revenues will pour in from—you guessed it—product-name placement. Citizen Explorers will likely embark on their flights sporting Eagle Creek space-sickness bags, Adidas Skywalkers, and Calvin Klein One helmets ("A helmet for a man and a woman").

At this point, space tourism grows exponentially. Empty first-stage fuel tanks—left in orbit by selected spacecraft—are captured and reconditioned, forming the core of an orbiting Space Hotel. Life-support systems and minibars are brought to the site by a "heavy lifter": a huge, reusable booster on a par with the *Saturn V*. Such rockets will be built by industry, solely to support space tourism. But once they *are* built, their uses are legion. Leased by NASA, they become workhorses for long-overdue missions: settlements on the Moon, and the human exploration of Mars.

This brave new future could be upon us, says Aldrin, by the year

2020. At that point, the fun really begins. With an orbiting hotel in operation, work begins on the "Lunar Cycler": a spacefaring cruise ship that uses the gravitational pull of the planets—the so-called "slingshot effect"—to maintain a continuous loop between the Earth and Moon.

Aldrin demonstrates the concept with condiments: a Heinz ketchup bottle is the Earth, a mustard jar the Moon, a bottle of Tabasco the spacecraft. Passengers are shuttled aboard the cruise ship while it's coasting in Earth orbit. The Lunar Cycler then whips around the home planet, speeds into space, rimshots the Moon's gravity well, and returns to Earth orbit a week later. Far-fetched as it sounds, the math is relatively basic. Aldrin—once known in NASA as "Dr. Rendezvous"—has worked out the details.

Nor has he stopped there—for after the Moon comes Mars. The first Mars Cycler will take only scientists on its two-year mission to the Red Planet; but when the ship loops back to Earth for its four-month maintenance cycle, the interest will be intense.

"Can you imagine, in 2030, taking a space cruise on the very ship that carried the first human beings to Mars?" Aldrin stares at me, stone sober. "I can't believe that people wouldn't line up for that possibility."

And people will—if the response to Aldrin's international appearances is any indication. Girdling the globe on a grueling schedule, Aldrin pitches his vision at any venue that will have him. The month before our meeting, he'd made two speaking trips to Europe; a few weeks after, he'd be the featured guest at the National Press Club in Washington.

Unfortunately, wishing on a star—even at the National Press Club—doesn't make something so. Aldrin's ideas are compelling, and his science is robust, but the obstacles he faces are daunting. To begin with, there's the matter of investment. If private companies aren't ready to design LFBBs individually, they're unlikely to hand Aldrin the money. And though he's personally approached a handful of venture capitalists, Aldrin finds himself trapped in a time-worn Catch-22: the big players want to know who else is investing, before they put their own ante up. At present, *StarBooster*'s bottom line is decidedly sub-orbital.

Finally, the discouraging fact remains: most American citizens are quite content to "explore strange new worlds" simply by turning on their televisions. Though opinion polls show large public *enthusiasm* for the space program, only a small minority of voters favor its *expansion*. In recent polls, only 8 percent said they would increase funding for space exploration. Faced with other choices—like social programs—most Americans put space exploration on their list of budgetary *cuts*.

Call it a lack of imagination—or call it democracy—but political will depends largely on public support. No matter how good the prospects for space tourism are, NASA's desire to build new boosters and space shuttles is a long way from reaching escape velocity.

. . .

As we return to Aldrin's suite, the gibbous Moon hangs over Wilshire Boulevard. He appears not to notice. I ask if the significance of the Moon landings—an eleven-year effort comparable to building the pyramids—has changed over the years.

"I think the lunar landing has mellowed with time," he says. "It's grown into peoples' minds, as history. Like when I'm talking to someone, and I realize I'm describing something that happened before they were born.

"But Bucky Fuller acknowledged that there was a difference between the people who grew up before Apollo, and those who grew up afterwards. Before, we lived in a world that had restrictions, limitations. The people who grew up afterward have a sense that almost anything—even something as bizarre as going to the Moon—is possible."

Yet Aldrin's own memories of the Apollo era remain bittersweet. "Going to the Moon is not a rememberance filled with great happiness," the former astronaut admits. "It was a traumatic period of my life. We succeeded in what we were doing—but there were some rough edges."

"So looking up at the Moon isn't like seeing a picture of the Eiffel

Tower, and longing to be in Paris?"

"That's what people *think* I should think. But I've got to balance the romantic image with being honest. There's not a longing; there's an identification. When I look at the Moon now, it's no longer a stranger. It's a friend. I've seen it up close, in different, discrete phases. Of course it's still beautiful, and I appreciate it as much as anybody. But we've got experiments up there. It's dirtied our boots."

FLYING HORSES OF THE HIMALAYA

In the spring of 1990, I got a call from a guy in Santa Monica. His name was Joe Robinson, and he was consumed by the idea of launching a literary, rough-edged travel magazine "for the rest of us." Robinson was a die-hard entrepreneur; he picked my brain, put together an energetic team of believers, and overcame innumerable obstacles to put *Escape* on the newsstands. It lasted from 1993 until 1998, an uneven but always high-spirited contender among the travel pulps, groping for a toehold until financial rock falls knocked it into the abyss. This short offering, which Joe renamed "Airway to Heaven" ('nuf said), appeared in the Summer 1995 issue.

VIEWED FROM SPACE, the atmosphere of our planet appears as a micro-thin coating: a gleaming layer of translucent nitrogen, oxygen and hydrogen swirling with vapor and storms. More than any other element on Earth, air is the principle that sustains all life. *Prana* in Sanskrit, *ch'i* in Chinese and *lung* in Tibetan, the winds that flow over our oceans and continents flow through our bodies as well, nourishing with their simple molecules the most complex life forms in the universe.

From the sails that carried the Polynesians to Hawai'i to the high-tech turbines atop California's Altamont Pass, the immense energy of moving air has given rise to countless inventions designed to exploit the most plentiful of all natural resources. Many of these tools, like the kite and whistle, are almost universal. On the Asian continent, though, a unique and inspired use is made of the wind: it is a vehicle for prayers.

Prayer-flags—or *lung-ta*, a Tibetan phrase meaning "wind horse"—probably originated in the central Himalaya, where warm surface air rising toward the roof of the world provides an almost continual current of primordial energy. Placed on roofs and hilltops, strung across rivers and on high mountain passes throughout Nepal, Tibet and Sri Lanka, the flags are usually arrayed on long cords, in sets of five. The traditional colors—blue, white, red, green, and yellow—symbolize the five primary elements, as well as the rainbow.

The gauze-like flags, usually made of cotton or paper (although long-lasting synthetics have recently come into vogue), are printed at monasteries and sold outside important Buddhist shrines and temples. They almost always portray a central figure. Sometimes this is a particular deity: the compassionate protector-goddess Tara, or Padmasambhava, the lotus-born sorcerer who brought Buddhism to Tibet. Most often, though, the image is of the proud Wind Horse itself, carrying on its back a gift of sacred *norbu*: wish-fulfilling gems. This image is always surrounded by Tibetan mantras, or prayers, which are "recited" every time the flag flutters in the breeze. The prayers vary in length and eloquence, but their theme is generally the same:

Let Buddha's doctrine prosper!
May we be freed from all injuries,
and be favored with the real gift which we earnestly seek!
May life force, body, speech, merit and reputation prosper!
Victory to the gods!
Om mani padme hun!

The wind horse, meanwhile, has its own task to perform. Invocations inscribed upon the flags beseech the animal to pull up the mythical *mu*: an invisible cord by which the human spirit approaches Heaven.

The sight of freshly hung prayer-flags whipping in a gale, vivid against a backdrop of snow-capped peaks or neon-green hillsides, is never forgotten. One can actually see the prayers rippling into the atmosphere, rising like heat waves off a sun-baked highway. Even more electrifying, though, is the sound: the deafening hoofbeats of a thousand wild horses, galloping into the wind.

BHUTAN: OFF THE YELLOW BRICK ROAD

National Geographic *Adventure* launched in 1999, the venerable Society's long-overdue answer to rough-edged monthlies like *Outside* and *Men's Journal*. This story was lobbed into my court by Lisa Tabb, a visionary young editor/publisher who had spearheaded a number of maverick travel 'zines (*Just Go* and *EcoTraveler* among them) and had just been hired as *Adventure's* West Coast editor.

As is evident in this excerpt, I found Bhutan a strange and unsettling place—very unlike Nepal, India, or Southeast Asia, where unexpected encounters and spontaneous travel plans can lead you into a metaphorical (or literal!) poppy field. On the other hand, it's a huge relief to realize there's at least one place in Asia where conservation and cultural integrity are more important than fast profit....

"ARE YOU GOING UP?"

The traditional yak herder's greeting, delivered in the dialect of Bhutan's Dhur Valley, seems absurd as a line from a Marx Brothers film. The country's terrain, one quickly discovers, climbs like an escalator—from the lowland jungles in the south to the crystalline peaks lining the border with Tibet. As we pass the herder, we're climbing toward a ridge—with the steep part ahead of us.

Are we going up? Of *course* we're going up," I want to answer. "There's nowhere to go *but* up." Instead I smile, and offer the ritual response: "Yes—going up. Are you going down?"

The herder nods cheerfully. "Going down."

We watch him go, and resume our panting ascent. We're headed higher still; much higher. Today we'll climb through virgin forest, camping below the tree line. Our ultimate destination, still three days away, is the base camp of Gangkar Punsum: the highest unclimbed mountain in the world.

. . .

"Bhutan is a destination apart—a Himalayan kingdom like no other." That's what I'd heard from just about everyone: trekkers, bird watchers, mountaineers, bicyclists, Buddhist pilgrims, rafters, and cynical old Asia hands who'd watched places like Nepal and Thailand become gory casualties of greed and globalization.

A rap like this is usually too good to be true: if the buzz is out, count on it, the hordes have already arrived. In the "Land of the Thunder Dragon," though, the rule doesn't hold. Bhutan may be a tiny, landlocked country (the population is about the same as San Francisco's), but its rein on development is impressive.

I realized this in Paro, the moment I stepped off the plane. The air was lucent, suffused with ions and chlorophyll. The unterraced hills were thick with pines. And the Paro Chhu—the twisting river we followed to the bite-sized capital of Thimpu—looked clean enough to bottle.

None of this happened by accident. If Bhutan has avoided environmental ruin, it's because the country's leadership has refused to sell off its natural heritage for a handful of beads and trinkets. The backbone of national policy is "Gross National Happiness": King Jigme Singye Wangchuck's Buddhist conviction (instilled by his father) that quality of life must be Bhutan's highest priority. Preserving his nation's culture and character, the 44-year-old king insists, is infinitely more important than any short-term gain.

The policy is popular among the Bhutanese—and it seems to be working. Unlike its Himalayan siblings, Bhutan has managed to protect its heritage. While Kathmandu stews in pollution and Tibet becomes a Chinese theme park, Bhutan's culture and ecology remain unspoiled. This is not to say there isn't "progress." There's a free (though royalist) press, and in 1999 the kingdom launched its first television station (satellite TV was already available). The Internet was recently made available.

But the cold fact is that Bhutan is girdled by trouble spots: Tibet, Nepal, Assam, and Sikkim (once a sovereign Buddhist nation itself, now part of India). King Wangchuck's determination to preserve Bhutan's cultural unity is more than savvy; it's a necessity. Without intense national pride and self-reliance, tiny Bhutan would be devoured by the behemoths that surround it.

The current of nationalism is obvious immediately. The first thing you notice, right at the airport, is the dress code. Thimpu's shops could make a fortune importing Old Navy T-shirts and Gap sweats. But Bhutan's citizens are compelled, by law, to wear traditional clothing (the robe-like *gho* and *kira*) while in public. The effect is striking, and provokes a mixed reaction. At first, I bristled at the idea of a dress code; how dare the government tell people what to wear? But ghos and kiras are beautiful—and they serve a multiple purpose. For one thing, they keep local tailors in business. For another, they impart a sense of solidarity: they remind the Bhutanese that the guys walking around in T-shirts and jeans are outsiders—and they remind outsiders that Bhutan hasn't sold out its traditions.

The strategies for safeguarding the environment are more subtle. Bhutan has few cars and a single, remote airport. Appropriate technology is encouraged and subsidized. Plastic bags, the curse of the developing world, are banned. When it was learned that the migratory cranes of Phobjikha Valley were disturbed by the region's new electrical wires, the locals tore them down and went solar.

Tourism receives the same kind of scrutiny. Since Bhutan opened to travelers in 1974, numbers have been tightly controlled. In 1998, half a million foreigners swarmed into Nepal; Bhutan hosted 6,000. "High quality, low volume" is their slogan. And at $250 a day (which includes in-country transport, lodging and all meals), you're not going to see many shoestring travelers—not even on popular routes like the Chomo Lhari trek.

I'm out to do more than trek. My goal is to see if the hype about Bhutan is true—and to discover how much of an "adventure" you can have in a country that monitors tourism so closely. The "perfect" Bhutan visit, for us physical types, includes trekking, sightseeing, and whitewater. Though it took some juggling, Geographic Expeditions created an itinerary that covers all three. My goal isn't to check out the well-worn routes, though, so much as test the edges. I'm looking for places where adventure travel is carving a foothold; places where Bhutan's government is seeking a compromise between isolation and inundation. Gangkar Punsum—Bhutan's highest and most elusive peak—lies as close to that edge as you can get.

Bhutan's drenching monsoon and harsh winter follow on the heels of each other, so the trekking season is short: six to eight weeks, compared with nine *months* for Nepal. Since it's late October, we head for the mountains first. This means a week long drive through lush, wooded countryside, including a few days of acclimation in Thimpu. By the time we start walking, the air holds a definite chill.

. . .

Gangkar Punsum literally means "The White Mountain of the Three Brothers." Three major rivers originate from the triple peaks of the 24,741' massif, which rises like an ice-bound barge on the country's northern border. Like all of Bhutan's mountains, Gangkar Punsum is sacred: an abode of the gods. But unlike in Nepal or China—where dozens of expeditions each year pay huge mountaineering fees—Bhutan's peaks are not for sale. Sacred means off-limits. They cannot be climbed.

There were at least four attempts on Gangkar Punsum before the government forbade climbing in 1988. None were successful. The most famous of these was led by British adventurer Steve Berry in 1986; high winds drove his team back. (His hard-to-find book, *In the Land of the Thunder Dragon*, details the effort.) Nearly all these previous expeditions, however, reached the mountain from the west. Our own five-day approach, ascending the southward cascade of the Chamka Chhu to an alternate base camp, traverses a zone restricted by the military until 1998. In October of that year, Geographic Expeditions entered the area with an 11-person reconnaissance trek. A year later—just three weeks before our own expedition—climber John Roskelley returned with a group of 17 trekkers. Roskelley had failed in his 1985 bid to summit the mountain. It had taunted him once again, offering days of torrential rain.

Our team is much smaller: eight people, eight horses, and a self-assured Tibetan mastiff named Yellow-Eye. The humans include two camp hands; a pair of local horsemen; a terse, hard-drinking local guide and horse contractor named Sherub-la; and French photographer Matthieu Paley. Paley is a wildlife fiend, fresh from a snow leopard project in Pakistan. He carries a chunk of dried leopard dung in his pocket, comparing it hopefully to every spoor he finds along the trail.

The most important member of our party, as far as the Bhutanese government is concerned, is Kesang: our official Tourist Authority liaison. Every group visiting Bhutan, however small, is accompanied by such a guide. In some respects, we're lucky. Kesang is smart and athletic, an expert archer who takes real pride in Bhutan's traditions. In other respects, a chaperone of any kind is a ball and chain. Paley and I are accustomed to free reign; and Kesang, however good his intentions, is paid to breathe down our necks. We accept the relationship, but we don't kid ourselves. Kesang's presence will keep us at arm's length from the Bhutanese. These guides, bottom line, are a firewall between the tourist industry and Bhutan's indigenous culture.

The trail ascends through vast thickets of pine and bamboo, gnarled rhododendrons, woodpeckers rattling in the trees. Fronds of juniper flag the trail. Tomorrow should take us over the highest pass of our journey: the 15,570' Tholey La. Sherub-la hums a Buddhist prayer as he sets the pace, half a minute ahead of me. His voice is a low drone, barely audible above the river.

There are no airplanes above, few bootprints below. With the population so sparse, there's no deforestation to speak of. There is, unfortunately, mud: buckets of it, churned into sludge by countless yaks on their way to winter pastures. Trekking soon becomes a meditation in rock-hopping—with ankle-deep slime the penalty for distraction.

Bhutan's wonderland reputation seems well-deserved. The country—what we've seen so far—is virginal compared with its Himalayan neighbors. There are no power lines, no biscuit wrappers in the bushes, no crowded lodges offering video screenings of *Men In Black*. One hears it said that Bhutan is like Nepal before tourists discovered it. I'd go further; the landscape is so lush and primordial it evokes a Nepal before the *Nepalese* discovered it.

By late afternoon we're above the tree line, camped with the yak herders at Thashisa: a village whose name, ominously, means "where the horse died." The river flows blue through here, level and slow. The bare, snowy hills, flecked with granite, look like frosted licorice.

I join Kesang and Sherub-la in a stone hut belonging to a leather-skinned patriarch named Letoh. The sooty interior smells keenly of yak cheese; woven baskets packed with butter and flour are stacked against the walls.

Letoh is restless; he's been too long in Thashisa. According to clan rules—based on the lunar calendar—his family cannot leave these summer pastures until a specific group of herders returns over the Tholey La. A few weeks ago, a freak storm dumped six feet of snow on the pass. The yaks in question are long overdue. Meanwhile, the elderly Letoh—whose two hundred beasts are present and accounted for—is marooned.

And so, for that matter, are we. For unless the yaks are able to make their way over the pass, there's no chance our horses will make it. No one wants to say it, but the import of Letoh's dilemma is clear: our attempt to reach base camp may be doomed.

· · ·

We wake to a frigid morning. Crusts of ice break under our feet, and the mud and dung we tramped through on our way into Thashisa has frozen into an ugly brown meringue. After a breakfast of pan-

cakes we set off through a gray-walled canyon, where shaggy rhododendrons hang limp against the cold. Three hours bring us to the
snow-buried huts of Lazoor. I examine the pass through binoculars.
Bad news: there's no sign of the yaks.

The horses are an hour behind us, picking their way. Kesang wants
to power up the pass solo, to gauge conditions on the trail. "There is
no use." Sherub-la vetoes him soberly. "A man can make it; but if a
horse cannot, what to do?"

Our wizened guide squats on the ground, sewing a chain of prayer
flags. It's an optimistic gesture; the red and white banners, inscribed
with Tibetan mantras, are meant to be tied atop the pass.

When our caravan arrives, a decision is made: we'll begin the
ascent, and see how far we get. After half an hour, the plan seems ill-
advised. The trail is a stairway of quick, precipitous switchbacks,
strewn with snow-covered stones. I ask Sherub-la if we can send our
strongest horse ahead to break trail. "Yaks are smarter than horses,"
he says, shaking his head. "The horse may step in the snow, fall into
a crack, and break its leg."

If going up is a horror, the thought of retreat is unbearable. It also
seems inevitable. At 15,000 feet, the snow deepens abruptly. The
lead horse falters; breath steams in jagged bursts from his nostrils.
Sherub-la takes one look at him, and walks toward Kesang. I've
watched enough baseball to read his expression. But as we're steel-
ing ourselves for the showers, our teenage cook cries out with joy: far
above us, two yaks stand silhouetted against the sky.

The normally reserved Sherub-la shouts with glee. Matthieu and
Kesang howl; I throw my arms around the bewildered Yellow-Eye.

We move to higher ground, and wait for the herds to descend.
While lunch is prepared, Sherub-la recites prayers over his carefully sewn flags. He sprinkles them with rice, swallows a few pellets
of bitter ritual medicine, and offers a peg of brandy to the protector
gods of the valley. Then he passes the bottle.

Atop the Tholey La, the mountains fan around us like shark fins.
We remove our hats, and echo Sherub-la's call of victory: *"Ha gyel
lo!"* The gods are great! Within minutes, his prayer flags are whip-

ping in the wind.

We fly down in reckless bounds, diverting off the switchbacks and sinking into waist-deep snow. Yellow-Eye lopes after us, and disappears into a drift. In minutes, we've lost a thousand hard-won feet. As we approach our destination—another herder's camp, frantic with the chores of departure—Kesang predicts our fate. "We will definitely make it to Gangkar Punsum—110% sure," he pronounces confidently. "I guarantee."

Matthieu and I eye each other warily, fearing a jinx. Kesang should know better. There are no guarantees in the mountains.

. . .

All along the trek, we encounter myriad signs of Bhutan's Buddhist faith: prayer flags bristling on ridges; *chortens* piled with small clay icons; house-sized boulders incised with the mantra of Guru Rimpoche, the mystic saint who introduced Buddhism to Tibet and Bhutan in the eight century. My personal favorites are the prayer wheels. The painted cylinders, filled with handwritten mantras, are turned by the tireless energy of streams and tributaries. There's something poignant about these devices; it's like getting the Earth to pray for itself.

We wind through a forest thick with giant ferns. Beside us, the Chamka Chhu is mouthwash blue and terrifically wild. "Today we see Gangkar Punsum naked," Sherub-la states. Minutes later, we enter a clearing. The mountain, a broad wall spiked with three distinct summits, rises up unobscured.

We ascend steadily, pacing ourselves in the thinning air. Today's climb, though more gradual than the ascent to the pass, is much longer. The trees vanish, giving way to raw vistas of rock and snow. The temperature drops 20 degrees. There's no visible trail; we mince across uneven ground, poking with sticks to find our footing.

An hour later, the horses quit. They simply stop, noses down, and make their intention plain. Why here? It's a mystery. The trail ahead— river, stones and snow—is nasty, but no worse than what they've already done. Sherub-la confers with the horsemen, and returns with a grim verdict. This is it: the end of the line.

I look at him like he's crazy. It was a brutal hike from those last huts; we haven't come this far to be waylaid by a few skittish beasts. Matthieu and I huddle, and return with an alternative.

"Here's the plan," I say. "We'll unload our essential gear, send the horses back, and continue—on foot—to base camp." There's a brief silence. We're not the most popular guys in the valley, but we're holding the purse strings. Kesang doesn't argue, and the others reluctantly agree. After half an hour, five of us—including Kesang, Sherub-la and Samten, the head cook—begin the final approach to base camp.

I soon appreciate our folly. Trekking companies tell you to bring a duffel bag—they tie easily onto horses. But they don't figure on you carrying the damned thing yourself, stumbling along like Jack Lemmon in *The Out-of-Towners*.

And we're definitely from out of town. The snow deepens with every step. Just below lies a jumble of boulders, balanced above an icy marsh. My duffel, slung by its handles around my shoulders, swings me like a pendulum. I fall a dozen times, breaking through the crust of snow and plunging into the glacial streams below. Snowshoes might have been wise... had anyone known. But part of Bhutan's appeal, ironically, is its lack of infrastructure. Though it's been three weeks since Roskelley's group returned down this valley in a snowstorm, news about the conditions never reached our outfitters in Thimpu.

Two hours of anus-clenching boulder hopping brings us to the abandoned huts of Bumarpa. Sherub-la snags the largest one for cooking, while Matthieu and I pitch camp in a doorless refuge with loose stone walls, snaggled roof planks, and a filthy dirt floor. A place like this needs a name, and Matthieu quickly obliges. "The Hell Shack," he suggests. It works for me.

Samten boils noodles for dinner. That's it: noodles. He has not, in the interest of saving weight, brought so much as a tomato. Kesang, on the other hand, has packed in a fifth of Johnny Walker. We're glad to see someone has his priorities straight.

After a few drinks, Matthieu and I trudge dizzily home. The stars are diamond sharp, and the Milky Way streams across the zenith like a celestial reflection of the Chamka Chhu.

. . .

Matthieu rests fitfully. He's listening for a dreaded sound: the low, keening whistle that signals the approach of the *migoi*, Bhutan's breed of abominable snowman. He's obsessed with the monster, convinced it will come for him in the night. Here, at base camp, we're utterly vulnerable. Matthieu is afraid; very afraid.

He has reason to be. To begin with, we're the freshest meat around. But the real source of his terror is an experience he had a week ago when, driving toward central Bhutan, we'd spent a night in Trongsa.

Trongsa lies seven hours east, by car, from Thimpu. Aside from its textile-and-tuna bazaar, the main attraction is a magnificent *dzong*. Dzongs are found in many of Bhutan's historic cities—they're both monasteries and administrative centers, demonstrating the close link between religion and politics in this Buddhist monarchy—but Trongsa's may be the most impressive in the country. It's a sprawling white fortress, perched high above a seemingly infinite valley.

Foreigners are forbidden in most of Bhutan's dzongs, except with official permission. One morning, though—while Kesang was still sleeping and before the guards took their posts—Matthieu passed the site while taking photographs. He spied an open doorway and stood paralyzed, unsure whether to proceed. Suddenly he heard a whistle; a monk loomed in an upper-story window, beckoning him inside.

Following the drone of chanting, he made his way through the door and into the monastery. After crossing a small courtyard—careful to stay out of sight—he climbed a narrow stairway. Now he was at the entrance of the main *lhakhang* (chapel), surrounded by the un-earthly din. At that moment, he looked up—and saw, hanging in the shadows, three flayed skins. Each had black hair, dangling limbs and long, splayed fingers. He tried to photograph them, but his hands shook violently. He fled from the dzong, and appeared at breakfast with wild eyes.

The sight had unnerved him completely. It was possible these were human hides—that in itself was a nightmarish thought. More likely, though, they were the skins of migoi. He'd read, in a 1962 National Geographic, that some dzongs claimed to possess such hides. Could the creatures really exist? Matthieu was now certain that they did. He also believed that, somehow, stumbling upon the forbidden sight had cursed him—and that the migoi could smell his fear.

"Did you hear that?" Matthieu sits up with a start, breathless. It's 2 a.m.

I grunt a negative, and fall back to sleep—snoring, so I've been told, with a low, keening whistle.

. . .

Dawn is silent and clear. We dress quickly, and begin walking while the snow is still firm. The scenery around us is otherworldly. I feel like a space traveler, crossing the polar caps of Mars. There's very little life. We see only a few quick birds, and some fragrant shrubs sheltered by gleaming white islands of granite. Leathery, rust-colored lichen covers the rocks.

In dry conditions, the main Gangkar Punsum glacier is two hours away. We stay above the river, crossing avalanche scree and frozen marshes on numbing feet. By nine o'clock the crust has thinned, and every step is a gamble. We sink to our waists in the softening snow. Despite our resolve, the effort and altitude wind us. We can go no further.

A short climb affords us a magnificent view of the three-pronged massif. The flank of Gangkar Punsum is shrouded in clouds. I shed my pack on a dry boulder, taking in the majesty of the scene. Knowing it's unclimbed gives Gangkar Punsum an aura of mystery—like the Moon, before the Apollo astronauts turned it into a used car lot.

But even Gangkar Punsum may not remain unspoiled forever. At least one American climber is seeking a permit. He hopes to reach the false summit, then descend from that point "as a sign of respect for the mountain." Another threat is the Chinese, who might some-day issue permits to climb the peak from their side of the border.

For my part, I agree with Bhutan's policy. I strongly believe—for spiritual as well as poetic reasons—that there should remain at least one mountain, of real height, that remains forever unclimbed. If Gangkar Punsum goes, what will that leave us? Forbidden peaks are an endangered species—and, below a certain altitude, there's no real impact to the gesture.

For now, though, this whole valley demonstrates the strength of Bhutan's convictions. As we hike back to base camp, our experience seems an apt reflection of the Kingdom's attitude to the outside world. Gangkar Punsum lets us get close—but not too close.

. . .

With permit fees pushing $2,000 a week, Bhutan is basically a trophy destination. The average tourist is over forty, moving through the country on a fixed itinerary. There are specific must-sees, and the roads that link them are a minivan Habitrail. As adventure travel expands, the age demographic may change—but the Tourism Authority will always monitor where people go, and what they're allowed to see.

As a result, there's something Oz-like about Bhutan; not so much in the presence of a Emerald City or Scarecrow, but in the fact that one is compelled to follow the Yellow Brick Road.

Matthieu and I emerge from the Gangkar Punsum trek onto the rolling streets of Jakar—the administrative (and therefore religious) center of Bhutan's expansive Bumthang region. As we've gotten back a day early, we find ourselves in possession of an awkward commodity in this country: free time. We soon fill up on Jakar's monasteries and fortresses; most of them don't even admit foreigners. By late morning, we've had it.

I'm fresh out of ideas, but Matthieu kites an alternate plan. Since we have a free day—and since it's en route to our next destination—why not spend a second night in Trongsa? He keeps his voice casual, but I guess his plan: to revisit the Trongsa Dzong, and solve the riddle of the migoi skins. Kesang wearily agrees. It's the path of least resistance, and that much closer to his home in Thimpu.

A harrowing, four-hour drive takes us from Jakar to Trongsa. The road, slippery with snow, skirts an unprotected precipice. Huge Tata trucks blow by, paintings of the Buddha above their windshields. My thoughts turn to Woody Allen: *Never trust a driver who believes in reincarnation.*

We arrive after dark, and fall straight into bed. When I awake, before dawn, Matthieu is already gone. But I make my own way to the dzong, find the side door, and hurry through the courtyard he had described. I find him around a corner. He's sitting on a low stone wall, with novice monks tugging at his beard.

There's no way the monks will let us near the lhakhang without a good reason. Raiding lost migoi hides might not fill the bill. But the sound of chanting fills me with reverence, and I realize there are very legitimate reasons to visit the chapel. I tell the monks—quite honestly—that I wish to make an offering to the Buddha.

"This way, please." We're led up a flight of worn wooden steps, to the entrance of the main prayer room. Matthieu nudges my arm. I glance above me, and there they are: three flayed skins, barely visible in the dim light! The locks of hair, long, limp fingers and parched skin fill me with horror, and I instantly understand why Matthieu was haunted by the sight. "My God," I whisper. "Those are *human* skins...." We stare with fascination as the sound of *kangling*—thighbone trumpets—issues from the chapel. I want to examine the hides more closely, but the monks beckon us inside.

When we emerge, a senior lama is waiting for us. We prepare to be ejected—or worse. But Bhutan's monastic community, it turns out, has its own way of dealing with tourists. The lama pumps our hands, praising our efforts to find the "real" Bhutan. He calls for tea and biscuits. Before long we're surrounded by adolescent monks, who pepper us with questions about Tiger Woods, Bill Clinton and the NBA.

My own curiosity, though, remains unsated. I take a breath, and face the head lama. "What," I ask, pointing upward, "are those skins doing here?"

"Those?" The lama laughs, then turns dead serious. "They're devils!" He stands on a bench, and pulls one by the arm. The face swings into view. The eyes, I realize, are drawn with crayon; the hair is a patch of horsehair. "Bad creatures! For our rituals!" It's true: the "skins," cut from pinkish cloth, symbolize greed, anger and envy— the demons of the Buddhist hell realms.

I glance at Matthieu; he's weeping with relief. For my own part, I'm a bit disappointed.

THE UNION OF THE SUN
AND THE MOON

During the round-the-world pilgrimage described in *The Size of the World*, there was one obstacle, one stumbling block, that frustrated my every effort at diplomacy: the Islamic Republic of Iran. As some readers will recall, I expended enormous effort and anxiety in an attempt to win passage through that nation—all in vain.

Five years later I learned that a small group of Americans, under the auspices of Geographic Expeditions, was traveling to Esfahan to view a solar eclipse. With support from Salon and an Internet start-up called the Adventure Zone Network (of which I now own 40,000 shares of worthless stock), I joined that expedition. Even this was touch and go; a week before our departure, religious conservatives launched a violent crackdown on liberal students. Fortunately, the situation calmed down enough to satisfy Geographic's directors. These dispatches appeared on *Salon* in August 1999; my video footage of the trip may still be viewed (with a DSL line and military-grade computer) on www.AZN.com.

Dispatch 1: Letter from Teheran

THIRTY MINUTES BEFORE Lufthansa flight 600 landed in Tehran, an
odd transformation took place. As if on cue, the four or five dozen
women in the cabin—women who'd left Frankfurt in tanktops and
halters, blouses and shirts—rose from their seats, and pulled plastic
bags from the overhead bins. Each bag contained the same two items:
a broad black scarf, called a *rusari*, and a *roupush*, or oversized
trenchcoat. By the time we strapped in for landing, every passenger
of the female persuasion (girls under nine excepted) had covered her
hair and skin completely, leaving only her face showing.

This sudden reverse metamorphosis—butterflies back into their
cocoons—was so striking that I almost laughed. The change was especially dramatic in the woman sitting next to me. This was Sophia,
an Iranian by birth who had been living in Hawaii for two years.
Sophia's manner, so lively and playful during the five-hour flight,
now took on a somber and wary mien. She was doing something she
hated to please someone else: someone who could not be pleased.

Naturally, I was fascinated. Everything about Iran fascinates me.
I've attempted to visit this country twice; twice was my visa application rejected. This time, I applied as part of a small group arranged
by San Francisco's Geographic Expeditions. Our chief purpose is to
observe the last total solar eclipse of the millennium, which will throw
a giant shadow across south Europe, Turkey, Romania, Iran and north
India on August 11. Weather permitting, we will witness totality in
Esfahan—the legendary city which was the jewel of 16th and 17th
century Persia.

I've never seen an eclipse before, and I've never been to Iran
before, so the trip seems a good opportunity to experience two legendary states of darkness. Not that I personally think of Iran as a
dark place—on the contrary, I associate it with Rumi, Omar Khayyam
and the great Persian poet Hafiz. But let's not kid ourselves. Since
1979, Iran has been an Islamic republic under the strict supervision
of stern-faced ayatollahs, and the official line is a rhapsody on the
theme of Great Satan.

These days, though, we're more of a bite-sized Satan. For Iran, like much of the developing world, is awash in contradictions. This fact has emerged in nearly everything I've encountered here—starting with the women on the plane. Like much of Iranian society, they seem to be living with their heart in one place and their hand in another; pulled between the poles of enthusiasm for the new and fear of the old. As Sophia said to me before we parted: "Of course we hope things will change. But I doubt they ever will." Saying this, she bundled up her roupush and stepped outside—into 107-degree heat.

This social ambivalence became even more apparent after we deplaned. Our eight-member group was met by emissaries and herded into a lavish waiting area filled with comfortable couches, mirrored tile and skittering woodwork. This was, a brass sign proclaimed, the CIP lounge.

"CIP?" I looked quizzically at Sanjay Saxena, our Delhi-born expedition leader. "Shouldn't it be VIP?"

"No," he replied drolly. "As far as Iran's concerned, we're CIPs: Commercially Important Persons."

We would wait a few minutes, we were told, while our luggage passed through customs. In fact, it was two hours. During the interval, we were fed strong tea and served small, creamy cakes. An elderly man with a white mustache took pains to put us at ease. He offered a newspaper—the *Iran Daily*—which I opened greedily. Atop page three, I spied a short column called "Let's Memorize the Quran."

"Good idea," I thought to myself. I was genuinely intrigued; I know virtually nothing of the Koran (as westerners prefer to spell it), and was grateful for the opportunity to increase my knowledge. The passage, I noted, was from Sura 5, 51:

"O you who believe!" it began. "Do not take the Jews and the Christians for friends; they are friends of each other; and whoever amongst you takes them for a friend, then surely he is one of them; surely Allah does not guide the unjust people."

Whoops. I turned quickly to another page, and scanned a more hopeful story:

IRAN LIFTS BAN ON WESTERN MUSICAL INSTRUMENTS

TEHRAN (Reuters)—Iran has lifted a two-decade ban on the import of Western musical instruments, which it has long seen as decadent and corrupt, a newspaper said on Wednesday.

The moderate Iran newspaper said a state organization affiliated with the culture ministry had given the green light for the import of... flutes, pianos, classical guitars, harps, drums, saxophones and organs.

I was pleased to see that the ban on accordions remains in effect. Just below, I spied this unlikely headline:

AFRICAN QUEEN PLIES MICHIGAN WATERS

BAY CITY, MICHIGAN (AP)—The boat that once carted Humphrey Bogart and Katharine Hepburn around on the silver screen is plying Michigan waters. The *African Queen*, from the movie of the same name, will offer rides on the Saginaw River as a fundraiser for the Saginaw Valley Naval Ship Museum Committee....

My reading was interrupted by two customs guards, who approached a member of our group with apologetic smiles. The officers muttered something to Ali, our local guide, who translated for our unfortunate companion.

"The agents wish to inform you that they found a bottle of Absolut Citron in your luggage. They invite you to watch them pouring it into the toilet, to assure yourself they are not stealing it."

"No problem." His eyes lit up. "Can I take a picture?"

This was a stroke of genius. I could already envision the billboard, easily visible on the Bay Bridge approach into San Francisco: "Absolut Islam." Predictably, however, the answer was no.

. . .

Most of us have read or heard the recent reports of students riots in Tehran, the worst since the fundamentalist revolution that installed the late Ayatollah Khomeini twenty years ago. The students were protesting the closure of a liberal newspaper, *Salam* (which means "Hello," or "Peace"). The newspaper was not publishing op-ed pieces urging men to run out and rent *Debbie Does Dallas*, nor inciting women to storm the segregated swimming pools. The publisher was merely supporting the agenda of Iran's reformist President, Muhammad Ali Khatami, who has excited the popular imagination with his policies favoring personal privacy and a more lenient interpretation of Islamic Law. Khatami himself, ironically, is a former journalist. But the unfortunate truth is that, though he received 70% of the 1997 vote, Khatami has little real power. It might help to imagine him as the head of a small Medieval fiefdom, promising to reform the will of a Pope.

Be that as it may, it was a shock to walk down the streets of Tehran on Friday—the Muslim Sabbath—and feel no sense of menace at all. Everyone I met was helpful and hospitable, and quite eager to talk about Iran/American relations—within limits. Even my taxi driver, who spoke perhaps ten words of English, pumped my hand when he heard where I was from.

"Oh, America! Very good! JFK, very good!"

"What about Bill Clinton?" I ventured.

"Very good, very good!"

"George Bush?"

"Very good!"

"Ronald Reagan?"

"Sorry..." he shrugged. "No English."

I spent much of the day strolling around. There isn't much to see in Tehran—the museums are about the only things open on Friday—but it's a good day for protests, and I was hoping to run into some kind of trouble. No such luck. The closest I came was outside the defunct American Embassy (now a military training school), where I tried to photograph a gaily lettered mural saying "Down With U.S.A." A guard politely hurried me along. It's a good thing he did, or I probably would have missed all the other anti-American murals along the side of the building. I was especially moved by one plaintive message, illustrated by a scowling Khomeini:

On the Day the U.S. Praises Us We Should Mourn

One thing that stuck in my mind was the Iranian movie posters. Think about it: how many films in developing countries, from Mexico to India, rely on the thinly disguised charms of a buxom love interest? In Iran, of course, you see nothing of the sort. The women wear rusaris, even in the movies. This leaves little with which to inveigle the typical male viewer, so the same formula is repeated time and again: a single man poised heroically against an unseen obstacle, as a helpless-looking woman cowered beneath her scarf.

I dine alone this evening, typing up my notes in an ill-lit kabab salon as my fellow travelers painted the town. As I sit at my lonely table, a group of handsome Iranian men approaches me. They're burdened with heavy gear: lights, cameras, cables. "Excuse me, Sir." Those three simple words, ever concealing a hidden agenda!

"How may I help you?" I'm overly keen, eager to appear on a local film poster.

"We are with Iranian Television. We would like to make a film here, of you working on your computer. For TV. It will show that Americans are welcome in Iran. May we shoot you?"

"Why yes," I replied, touched. "No one has offered to shoot me all day." The producer smiled, and signaled to his crew. "Just one thing, though," I amended.

"Please?"

"No close-ups of the screen."

. . .

Dropping into bed, jet-lagged to the point where a toothbrush weighs eight pounds, I finally noticed it: the golden arrow on my hotel room ceiling. It was, inexplicably, a comfort. I shifted my pillow a bit, and slept with my head pointing in the direction of Mecca.

Dispatch 2: Shiraz, Iran
Poets and Patriots

Awoke this morning to the most terrifying sight I might ever have imagined in Iran: clouds. The total solar eclipse is but a few days away, and the sky is covered with a thin, but opaque, layer of fluff that may well obscure our viewing. This is painfully ironic, as the very reason Geographic Expeditions chose Iran for its eclipse expedition was that NASA predicted a 98% chance of clear skies over the Middle East—as opposed to around 50% in Europe, and around 80% in Turkey.

The one ray of hope is that we are currently in Shiraz, about 550 miles south of Tehran, not far from the Persian Gulf. Esfahan, where we will observe the eclipse, is halfway to Tehran, on the inland side of the Zagros Mountains. It's much less likely to be cloudy. Still, the sight gave our small group a scare, and we spent breakfast debating, half-jokingly, whether we might consider catching a flight back to sunny Bucharest.

. . .

Shiraz is one of the most ancient cities in the world; there are reliable records of complex trading societies existing here for more than 25 centuries. The ruins of Persepolis, a sort of Persian New Year's resort palace that had been under construction for two centuries when it was sacked by Alexander the Great in 331 BC, lie about 30 miles north. Further north is Pasargadae, where the Persian empire was born three centuries earlier. There's not a heck of a lot to admire in these ruins, and the once-sylvan landscape is now parched and bare, but one definitely gets the impression of antiquity. It makes a place like New York or San Francisco—the whole of North America, practically—seem awkwardly adolescent.

And Shiraz is one of those places where the *idea* of Persia—Persia as a state of mind—takes on real meaning. The name, for one thing. Shir Raz: City of Mystery. It was known for centuries as a place of nightingales, roses and poets. The Syrah grape originated here, and the local wine was the favorite of such poet/mystics as

Sa'adi, Hafez and Omar Khayyam. These days, of course, the strongest drink you can buy is nonalcoholic beer.

There are 16 universities and 59,000 students in Shiraz. More than half of them are women. And quite a few of them seem to be poets—or at least of poetic temperament. One certainly concludes as much after watching an endless stream of black-shrouded females prostrate themselves, weeping, upon the tomb of Hafez.

Both Hafez (born in 1324) and Sa'adi (1210) lived and died in Shiraz. Between them, they more or less represent the pinnacles of Persian literature. Sa'adi was a practical sort of writer who, like Shakespeare, added a vast number of colloquialisms to his culture. "I complained that I had no shoes," wrote Sa'adi, "until I met a man who had no legs." Or, "You have two ears and one mouth—so best to listen twice before speaking once." In short, he was full of the sort of phrases which parents use to torment their children.

Hafez, on the other hand, was a lyrical mystic. As a young man, he could recite the entire Quran by heart. Hence the appellation *hafez*, which literally means, "One who remembers." One of the wits in our group asked Ali, our imperturbable guide, if he knew the word for "One who forgets."

"It's very interesting," Ali replied. "The word, also from Arabic, is *ensun*—which also means 'human being.' For it is said that all humans once knew God and His teachings, but have forgotten them."

There is a tradition, at the tomb of Hafez, that the visitor make a wish, open at random a volume of Hafez, and place one's finger upon the page. Thus is one's fortune revealed. Ever a sucker for such omens, I strode over to the little bookshop and located a copy of "Hafez in English." I performed the rite without delay, with the following result:

> *'Twas morning, and the Lord of day*
> *Had shed his light o'er Shiraz' towers*
> *Where bulbuls trill their love-lorn lay*
> *To serenade the maiden flowers.*

The message, which reminded me powerfully of *Jabberwocky*, seemed to indicate no relief in my struggle against jet lag.

There are many lovely mosques and mausoleums in Shiraz. The most beautiful is undoubtedly the Bogh'é-yé Shah-é Cheragh (I only ever learned the 'Cheragh' part). The history behind the personage honored in this shrine (i.e., the brother of the eighth grandson of the Prophet Mohammad) is maddeningly complicated, but he was called the King of the Lamp and died (or was poisoned, like his brother; one never knows for sure in Persia) in 835.

Let me interject that for an *ensun* such as myself, there is a tremendous amount of history to be overlooked if one is to enjoy Iran. The string of eras, dates, deeds, sackings, sieges, poisonings, seductions, dynasties, Imams, Alis, eighth-grand-brothers and rulers named Xerxes is enough to make you throw your guidebook at the wall.

This frustration evaporates instantly, however, the instant one steps, shoeless, into that Cheragh place. It is unbelievable. My friend on this journey, Sam, told me he'd seen the place featured in a film called *Baraka*, but I cannot imagine a film could do this shrine justice. The entire interior is an intricate mosaic of tiny mirrors, covering every inch of the high walls and vaulted ceilings. Chandeliers hang in their midst; morning light pours in through colored glass.

Sam and I entered during a mid-morning call to prayer, and stood with our mouths open. It was like falling into a kaleidoscope loaded with diamonds. I might have stayed forever, but we suddenly found ourselves surrounded by several hundred Iranian schoolboys. Mirrors, they see every day. Two Americans—now that's something. They massed around us, their notebooks open, begging for autographs.

. . .

In the Shiraz bazaar—not the main bazaar but the "nomadic" bazaar, where women from the country shop for colorful dresses and lively appliqué rusaris (the code of dress is less strict for women who have to milk cows)—a cloth seller asked me about my impressions of Iran. "Is our country," he asked, "as you expected from reading the newspapers in America?"

I told him that it was not. From everything I have experienced, Iran is one of the most hospitable countries on Earth. Everywhere we roamed the locals asked after us, and welcomed us sincerely. One never forgets where one is—portraits of the ayatollahs hang everywhere, frowning above the masses on their clouds of beard—but there is no air of religious fanaticism or prejudice. I'd be willing to bet that Salman Rushdie could wander the bazaars unmolested.

On the other hand, it's not as if there is no reaction at all. At the mirrored mosque, a man approached and began haranguing me in Farsi. Ali, translating, explained that the individual wanted to know why America feels the ever-present need to meddle in the affairs of other nations; why it supports only those countries in which it has a vested commercial interest; why there is so much intolerance of the idea that a country like Iran or Cuba might pursue an alternate system of government.

These were pointed questions, and I did my best both to defuse them and answer them honestly. I think we were able to agree, by the end of our conversation, that the winds of change may be blowing, at least as far as American/Iranian relations are concerned. Over 20,000 tourists are visiting Iran for the eclipse, and the numbers will stay large as the true season begins in the fall. In 2002, New York's Asia Society is sponsoring an enormous show of art of Persia's Safavid Period (1502-1722). Most of all, of course, there is the optimism generated by President Khatami—and by the fact that he was elected with so much of the popular vote.

There's no question that Iran is in the midst of an exciting and delicate time. It seems the entire country is holding its breath, waiting to see what the ultimate outcome of July's student demonstrations will be. I wrote briefly of the contradiction inherent in Iranian social life; of the fascination, attraction and loathing Iranians feel toward America and the West. The word I used was ambivalence, but Persians are more severe with themselves. "We're a nation of hypocrites," one fairly conservative individual told me. "We know this. But as the political tide shifts, you will see that more and more people come around to Khatami's side."

People are fed up with the inflexibility of religious law, he suggested, and would love to see a change. When I asked why President Khatami had not taken a harder line—why he so quickly capitulated to the Supreme Leader by condemning the protests—my friend laughed. "It's because he is smart. Change must occur very slowly, very carefully," he said. Things in Iran transpire at their own pace, and cannot be pushed. "If there is one wrong move, the entire process of reform will crumble."

Iran could have played it safe, and kept its doors more carefully guarded during the eclipse. The very fact that the government allowed so many thousands of Japanese and European tourists to enter—as well as our small American group—is a sign that the fist of suspicion may be opening. I would not be at all surprised if Khatami turns out to be the Gorbachev (or at least the Khrushchev) of Iran.

. . .

It is considerably later. I'm sitting at the traditional outdoor teahouse that adjoins Hafez's tomb, sipping smoke from a hubble-bubble: a traditional Persian water pipe. The glances of the locals, curious but not disapproving, indicate that, despite the occasional choking fit, I am not disgracing myself.

It is moments like these, really, that represent the soul of travel; moments when one breaks from the tourist circuit and finds an alcove of peace and contemplation. Time slows down, and the essence of an unfamiliar culture surrounds you without planning or artifice. These are the times when one can imagine spending weeks, or months, in a city like Shiraz—meeting the living poets, and cultivating a real understanding of the people who make this their home.

The smoke bubbles pleasantly as I draw through the pipe; there is a lovely cherry flavor to the tobacco. Nearby tables are filled with men and women reading newspapers, doing crosswords (in Farsi; a daunting feat) and chatting over tea and cake. It is a measure of Iran's sophistication that my laptop draws nary a glance.

In a few hours I will board an Iran Air jet—a tired Soviet passenger plane, worn out from years of misuse by Aeroflot—and journey north to Esfahan, for the rendezvous of the sun and moon.

Dispatch 3: Esfahan, Iran
Kusoof! Kusoof!

Part I: Celestial Mechanics

During my travels in Iran I've been reading *Samarkand*, an historical novel by Lebanese journalist Amin Maalouf. Set in 11th century Persia, the book recounts the times of the poet-philosopher Omar Khayyam, whose most tumultuous years began and ended in Esfahan.

Aside from drinking about half the wine available in the city, Omar of Nishipur—who, despite his near heretical views, enjoyed royal patronage—realized his dream of building an astronomical observatory; he was accomplished in the arts of astronomy as well as astrology. One of his goals was to measure accurately the length of the solar year. Not only did he succeed, but the system he developed came into use during his own lifetime, on March 21, 1079. "This officially carried the name of the Sultan," writes Maalouf, "but in the street, and even in certain documents, it was enough to mention 'such and such a year in the era of Omar Khayyam.'" A modification of his calendar remains in use today.

Khayyam's legendary observatory no longer stands; it was destroyed by the invading Mongols, four centuries before Esfahan became the baseline of Persian civilization. It is astonishing to walk along the shaded streets, through the four-kilometer long bazaar, in the shadow of the magnificent 17th century Mosque of Emam, and realize that none of this (except for parts of the bazaar) existed during Khayyam's time.

(Speaking of the bazaar... During my morning stroll through the millennia-old labyrinth, I ran into a 16-year-old boy who cornered me as I bargained for the local version of a Dairy Queen cone. Like many young Iranians, he was keen to practice his English. His opening gambit was potentially awkward—"Excuse me, please, but why does America think it is king of the whole world?"—but we soon settled into a discussion about the charms of Esfahan. The definitive statement came after I suggested that Esfahan is more beautiful than

Shiraz. The boy frowned. "Esfahan," he declared, "is more beautiful than Chicago.")

One thing the Persians of Khayyam's era held in common with present-day Iranians is a fascination with the heavens. Nine centuries after Khayyam performed his calculations for the Seljuk court, the city of Esfahan has gone eclipse-crazy. Eclipse banners line Chahar Bagh, the main boulevard; posters showing the fabulous blue dome of Emam Mosque surrounded by a solar corona hang in every window. At ten this morning, with the event only 30 hours away, I wandered into a *madrasé*—an Islamic university, comparable to a yeshiva—and was immediately surrounded by turbaned clerics who called to me excitedly: *Kusoof! Kusoof!*

It is an expression I've heard a great deal these days. The literal meaning, as clearly as I can tell, is "the union of the Sun with the Moon."

It's out there somewhere, our Moon, moving inexorably toward its Wednesday rendezvous. Totality will occur at 4:40 p.m. This will be the first total solar eclipse to pass over Persia since the 1950s, long before the birth of more than two-thirds of the population. Eclipses are cyclical; they happen in the same places every 35 years or so (the next one to darken the U.S. will occur in 2017). But this is the last such event of the millennium, and tourists from around the world have converged on this ancient caravansary town to witness the spectacle. During the past week we've met groups from Japan, Italy, Spain, France, and England. We seem to be the only Americans. I did, however, hear a strange rumor—I have no reason to believe it is untrue—that this afternoon's flight from Tehran to Esfahan will carry a group that includes moonwalker Neil Armstrong (I can't seem to shake these guys).

The dire predictions of comet-watchers, asterophobics and dusty infidels like Nostradamus phase the locals not at all. The Imams I spoke with have no qualms about the eclipse. They will, however, recite special prayers, "like when there is an earthquake." So one doesn't quite know what to expect.

It is true that Nostradamus, who has often been off in his predic-

tions by only a letter or two, predicted that a "King of Terror" will
arrive from the skies just about tea time tomorrow. But the slightest
error in interpretation could give his words a very different meaning.
Both Yeats and Rilke, after all, equated terror with transcendent
beauty. As my astrologer friend Rob Breszny prefers to think, this
millennial eclipse may just as well deliver a breakthrough in human
consciousness. Reason enough, I reckon, to be smack in its path.

The weather, incidentally, is perfect. Not a cloud in the sky. The
only question is exactly where to observe the eclipse from. Sanjay,
our leader, seems partial to driving out of town and setting up camp
on the mesa of nearby mountain. He has a point; it would be fantastic
to see the shadow of the Moon race across the landscape as a 100-
second sunset occurs in every direction at once. For my money, though,
it could be equally spectacular to watch the phenomenon darken the
crowded plaza in front of the city's revered 17th century mosque.

In any case, the level of excitement is growing by the hour. Odd,
how the Sun and Moon know nothing of this; to the players themselves,
this is no more than the impassive dance of celestial mechanics.

Part II: In the Shadow of the Moon

The longest period of totality in Iran will be one minute and 58
seconds, but the figure reduces dramatically as one moves even slightly
away from the center line. Esfahan is 15 miles from that line, and
totality here will run only 1'38". After paying a fortune and lugging
their cameras and telescopes halfway around the world, many of the
Geographic clients were understandably eager to drive toward the barren southwest, wringing as many seconds out of totality as possible.

I stayed behind in Esfahan, setting up camp in Emam Khomeini
Square. Built in 1612, the vast plaza—alive with fountains and lined
by craft shops—served as the center of Safavid Dynasty Persia. As I
stood by the fountain in front of the cream-colored dome of the
"Women's Mosque," the high minarets of the Masjed-è-Emam gateway loomed to my left. High behind them, the impassive sun burned
through the afternoon haze. A few fluffy clouds flirted nearby, providing an unneeded element of suspense.

At 3:15—the moment of "first contact" between the Sun and Moon—there was a murmur from the hundreds of people assembled in the shade of the mosque. Though crowded, Khomeini Square was not the crush I'd expected. I wondered if everyone really had fled, driving across the plains in pursuit of longer-lasting shadows.

The situation soon changed. By 4:15—fifteen minutes before totality—the plaza was filled with thousands of locals, the vast majority too young to recall the last eclipse here 45 years ago. Iranian television and radio had been vigilant—they'd broadcast warnings and instructions every ten minutes—and no one was seen without a shadow box or mass-produced sun-viewer. Some people had built ingenious contraptions for observing the crescent sun. The simplest were small mirrors, which threw images of the orb across the walls of the mosques and palaces. The crescent, let me remind you, is the emblem of Islam, and I doubt the symbolism was lost on this crowd.

The atmosphere was charged and giddy. It was probably the closest Iran will come to Woodstock: T-shirts, overpriced soft drinks and all. There were a few pointed differences: devout Moslems spread woven mats on the grass and prostrated themselves, reciting the appropriate prayers; a small, spontaneous, and very short-lived anti-American demonstration erupted near the Ali Ghapu Palace.

The Women's Mosque is famous for changing color through the day. During the last five minutes of sun, the dome hurried through a full day's work—glowing first peach, then honey, then amber. As the world darkened, a terrified thrill swept through the plaza. Thirty seconds before totality a collective cry rose from the crowd, mounting to a fevered climax. I think I yelled myself as the last sliver of light winked out. The ground rippled with a weird diffraction pattern, and the Sun disappeared behind the Moon.

It was otherworldly, magnificent beyond compare. Venus burned near the zenith, and the cooperative clouds took on a wine-dark glow. The automatic lights crowning the minarets flickered on. A mane-like corona twisted wildly from the sun, while bright red flares danced around its edges. I tried to view the effect with binoculars, but it was impossible; this was my first eclipse, and my hands were shaking uncontrollably.

There was a sudden, timeless silence. Then, from every direction, came the familiar Persian expression of delight, reverence and awe: *Ma'sha'Allah*! What wonders God has willed!

Never, I reflected, were words more truly spoken.

Ninety-eight seconds is not a long time. Before we knew it, Bailey's Beads shimmered around the occulted disk, and a wink of sunlight appeared at the Moon's southeastern edge. Venus blinked out; in an instant, the plaza was flooded with light. I got the impression that people couldn't decide whether to cheer or moan. Our collective moment had ended; there was nothing to hold us from business as usual.

Yet we had shared something extraordinary; something that can hardly be described, and could barely be believed. I filtered out of the plaza with thousands of Iranian men, women and children, shaking hands and slapping backs, feeling the sort of solidarity usually brought on by moon landings, Superbowls or earthquakes.

Somehow, the news from Iran will never read quite the same to me again.

Dispatch 4: In the Air
Ayatollah You So

How quickly it's all behind me. Back in the sterile and neutral environment of the Commercially Important Persons lounge it all seemed like a dream, a brief diversion from purgatory. And this plane, despite a completely unexpected and miraculous upgrade to Business Class, is no better....

Wednesday. What I forgot to mention was the almost tangible quality of light; how, in those last minutes before totality, it seemed as if the Earth had turned to face a direction I'd never seen it face before. The word "soft" seems inadequate, but there was a foil-like plasticity in the atmosphere, as if the very nature of light were being bent.

Later that night, my American-Iranian friend Saied and I wandered around Esfahan. As the nearest tea house was full (mostly with women, I noticed) we squeezed onto a bench with a young Esfahani university student and his local family, drinking hot tea in tiny glasses and drawing from a collective hookah. After that we took a taxi to the square. What kind of life do these Iranians lead? It was nearly eleven, but every grassy patch was filled with couples, families and friends, picnicking next to the lawn lamps. I felt a great sense of affection for the place, as well I should—the afternoon's eclipse was certainly a rite of passage. The entire trip to Iran, completed with élan in the midst of so many doubts and obstacles, was a rite of passage.

...

The group spent Thursday in Tehran, after a gallingly early start. Right off I phoned Ali, a civil engineering student I'd met at the Café Naderi last week. Joined by Sam, we shared tea and a hubble-bubble filled with apricot flavored tobacco in the Kowasa Hotel's cafe.

At that moment I knew that I loved Iran as much as any place I'd ever visited. The realization was bittersweet. It was unfair and absurd that I could not extend my stay, and develop a more intimate relationship with Esfahan—a city in which I could easily live for months. (God knows what kind of shape my throat would be in afterwards; those hubble-bubbles are addictive.)

The day's highlight came in the evening, as we shopped for nuts and music along one of the city's crowded avenues. It seemed the whole population was on the hoof; Thursday evening is Friday night in Tehran. I walked with my video camera on, recording the throngs of pedestrians, the crazy traffic, the film marquees and store windows and neon signs. There was no sense of hostility, small-mindedness, or religious fervor whatsoever. People spoke English in ambitious, halting phrases. They were genuinely curious. Even their political questions were direct and courteous. They took our hands, welcoming us to Iran. The ubiquitous photographs of Khomeini and Khameni seemed superfluous, like the obligatory portraits of royalty hanging all over Nepal.

"Five years," I reassured Ali, an Iranian Turk who despises his country's leadership. "Give it five years, and the hejab will disappear. Five years, and Iran will be open up to America—and swarm with tourists." In one week it had become impossible for me to understand how the United States and Iran have mixed themselves up in such a tragic and ludicrous relationship. I actually felt *lucky* to see Persia under shari'a and the ayatollahs; the situation seems that fragile.

. . .

Shortly after our plane took off, I looked behind me and surveyed the rows in Business and Economy class. It took me a few seconds to realize why the scene looked so peculiar. The chadors and rusaris had come off; women in every row were bunching their scarves, and shaking their hair free.

Five years. Not without some bloodshed, and a few frightening setbacks, but five years. Persia will be back. I'm-a telling you so.

. . .

Afterword: Okay; I know; I may have to revise that estimate. Recent events have placed the entire Islamic world into a new relationship with the United States, and it's too early to guess where Iran will shake out in the mix. Our government's overzealous response to the September 11th attacks—including racial profiling, the virtual closing of our borders to Muslim immigrants, and George W. Bush's reckless inclusion of Iran as part of an "Axis of Evil"—have alienated moderate Iranians, and made pro-Western sentiments more dangerous than ever. Still, it's important to remember that many educated Iranians, like their American counterparts, are well aware of the difference between a country's people and its bombastic leadership. With any luck, Bush's tactless remark will not reverse Iran's reformist trajectory. I remain hopeful that, when a future administration extends an olive branch to the people of Persia, they will accept the gesture with alacrity and enthusiasm.

ACKNOWLEGEMENTS

～

Many individuals have supported and inspired my work over the years. To begin with, I'd like to thank the skillful editors and agents who helped brainstorm, develop and disseminate these stories in this book: Heidi Benson, Susan Brenneman, Connie Bourassa-Shaw, Richard Conniff, Jim Cook, John and Susie Daniel, Morris Dye, Jane Dystel, Karen Evans, Donald W. George, Larry Habegger, Linda Halsey, Mark Jannot, Tracy Johnston, Randy Koral, John Miller, Cara Moore, Allen Noren, Peggy Northrop, James O'Reilly, Alexandra Pitcher, Charles Rappleye, John Rasmus, Amy Rennert, Trish Reynales, Joe Robinson, Mark Salzwedel, Joe Spieler, Lisa Tabb, Mike Urban, Laurie Wagner, Joan Walsh, and Nancy Zimmerman.

For technical assistance, my sincere gratitude to Mark Weiman and Roz Abraham at Regent Press; designer Lyn Bishop; Lowry McFerrin of ProForma Mactec Solutions; and Linda Watanabe-McFerrin, whose *Wild Writing Women* anthology spurred me into action. Thanks also to Theresa and Beverly at Palm Press, who unearthed Andy Sack's wonderful cover image.

Love and gratitude to Roz Greenwald, the adorable "Dr. Ruth" McVeigh, David McCutchen, Mary Roach, and Wesley "Scoop" Nisker, for support on so many levels. Tod Booth and Christopher Slater, my indispensible and (nearly) tireless assistants, helped me dog-paddle through a quarter century of articles and interviews; their patience, honesty and enthusiasm kept this project afloat. They were joined in their efforts by the lion-hearted Patty Spiglanin, a great friend and fearless critic.

In closing, I wish to honor the memory of three dear friends: Richard Kohn, Greg Keith, and Maia Hansen. Their warmth, humor, and wise literary advice are deeply missed.

. . .

STORY SOURCES